W9-AHK-461

The Demand for Money

The Demand for Money

Theories, Evidence, and Problems

Third Edition

David E. W. Laidler

University of Western Ontario—London

1817

HARPER & ROW, PUBLISHERS, New York
Cambridge, Philadelphia, San Francisco,
London, Mexico City, São Paulo, Singapore, Sydney

Sponsoring Editor: David Forgione
Project Editor: Eleanor Castellano
Cover Design: Hudson River Studio
Text Art: Reproduction Drawings Limited
Production: Debra Forrest Bochner
Compositor: Donnelley/Rocappi, Inc.
Printer and Binder: R. R. Donnelley & Sons Company

The Demand for Money: Theories, Evidence, and Problems, Third Edition

Copyright © 1985 by Harper & Row, Publishers, Inc.

All rights reserved. Printed in the United States of America. No part of this book may be used or reproduced in any manner whatsoever without written permission, except in the case of brief quotations embodied in critical articles and reviews.
For information address Harper & Row, Publishers, Inc., 10 East 53d Street, New York, NY 10022.

Library of Congress Cataloging in Publication Data

Laidler, David E. W.
The demand for money.

Bibliography: p.
Includes index.
1. Demand for money. 2. Demand for Money—Mathematical models. I. Title.
HG226.5.L35 1985 332.4'01 84-22585
ISBN 0-06-043827-4

84 85 86 87 88 9 8 7 6 5 4 3 2 1

Contents

Preface ix

I The Macroeconomic Framework 1

1 The Role of the Demand Function 3

Elements of Supply and Demand Analysis 3
The Case of Money 5

2 The Demand for Money in a Fixed Price Level Macroeconomic Model 8

The Fixed-Price Model 8
Shifts of the *LM* and *IS* Curves 13
Alternative Assumptions About the Interest Rate–Demand for Money Relationship 17

3 Price Flexibility in the Macromodel 22

Introductory Comments 22
Nominal Money and Real Money 22
The "Aggregate Demand" Curve 23
The Long-Run "Aggregate Supply" Curve 27
Aggregate Supply in the Short Run 29
Questions About the Demand for Money 32

II Theories of the Demand for Money 37

4 A Brief Overview 39

Methodological Considerations 39
Alternative Theoretical Approaches 40
Concluding Comment 42

5 The Classics, Keynes, and the Modern Quantity Theory 44

Irving Fisher's Version of the Quantity Theory 47
The Cambridge Approach 47
Keynesian Theory 50
Friedman and the Modern Quantity Theory 54

6 Further Developments in the Keynesian Approach to the Theory of the Demand for Money 59

Introductory Comment 59
The Transactions Motive 59
The Precautionary Motive 64
The Speculative Motive 69
Conclusions 77

III Data Problems and Econometric Issues 79

7 Measuring the Variables of the Demand for Money Function 81

Introductory Comment 81
The Measurement of Money 81
Income and Wealth 86
Expected Income 88
Returns on Alternative Assets 90
The Own Rate of Return on Money 93
The Expected Inflation Rate 94
Other Variables in the Function 96
Concluding Comment 97

8 Some Econometric Issues 98

Introductory Comment 98
The Identification Problem 98
Simultaneity 102
The Period and Frequency of Observations 103
Adjustment Costs and the Short-Run Demand-for-Money Function 105
Problems with the Lagged Dependent Variable 107
The Individual Experiment and the Market Experiment 110
Concluding Comments 114

IV The Empirical Evidence on the Demand for Money 115

9 An Overview of the Evidence 117

The Issues to be Addressed 117
A Summary of the Evidence 118

10 The Influence of the Opportunity Cost of Holding Money 121

Early Work on the Role of the Interest Rate 121
More Recent Results 123
Negative Results on Interest Rate Effects 124
Econometric Issues 126
The Own Rate of Return on Money 127
The Liquidity Trap and the Stability of the Interest Rate–Demand for Money Relationship 128
The Choice of Interest Rate 131
The Role of Expected Inflation 133
Concluding Comment 134

11 Other Variables and the Question of Stability 135

The Influence of the Price Level 135
The Choice of a Scale Variable 138
The Real Wage, Economies of Scale, and Institutional Change 143
Recent Instability of the Demand-for-Money Function 145
Concluding Remark 151

12 Tentative Conclusions 152

Introduction 152
Implications of the Evidence for Theories of the Demand for Money 152
Implications of the Evidence for Macroeconomics 155
Interpreting Recent Instability in the Demand-for-Money Function 158
Concluding Comment 161

Bibliography 163

Index 173

Preface

The purpose of this third edition of *The Demand for Money* is the same as that of earlier versions of the book: namely to provide a coherent guide to an important segment of the literature on macroeconomics which is accessible to undergraduate economics majors but which will also be useful to graduate students and even to academic and other professional economists.

Anyone familiar with earlier editions of this book will immediately notice two changes in this one. One word—*problems*—has been added to the title, and many more than one word have been added to the text. Of course, these two changes are completely interdependent. The first edition of this book was written seventeen years ago, when empirical work in macroeconomics, though long past its infancy, nevertheless was rather new. Macroeconomic theory had an agreed framework in the form of the *IS-LM* model, and debates in the area were largely about the quantitative significance of particular parameters of that model. Against this background competing hypotheses about the demand for money could be formulated, and econometric tests seemed capable of discriminating among them. Though empirical knowledge has advanced, and econometrics has been invaluable, its application to monetary economics has proved to be much more complicated than many of us thought it would be. At the same time developments elsewhere in economics have undermined the central position of the *IS-LM* model as an analytic framework.

This new edition of *The Demand for Money* reflects both of these facts. It lays more emphasis on the tentative nature of much of our empirical knowledge than did its predecessors and attempts to give a balanced account of more controversial material so that the reader may make up his or her own mind about certain issues. Hence its greater length and the extra word in the title.

Nevertheless, the book still retains its original outlines. It begins with an account of short-run macroeconomic theory which I hope is comprehensive enough to enable the reader to relate the book to what he or she has learned in intermediate macroeconomics. Although the *IS-LM* model is developed, this section now also contains an account of the elements of modern aggregate-supply-and-demand analysis. The second part of the book gives an account of various theories of the demand for money that is only marginally different from that appearing in the last edition. Problems of data and econometric technique have now become so important in monetary economics that one rather brief chapter in earlier editions has grown into a separate part of the book, containing two chapters dealing with these matters. This section is almost completely new, while the final section dealing with empirical results has been thoroughly revised for this edition and is, I hope, quite up-to-date. The reader is warned, however, that the literature of empirical monetary economics is now so voluminous that this section of the book does not pretend to offer a comprehensive literature survey.

As the reader of this book will discover, the demand for money is once more an acutely controversial area in macroeconomics, and the author of this book is involved in current controversies about the appropriateness of the "buffer-stock" approach to modeling the relationship in question. Although the approach is promising, it does not seem to me to be as yet so well established empirically that a supplementary textbook such as this should promote it to the exclusion of other points of view, and I have tried to avoid doing so. Therefore, though fellow advocates of the buffer-stock approach might be a little surprised at my reticence in this regard, I hope that those who disagree with the approach will find their views adequately represented.

More people have contributed to my thinking about the demand for money over the years than I could possibly acknowledge in this preface, but I owe special thanks to Robin Carter, Kevin Dowd, Joel Fried, and Peter Howitt who have discussed the subject matter of this book with me on many occasions, and having read this edition's manuscript offered me many useful suggestions.

DAVID LAIDLER

one

THE MACROECONOMIC FRAMEWORK

chapter 1

The Role of the Demand Function

ELEMENTS OF SUPPLY AND DEMAND ANALYSIS

We study the demand for any item mainly so that we may make predictions about the consequences of changes in its supply. This statement is as true of money as it is of anything else, although in the case of money, it is all too easy to lose sight of the simple principle which it expresses amid a mass of analytic complications. In order to illustrate this simple principle, we will first consider the market for some good, let us call it X. Assume that no buyer or seller of X is sufficiently important in his dealings that he alone can influence the price at which X trades. Assume second that expenditure on X is a sufficiently small part of expenditure in the economy as a whole that the market for X may be analyzed as if it operated in isolation from the markets for other goods. In such a market, the decisions of buyers and sellers are independent of one another and we may characterize the rules according to which those decisions are made in terms of a supply curve and a demand curve, as we do in Figure 1.1. The curves show that the quantity of X supplied per unit of time, per week say, will rise with its price (p_x), and the quantity demanded will decrease.

Since our purpose here is to illustrate the role of the demand function in economic analysis, let us look more closely at this latter relationship. To begin with, it is drawn on an "other things equal" basis. More specifically, elementary consumer theory tells us that, in addition to depending on its own price, the quantity demanded of X will depend on consumers' income and the prices of other goods. Hence our demand curve is drawn for given values of these variables. Moreover, our assumption about the relative unimportance of X as an object of expenditures enables us to treat these variables as influencing the demand for X by their effects on its demand curve, but as not being influenced by happenings in the market for X. They are, in short, *exogenous* variables in our analysis.

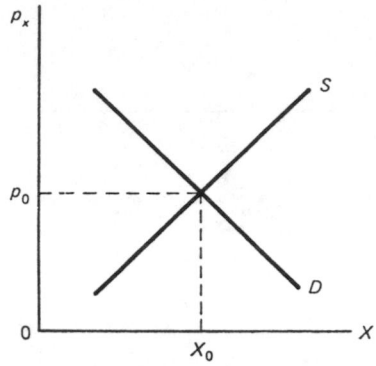

Figure 1.1 The supply and demand for a good X. p_0 is the equilibrium price of the good and X_0 is the equilibrium quantity bought and sold.

Our supply curve tells us the quantity of X which sellers will wish to provide at various prices, and our demand curve tells us the quantities which buyers will wish to purchase. Because exchange is voluntary, and because every act of sale is also an act of purchase, for these plans all to be realizable, for the market for X to be in *equilibrium,* the price of X must take a value at which these otherwise independent sets of plans are compatible with one another. That is, the value of this variable is determined at the intersection of the supply and demand curve. The price of X, one of the factors on which the demand for it depends, is thus determined within the model, it is an *endogenous* variable.

Now suppose that, for some reason, the quantity of X that sellers wish to supply at any given price increases by a particular amount, and that, whatever this reason may be, it does not also involve any change in the overall level of income prevailing in the economy or in the price of any other good. In such a circumstance, the supply curve of X will shift to the right from S_0 to S_1, and the demand curve will remain in place, as is shown in Figure 1.2. Plans that were compatible at the previously existing price no longer are. Clearly, in order to restore that compatibility, some variable (or variables) on which the quantity of X demanded depends must change. By assumption, income and the prices of other goods are given, and so in this case it is the endogenous variable, the price of X, that must change, falling, as is shown in Figure 1.2, from p_0 to p_1. Just how much the price of X will change in the face of a given shift in its supply curve

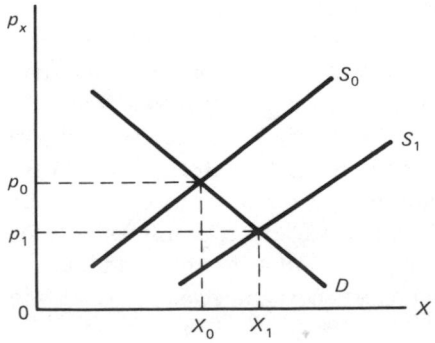

Figure 1.2 The effect of a shift of the supply curve on the price of X. As the supply curve shifts from S_0 to S_1, the equilibrium price of X falls from p_0 to p_1, and equilibrium quantity bought and sold rises from X_0 to X_1.

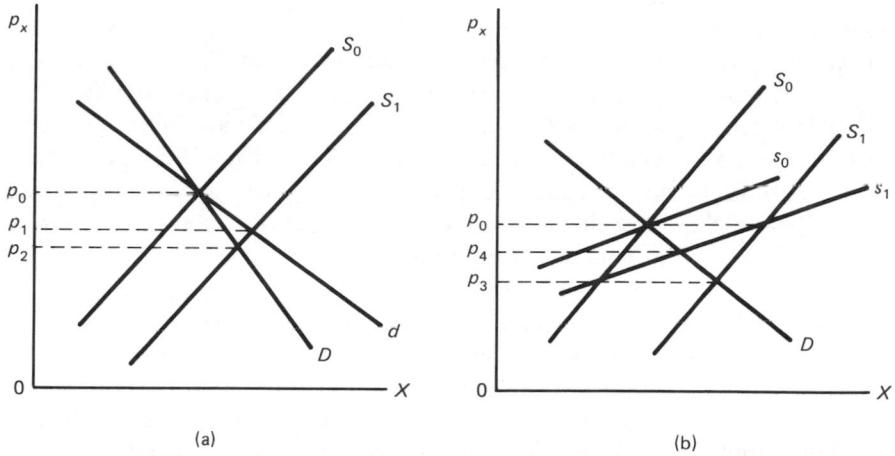

Figure 1.3 (a) The more shallowly sloped is the demand curve, the smaller is the effect of a given supply curve shift on the equilibrium price of X. If the demand curve is given by D, then when the supply curve shifts from S_0 to S_1, price falls from p_0 to p_2, but if demand is given by the more shallowly sloped d, the price falls only as far as p_1. (b) The more shallowly sloped is the supply curve of X, the less does its equilibrium price fall when the supply curve shifts to the right. The shift of S_0 to S_1 reduces equilibrium price from p_0 to p_3 but the equal rightward shift of s_0 to s_1 reduces price only to p_4.

will, among other factors, depend on the sensitivity of the demand for X to its price. If demand is rather sensitive to price, then the demand curve will be relatively shallowly sloped and price will fall relatively little; if it is insensitive, the demand curve will be relatively steeply sloped and price will fall by a relatively large amount. This is illustrated in Figure 1.3(a); and in Figure 1.3(b) it is shown that the slope of the supply curve is also a factor affecting the extent to which price falls in the face of a given increase in quantity of X supplied at any price.

THE CASE OF MONEY

The foregoing analysis could hardly be more elementary, and yet it illustrates all of those fundamental and general characteristics of supply and demand analysis that underlie economists' particular concerns about the nature of the demand for money function. First, it shows that, in the face of a shift in the supply function of a particular item, at least one, but of course not necessarily only one, of the variables on which demand depends must change. Second, it shows that the extent to which such a variable (or variables) will change depends on the nature of the relationship between the variable in question and the quantity demanded of the item under analysis. Third, it shows that the outcome of a shift in a supply function, heavily conditioned though it is by the nature of the demand function, does not depend solely on the latter. Other elements (in the foregoing simple case the slope of the supply function) must also be taken into consideration.

The case of money is a particularly important one for the application of these simple principles for a number of reasons. First, in virtually all contemporary economies, the nature of the supply function of money is such that, by manipulating variables that are directly under their control, the government can, within quite narrow limits, control the quantity of money supplied.[1] By manipulating the quantity of money supplied, the monetary authorities can therefore exert a systematic influence on at least some of the factors on which the quantity of money demanded depends. As we shall see in due course, among the variables that might influence the demand for money are interest rates, the level of real national income (and therefore employment), and the general price level. The importance of the behavior of these variables for the economic well-being of the community is surely quite obvious, and detailed knowledge of the demand function for money is an essential prerequisite to the active use of monetary policy.

As was suggested earlier, the analysis of the interaction of the supply and demand for money is, in general, a much more complicated matter than the elementary competitive market experiments we have just discussed, and the reasons for this are easily enough explained. What made our analysis of the interaction of the supply and demand for X so simple was the assumption that two of the three factors on which the quantity of X demanded could be treated as *exogenous.* Income and the prices of other goods were held constant, so all adjustment to changes in supply was concentrated on the price of X. As we shall see in due course, there might be circumstances in which the consequences of changes in the supply of money impinge on only one of the factors determining demand, but we cannot take it for granted that this is always the case. We must consider the possibility that all of the factors on which the demand for money depends will respond simultaneously to a change in its supply, and hence we must be prepared to analyze their interaction if we are to understand the consequences of a change in the supply of money.

We cannot carry out such analyses with the simple supply and demand apparatus deployed above. We need a model of the whole economy rather than of one isolated market in order to carry out this task. When we construct such a model, we shall find that we cannot answer all the questions we might like to ask about the consequences of changes in the supply of money on the basis of knowledge of its demand function alone. Such knowledge helps, and without it we could not get anywhere, but it will not take us all the way. Other properties of the economy are important too. Just why this is so, and what limits it might impose on our knowledge is best discussed in terms of a model that permits us simultaneously to analyze the interaction of the supply and demand for money and of the factors that underlie the demand for money. It is to the exposition of such a model that we turn in the next two chapters. As he works through that exposition, the reader should try to keep in view the main purpose of the

[1] To say that the authorities can control the money supply if they wish is not to say that they will in fact do so. For example, in an open economy, the government may decide to operate a fixed exchange rate for its currency. It can only implement such a policy by standing ready to buy and sell units of foreign exchange at a fixed price in exchange for domestic money, but if it does that, it clearly cannot control the amount of domestic money it issues.

exercise. First, it is to develop a framework in terms of which we may analyze the interaction of the supply and demand for money with a view to understanding the consequences, for the factors which determine the demand for money, of shifts in its supply. Second, in the light of that analysis, it is to enable us to formulate questions about the nature of the demand-for-money function, which will enable us better to understand the interaction in question.

chapter 2

The Demand for Money in a Fixed Price Level Macroeconomic Model

THE FIXED-PRICE MODEL

It is convenient to build a macroeconomic model in stages, and in this chapter we shall put together a structure that enables us to concentrate on the determinants of two of the three principal variables that are commonly thought to influence the quantity of money demanded, namely the level of real national income, and the level of a representative interest rate to which we shall refer simply as "the rate of interest." In order to construct this model, it will be necessary to treat the third of these variables, namely the general price level, as exogenously given.[1] We do this purely for analytical convenience, and not because we believe an exogenously given price level to be a characteristic of the real world we are ultimately interested in understanding. In due course, we shall relax this price fixity assumption, but for the moment we shall assume that all changes in the level of aggregate demand for goods and services are met solely by changes in output. This in turn must imply that there exist in our economy enough productive resources to meet any level of aggregate demand that may arise. Let it be stressed that this assumption too is made for analytic convenience and is not to be regarded as descriptively accurate.

In our economy, expenditure is made by households, in which case it is called *consumption,* by firms, in which case it is called *investment,* or by the government, in which case it is called *government expenditure.* Conventional assumptions are made about the determinants of these components of expenditure. Consumption is thought of as being an increasing function of disposable

[1] Because the model we are dealing with here has a fixed price level, it is unnecessary to deal with the distinction between the nominal interest rate, and the real interest rate, the latter being the nominal rate adjusted to account for the effects over time of inflation on the purchasing power of the capital value of bonds. With a fixed price level, there can be no inflation to make adjustments for.

income and, since it is for the moment convenient to deal with an economy in which there are no taxes, this means that consumption can be treated simply as a function of income. It is also postulated that the marginal propensity to consume is less than 1. Investment is thought of as being negatively related to the rate of interest, while government expenditure is treated as exogenous—that is, as a variable that may affect but is not affected by the other variables in the model. This income-expenditure subsystem of our model is in equilibrium when the level of expenditure in the economy, as determined by these functions, is equal to the level of income, and in Figure 2.1 the reader will find the system set out in familiar geometric terms. (*Note:* In labeling the figures in this book, subscripts in parentheses have been attached to many variables. This notation indicates that the variable carrying the subscript takes the value it does given that the variable in the subscript takes the value mentioned in the subscript. For example, in Figure 2.1 $Y_{(r_0)}$ indicates the value income takes given that the rate of interest takes the value r_0.)

Panel (a) shows the consumption function $C = c(Y)$ and the exogenous level of government expenditure $\overline{G}$, while the investment function $I = i(r)$ is plotted in panel (b). If it is assumed that the rate of interest is fixed at level r_0, the level of investment will be determined at $I_{(r_0)}$. In panel (c) this level of investment is added to consumption and government expenditure to produce

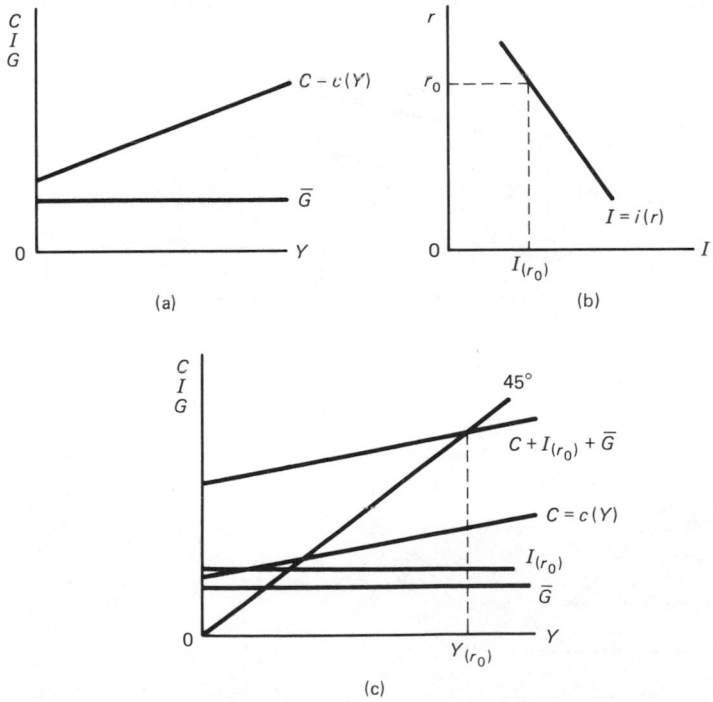

Figure 2.1 The simple geometry of income determination. *C* is consumption, *I* is investment, *G* is government expenditure, *Y* is income, and *r* is the rate of interest. *c* and *i* denote functional relationships, while the bar over *G* indicates that it is an exogenous variable.

the curve $C + I_{(r_0)} + \overline{G}$ which gives the relationship implicit in the model between the level of aggregate expenditure and the level of income. The 45° line plots all the points at which aggregate expenditure measured on the vertical axis can be equal to income measured on the horizontal axis. The aggregate expenditure curve crosses this line at the only point at which expenditure as determined by the functional relationships involved in the model is equal to the level of income. $Y_{(r_0)}$ is then the equilibrium level of income, but only so long as the rate of interest remains at r_0. If it takes some other value, so will the level of investment, and the equilibrium level of income will be different.

Implicit in the foregoing analysis is a relationship between the value of the rate of interest and the equilibrium level of income, and it is easy enough to make this relationship explicit. Figure 2.2(a) shows the relationship between investment and the rate of interest. Panel (b) shows various relationships between aggregate expenditure and income, each based on the same consumption function and level of government expenditure, but each assuming that the rate of interest takes a different value: r_1 is a lower interest rate than r_0, while r_2 is lower still. The lower the rate of interest, the higher the level of investment, as Figure 2.2(a) tells us, and the higher the level of investment, the higher the level of aggregate expenditure. Thus, in Figure 2.2(b), $C + I_{(r_2)} + \overline{G}$, lies above $C + I_{(r_1)} + \overline{G}$, which in turn lies above $C + I_{(r_0)} + \overline{G}$. Corresponding to each of these aggregate expenditure curves is an equilibrium level of income. As can readily be seen, the lower the level of the rate of interest, the higher this level of

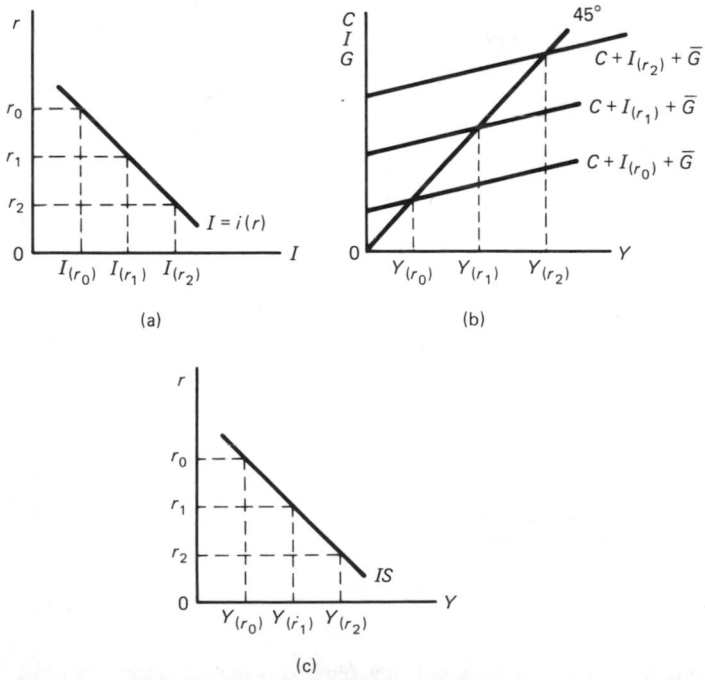

Figure 2.2 The equilibrium relationship between the rate of interest and the level of income implicit in the model of the real-goods market.

income. This relationship between the rate of interest and the equilibrium level of income is plotted as the curve *IS* in Figure 2.2(c). (*IS* refers to the fact that in a model without government expenditure any point along this curve is one at which investment is equal to saving. It is now general to use this label for any curve showing real-goods market equilibrium.)

The foregoing analysis at first sight presents us with a problem, for, as Figure 2.2(c) shows quite explicitly, the income-expenditure system with which we are dealing can tell us what the equilibrium level of income is if we know the rate of interest, or, for that matter, what the rate of interest is if we know the equilibrium level of income. The clue to completing our model, so that income and the interest rate are both determinate, lies in the fact that people not only make decisions about current flows of goods and services, about how much to consume, about how much to invest, and so on, but also about stocks, about how to hold their wealth. As we shall now see, it is at this point that the demand for money function appears on the scene.

There are many ways of holding wealth.[2] An individual can own consumer durable goods, corporate equities, bonds, and so forth, but for present purposes it is sufficient to assume that there are only two types of assets available—money and bonds. The problem facing individuals as far as holding their wealth is concerned is how to allocate it between money and bonds. If we take the level of wealth as given, then if money is not held, bonds must be, and the problem reduces to that of how much money to hold. The bulk of this book is devoted to examining various hypotheses about what variables are involved in this decision, but for the moment we merely assert a commonly held simple hypothesis about the determinants of the demand for money, already alluded to above, and see how it can be fitted into our model. It is usually argued that, at a given price level, the demand for money depends primarily on the level of income and the rate of interest, and that, if the price level varies while other variables remain unchanged, the demand for money will vary in exact proportion to the price level. This is equivalent to asserting that the demand for money measured in units of constant purchasing power, that is, the demand for *real-money balances,* as money measured in such units is usually called, does not vary with the price level.

Because money is a universally acceptable means of exchange, it is usual to argue that the demand for it increases with real income. Moreover, because bond holding is the alternative to money holding, interest income is forgone by holding money. The higher the rate of interest, the higher is the opportunity cost of holding money, and so, it is argued, the lower is the demand for money. As to the supply side of the money market, it is usual to assume as a first approximation that the quantity of money supplied is completely under the control of monetary authorities whose behavior may be treated as exogenous to the model. As with any supply and demand problem, we have equilibrium when the supply and demand for money are equal.

[2] Here we are referring only to what is nowadays called *non-human* wealth. The relevance of a more inclusive concept of wealth that encompasses human wealth to the analysis of the demand for money is discussed on pages 55–56.

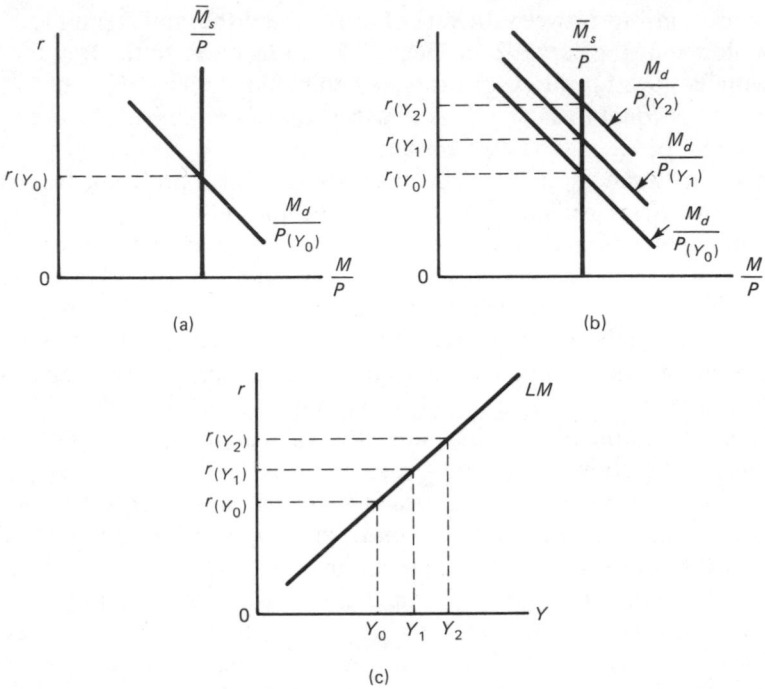

Figure 2.3 The equilibrium relationship between the rate of interest and the level of income implicit in the model of the money market. *M* is the quantity of money and *P* is the price level, so that *M/P* is the quantity of money measured in units of constant purchasing power. The subscripts *s* and *d* stand for supplied and demanded, and the bar over M_s indicates that it is an exogenous variable.

Figure 2.3 deals with all this in geometric terms. In panel (a) we graph the demand for money as a function of the rate of interest at the level of income Y_0. With a given money supply and price level, we have equilibrium when the rate of interest is equal to $r_{(Y_0)}$. Note, however, that we have here a problem analogous to the one we met earlier in the context of the market for current flows of goods and services. $r_{(Y_0)}$ is an equilibrium value only so long as the level of income is at Y_0, as Figure 2.3(b) shows clearly enough. Here Y_2 is a higher level of income than Y_1, which in turn is higher than Y_0. Since the demand for money at any rate of interest increases when the level of income rises, the whole curve relating the demand for money to the rate of interest shifts to the right as income increases. With a given money supply and price level, this involves the equilibrium interest rate rising. As far as equilibrium between the supply and demand for money is concerned, there is thus implicit in the model a positive relationship between the level of income and the rate of interest. This is plotted in Figure 2.3(c) and labeled, as is customary, *LM*. (*LM* refers to the fact that, at any point on this curve, "liquidity preference," a phrase which in this simple model is synonymous with "demand for money," is just satisfied by the supply of money.)

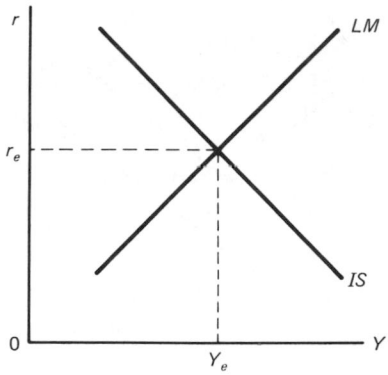

Figure 2.4 The determination in the complete model of the equilibrium levels of the interest rate and of income.

We now have two different equilibrium relationships between the rate of interest and the level of income. However, the people whose decisions underlie the consumption and investment functions are the same people whose behavior vis-a-vis wealth holding yields the demand-for-money function. The level of income and rate of interest involved in both sets of decisions are the same, and the economy as a whole can be in equilibrium only when their values lie on both the *LM* curve and the *IS* curve. Obviously this can occur only where the two curves intersect. In Figure 2.4 the two curves are plotted against the same axes, and the equilibrium level of income is given at Y_e with the rate of interest having an equilibrium value of r_e. These in turn imply equilibrium values for consumption and investment, as should be apparent. They also imply equilibrium money holdings, because, with the price level held constant, our model has now determined for us the values of the two other variables on which the demand for money depends.

SHIFTS OF THE *LM* AND *IS* CURVES

If the demand for money depends on the price level, real income, and the interest rate, and if we hold the first of these constant, then it follows that if equilibrium between the supply and demand for money is to be maintained, a change in the quantity of money supplied must cause the latter two determinants of the demand for money to change in some combination or other. The *IS-LM* system we have just developed enables us to make more precise statements about this matter. Figure 2.5 is essentially the same as Figure 2.3. In panel (a) we show the demand for money as a function of the rate of interest at two (rather than three in order to maintain geometric clarity) different levels of real income. We then consider what would happen if the supply of money were to be increased from $\overline{M}s_0$ to $\overline{M}s_1$. It is clear from panel (a) that, for any level of income, the rate of interest would have to fall in order to maintain equilibrium between the supply and demand for money. This in turn implies that the *LM* curve, which, in the initial situation, is at LM_0, shifts to the right to LM_1, as is

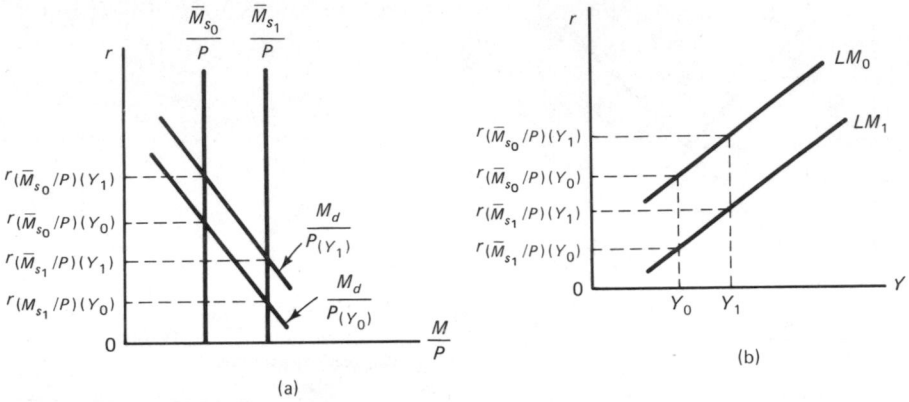

Figure 2.5 The derivation of a shift of the *LM* curve caused by an increase in the money supply.

shown in panel (b). By similar reasoning, it can be shown that a decrease in the money supply will shift the *LM* curve to the left. If, in Figure 2.6(a) we superimpose such shifts of the *LM* on a given *IS* curve, we may deduce how a change in the quantity of money will affect the level of income and the value of the interest rate. Clearly the precise amounts by which a change in the money supply will affect interest and output will depend on two sets of factors. First they will depend on the distance the *LM* curve shifts, and on its slope, which in turn depend on the demand for money function. Second, they will depend on the slope of the *IS* curve, which is determined by the properties of the consumption and investment functions.

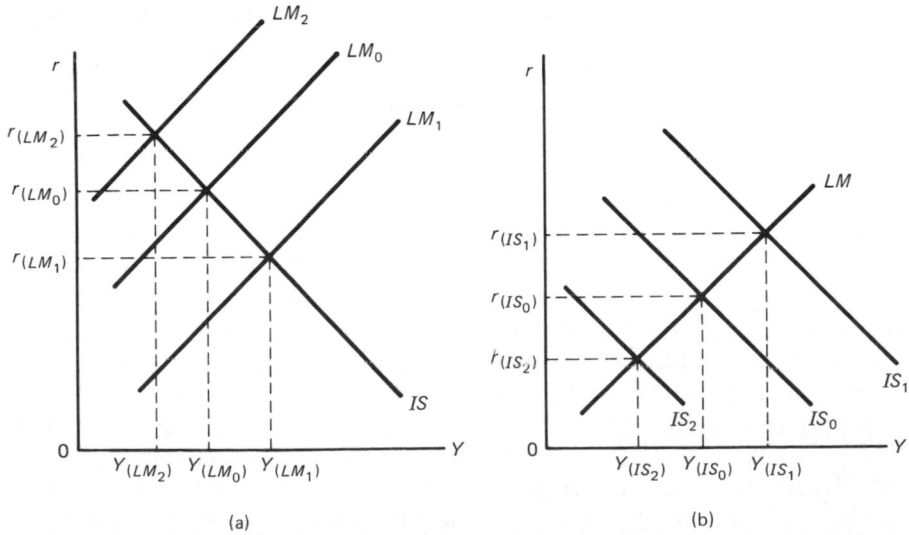

Figure 2.6 (a) The effect on the equilibrium level of income and the rate of interest of shifting the *LM* curve. The shift from LM_0 to LM_1 is the result of an increase in the money supply, and that from LM_0 to LM_2 of a decrease. (b) The effects on income and the interest rate of shifts of the *IS* curve to the right (from IS_0 to IS_1) and to the left (from IS_0 to IS_2).

We shall return to some of these matters in more detail in a while, but for now note that, as should be apparent from Figure 2.6(b), just as we need to know about the properties of the *IS* curve if we are to be able to make statements about the consequences of a shift of the *LM* curve, so if we are to say anything about the effects of a shift of the *IS* curve, we must know about the properties of the *LM* curve. Thus, knowledge of the nature of the demand-for-money function is necessary not only to enable us to make predictions about the consequences of a change in the supply of money, but also about the consequences of any factor that causes the *IS* curve to shift. A glance back at Figure 2.2 will be helpful at this stage, since it is there that the derivation of this curve is shown.

It will be recalled that the negative relationship between the rate of interest and the level of income embodied in the *IS* curve arises because investment is a component of aggregate expenditure, and because it increases as the rate of interest falls. Every point on the *IS* curve involves a given rate of interest generating a certain level of aggregate expenditure. Three factors can cause the *IS* curve to shift. If, as in Figure 2.7(a), the relationship between the rate of

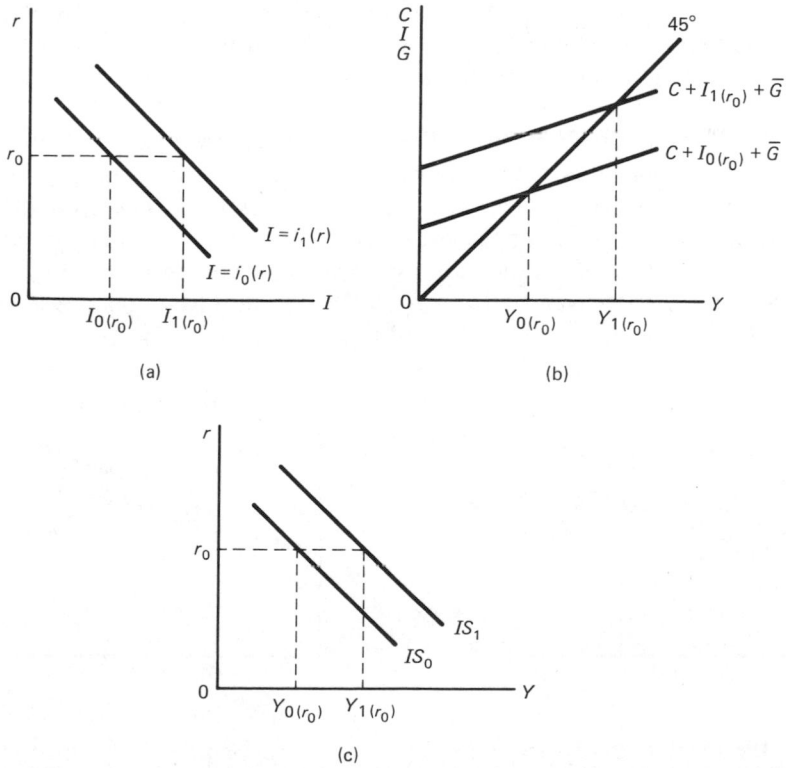

Figure 2.7 The derivation of a shift of the *IS* curve caused by a shift of the investment function.

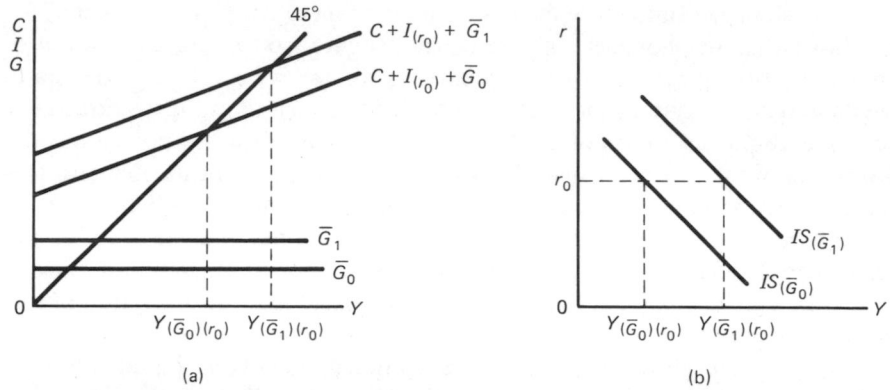

Figure 2.8 The derivation of a shift of the *IS* curve (b) caused by a change in the level of government expenditure (a). $\bar{G}_1 > \bar{G}_0$.

interest and the level of investment shifts to the right, this implies a higher level of aggregate expenditure at any level of the rate of interest [Figure 2.7(b)] so that the *IS* curve shifts to the right as shown on Figure 2.7(c). A similar argument obviously follows in reverse. If the level of government expenditure increases, again the level of aggregate expenditure increases for any given level of the rate of interest, so that the *IS* curve again shifts to the right. Figure 2.8 shows this. A cut in government expenditure has the opposite effect, as should be obvious.

The third factor, namely a shift in the relationship between consumption and income, needs looking at with a little care, since it is by shifting the consumption function that taxes have their main macroeconomic effect on the economy. Recall that consumption depends on disposable income and consider Figure 2.9(a) in which taxes are initially assumed to be zero so that the consumption function is first given by $C = c(Y)$. If a tax of a fixed amount T is levied, the level of income Y_0 will correspond to a disposable income of $Y_0 - T$

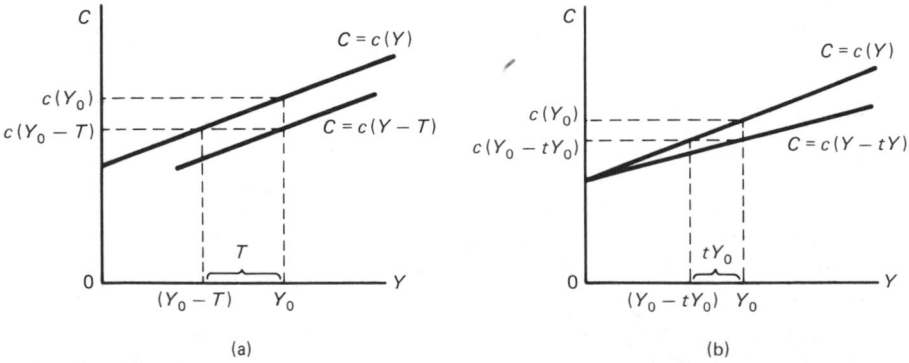

Figure 2.9 The effect on the consumption function of introducing (a) a fixed level of taxation T and (b) proportional taxation at the rate t. Note that a change in taxes is equal to an opposite change in disposable income, so that the effect of such a change on consumption at a given level of national income is to reduce it by the marginal propensity to consume times the change in taxes.

and consumption will now be equal to $c(Y_0 - T)$. A similar argument holds for any level of income. In the presence of a tax, the consumption function must be shifted to the right to $C = c(Y - T)$ by the amount of the tax in order that it will still enable us to determine the level of consumption given the level of before-tax income. This is equivalent to shifting the consumption function downward by an amount equal to the marginal propensity to consume times the amount of the tax, as should be clear from an inspection of Figure 2.9(a).[3]

In general, an increase in taxes shifts the consumption function downward and a cut in taxes shifts it up—shifting the aggregate expenditure curve in the same direction and by the same amount. Thus, an increase in taxes shifts the *IS* curve to the left, while a cut in taxes shifts it to the right. Although we have here discussed cuts in the *amount* of taxes, the same conclusions follow as far as an alteration in tax *rates* is concerned. A change in a tax rate can always be converted into a change in the amount of taxes paid by multiplying the change in the rate by the level of income. The only analytic difference here is that the shift in the consumption function is no longer a parallel one. This is shown in Figure 2.9(b).

The implications of the preceding discussion are straightforward but of considerable importance. Shifts in the investment function, which many economists would argue are both frequent and difficult to predict in the real world, influence real income and interest rates (in our fixed price level model) by causing the *IS* curve to shift. Governments implement their fiscal policies through changing their levels of expenditure and taxes, and changes in these factors also affect real income and the interest rate by shifting the *IS* curve. In turn, the manner in which *IS* curve shifts have their consequences divided up between the level of income and the interest rate depends on the slope of the *LM* curve. Thus, if we wish to be able to say anything precise about the extent to which fluctuations in investment will lead to fluctuations in real income, and therefore employment, or about the extent to which fiscal policy can be used to iron out such fluctuations, knowledge of the nature of the demand-for-money function is required, just as much as it is required if we are to be able to say anything about the consequences of monetary policy.

ALTERNATIVE ASSUMPTIONS ABOUT THE INTEREST RATE–DEMAND FOR MONEY RELATIONSHIP

It has been assumed throughout this chapter that the demand for money is stably and negatively related to the rate of interest. This is a key assumption in the derivation of the upward sloping *LM* curve on which so many of our conclusions rest. It has, however, been suggested by some economists that the demand for money is likely to be so insensitive to the rate of interest as to make it a reasonable approximation to treat it as not related to that variable at all. It

[3] The reader who wishes to understand what is going on should try to prove that an equal increase in government expenditure and taxes will shift the *IS* curve to the right by the amount of the increase in government expenditure, that is, that the balanced-budget multiplier is equal to 1.

has also been suggested, obviously by different economists, that when the interest rate is very low relative to its normal level, the demand for money is so sensitive to the interest rate as to make it worthwhile to treat the relationship in question as being one of infinite elasticity, a so-called *liquidity trap.*

This is not the place to go into the theoretical bases of these suggestions. They are taken up in Part II of this book, but it is worthwhile now to look at the effects which these different postulates have on the behavior of our model. Figure 2.10 depicts demand functions for money drawn on various assumptions concerning the role of the interest rate. Panel (a) depicts the usual case in which the relationship between the demand for money and the interest rate is assumed to be negative. Panel (b) depicts the case where there is no relationship between the demand for money and the rate of interest, but where the higher the level of income, the greater is the quantity of money demanded. Here the demand function becomes a series of vertical lines, those further to the right being associated with higher income levels. In panel (c) it is assumed that, at r^*, the demand for money becomes completely elastic with respect to the rate of

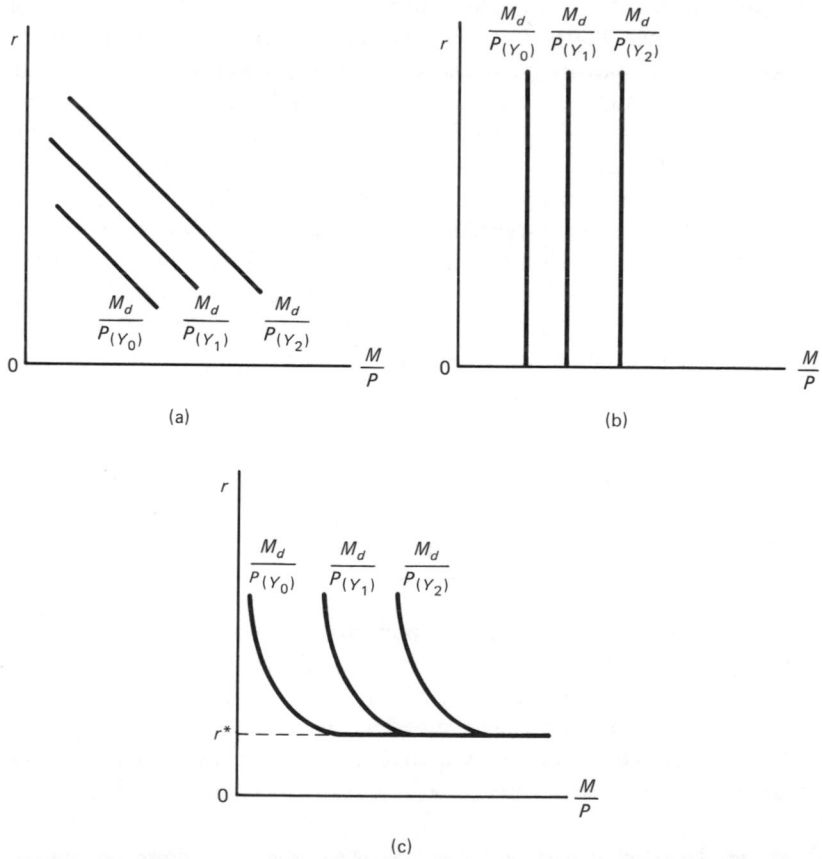

Figure 2.10 Demand-for-money functions drawn on different assumptions about the relationship between the demand for money and the rate of interest: $Y_2 > Y_1 > Y_0$.

interest. At interest rates greater than r^* the demand for money increases with increases in income, but the curves drawn for different levels of income all converge and become perfectly elastic at r^*, because at this interest rate level increases in the level of income are not capable of causing an already unlimited demand for money to increase further.

Let us now look at the implications of these hypotheses about the demand for money for the shape of the *LM* curve. The proposition that the demand for money is insensitive to the rate of interest implies that the *LM* curve is a vertical line, as shown in Figure 2.11(b). An equilibrium in which the demand for money is equal to a given money supply can occur at one, and only one, level of income if the demand for money is a continuously increasing function of that variable and depends on no other. The opposite extreme proposition about the relationship between the demand for money and the rate of interest—namely, that the relationship can be one of infinite rather than zero elasticity of demand—produces an analogously opposite implication for the *LM* curve. Though it is positively sloped above r^*, it becomes horizontal at that level of the interest rate. This is shown in Figure 2.11(c), while Figure 2.11(a) reproduces the *LM* curve used earlier.

Given the *LM* curves that they imply, we can investigate the consequences for the behavior of the complete model of these various assumptions

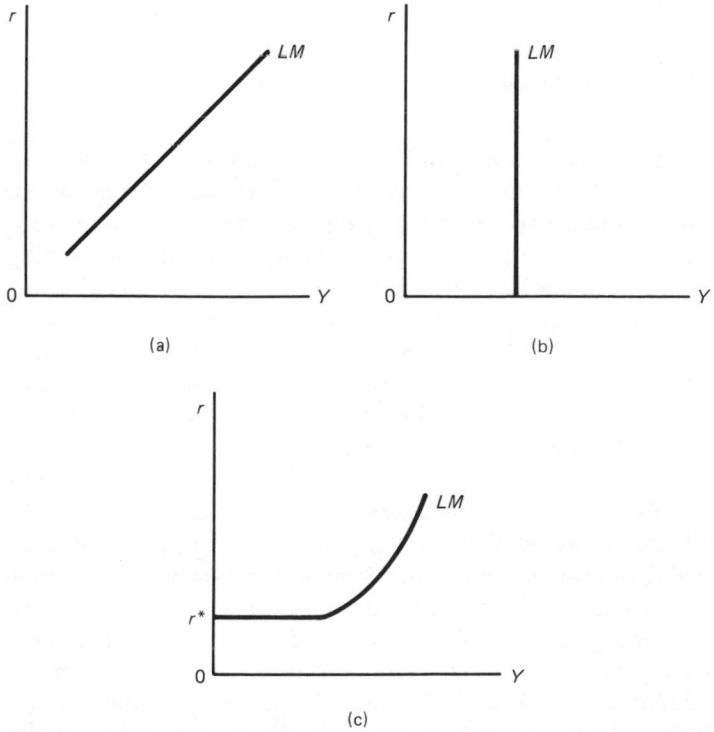

Figure 2.11 *LM* curves derived from the demand-for-money functions portrayed in Figure 2.10.

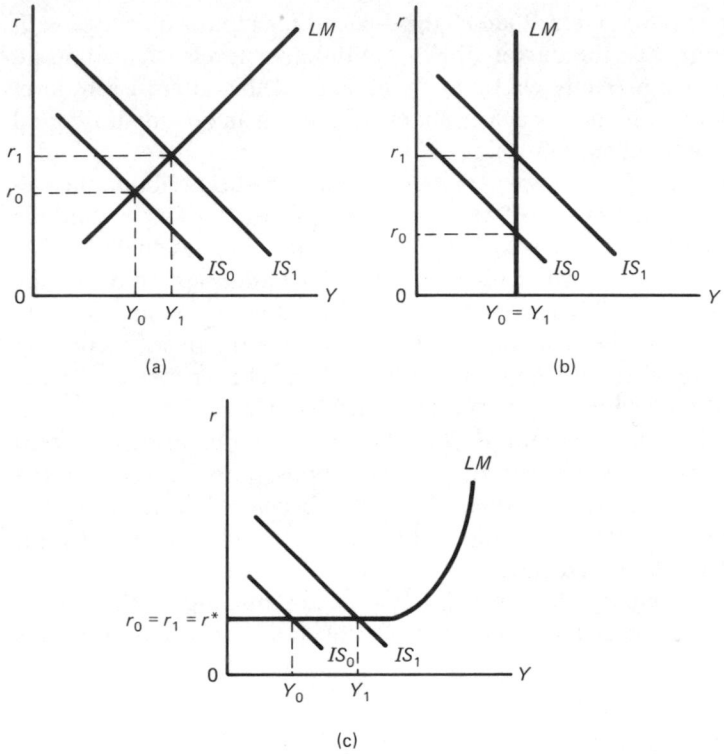

Figure 2.12 The effects of shifting the *IS* curve given different forms of the *LM* curve.

about the relationship between the demand for money and the rate of interest. Figure 2.12 deals with the effects of a shifting *IS* curve. As should be apparent, the results differ quite dramatically, depending on what form the *LM* curve is assumed to take. In panel (a) we present results based on an upward-sloping *LM* curve, which show that the level of income and the interest rate rise and fall together as the *IS* curve shifts. Panel (b) shows the results of assuming no relationship between the demand for money and the rate of interest. The only effect of shifting the *IS* curve in this case is to raise and lower the rate of interest. On the other hand, panel (c) shows that a horizontal *LM* curve involves all the effects falling on the level of income and none on the rate of interest.

Figure 2.13 deals with the consequences of shifting the *LM* curve. The upward-sloping *LM* curve case is displayed in panel (a) for purposes of comparison, while panel (b) shows that when the demand for money is completely interest-inelastic shifts of the *LM* curve influence both the level of income and the rate of interest. For a given shift of the *LM* curve to the right, the changes in both variables are greater than when there is zero interest elasticity of demand for money, but the resulting level of income depends only on the location of the new *LM* curve and not on any property of the *IS* curve. Panel (c) shows that when the demand for money is perfectly interest-elastic, so long as one is

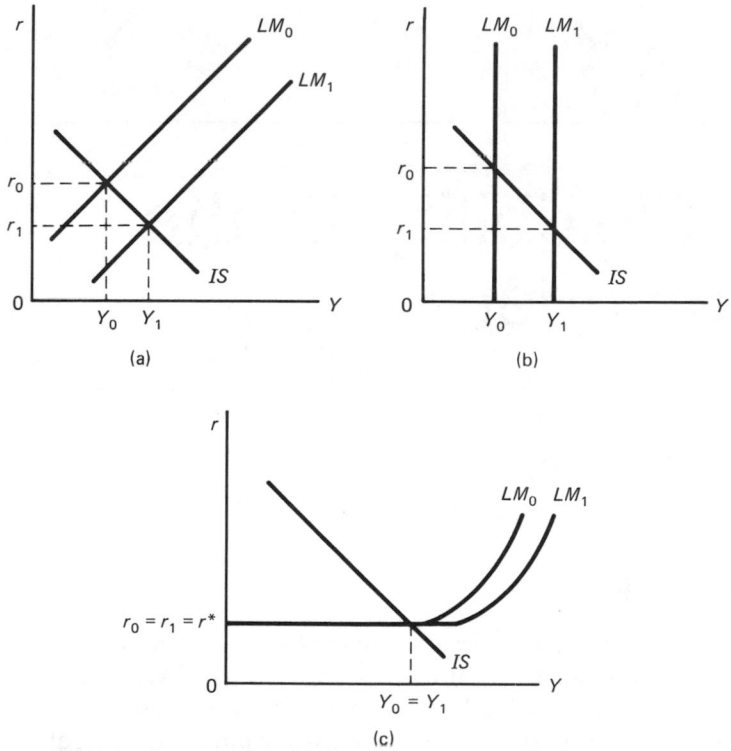

Figure 2.13 The effects of shifting *LM* curves of different forms.

operating in the region of the *LM* curve where the rate of interest is down at r^*, shifts in the curve alter neither the rate of interest nor the level of income, implying that in such circumstances changes in the quantity of money have no discernible effects on any of the variables that interest us. These last two results may be restated in terms of the simple principles of supply and demand analysis developed in the previous chapter. The first of them amounts to saying that if we remove the interest rate as a determinant of the demand for money and hold the price level constant, then real income is the only variable left to adjust when it becomes necessary to adapt the quantity of money demanded to a change in its supply. The second of them simply confirms that if at a particular level of the interest rate people are willing to hold an indefinitely large quantity of money, then, when the quantity of money supplied increases, there is no need for any variable to adjust in order to get it willingly held.

chapter 3

Price Flexibility in the Macromodel

INTRODUCTORY COMMENTS

Our analysis so far has enabled us to begin to show why the demand-for-money function is an important relationship. It has also enabled us to say something about specific aspects of the relationship, notably those involving the rate of interest, which might be worth particularly close investigation. However, all of our results have come from a model in which the price level is held constant; and not only is the price level an important endogenous, and far from constant, variable in the real world, but it is also, as we have already asserted, an important determinant of the demand for money. By treating this variable as an exogenous constant, we have considerably simplified our analysis of the interaction of the supply and demand for money, but there can be no guarantee that in simplifying our analysis we have not also rendered it misleading. The only way to assuage our doubts about this issue is to relax our assumption of a constant price level, and to see how this step changes the nature of our model.

NOMINAL MONEY AND REAL MONEY

If we are to deal with a flexible price level, it is important first of all to distinguish between *nominal money,* measured in units of current purchasing power, and *real money,* measured in units of constant purchasing power. As we shall show later, economic theory leads to the prediction that the demand for *nominal* money is proportional to the price level; and this in turn means that the demand for *real* money is independent of the price level, varying only with real income and the interest rate. A glance back at Figures 2.3, 2.5, and 2.10 will confirm that our analysis of the interaction of the supply and demand for money does in fact deal with money measured in real terms. When the price level is held constant, any change in the supply of nominal money is also a change in the quantity of real money, and so this just-mentioned property of our analysis did not need to be stressed earlier. It does now, because the supply of money the monetary authorities can control in any actual economy is the *nominal* supply. Given the *nominal* money supply, what the *real* quantity of money will be depends on the *price level.* For a given nominal quantity of money, the lower the price level, the proportionately higher will be the quantity of real money and vice versa. The effects on our *IS-LM* model of decreasing (increasing) the price level by a given proportional amount while holding the quantity of nominal money constant are identical to those of increasing (decreasing) the quantity of nominal money by an equal proportion while holding the price level constant. This must be the case because, as we have already seen, the variable measured on the horizontal axis of our demand for money diagram (e.g., Figure 2.3) is M/P, nominal money divided by the price level or, equivalently, real money.

THE "AGGREGATE DEMAND" CURVE

Our *IS-LM* model is capable of yielding implications about the interactions of the price level and the level of real income. For a given *IS* curve (with all that the phrase implies about the constancy of government expenditures and taxes, not to mention stability of the consumption and investment functions), and a given nominal money supply, Ms_0, and a given price level P_0, we have in Figure 3.1(a) an equilibrium level of real income Y_0. If the price level were to fall successively from P_0 to P_1 to P_2, the *LM* curve would shift rightward from LM_0 to LM_1 to LM_2 and the level of real income would increase from Y_0 to Y_1 to Y_2. In a manner exactly analogous to that in which we constructed our original *IS* and *LM* curves (see Figures 2.2 and 2.3, respectively) we plot in Figure 3.1(b) all pairs of real income and price level values generated in this manner in order to create what is usually called an *aggregate demand curve.*

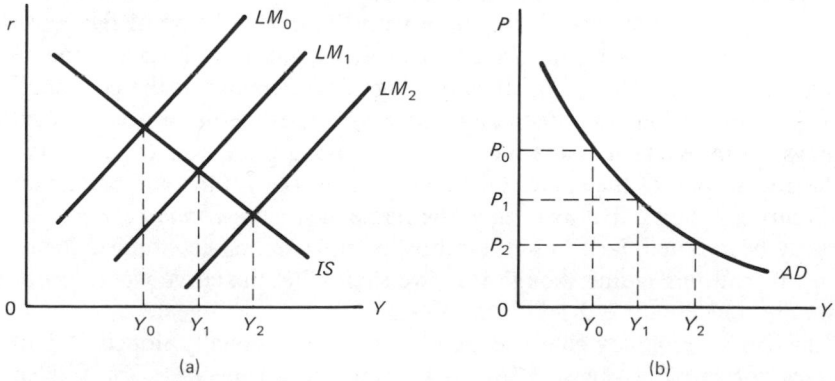

Figure 3.1 (a) For a given level of the nominal money supply M_{s0}, the lower the price level, the further to the right does the *LM* curve lie and the higher is the equilibrium level of income. LM_0, LM_1, and LM_2 are associated with successively lower price levels P_0, P_1, and P_2. (b) The curve *AD* ("aggregate demand") makes explicit the relationship between the price level and the level of real income implicit in panel (a).

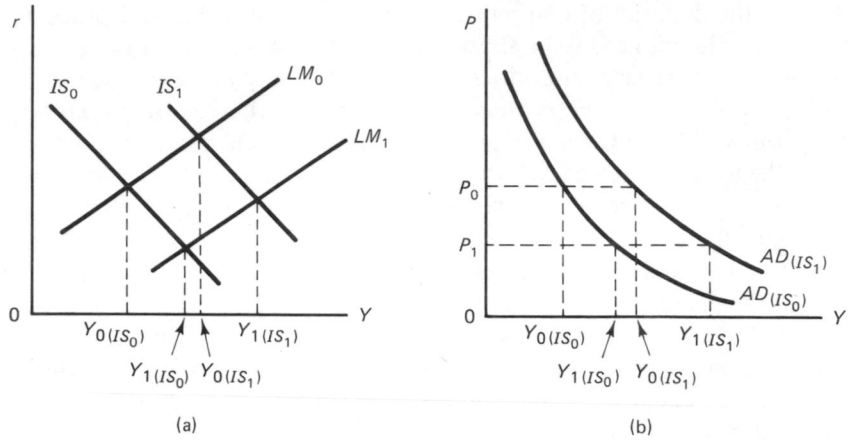

Figure 3.2 (a) The two *LM* curves LM_0 and LM_1 are drawn on the assumption that the nominal quantity of money is constant, but the price level P_0 underlying the former is higher than P_1 underlying the latter. The further to the right is the *IS* curve, the higher is the equilibrium level of income associated with a given *LM* curve. (b) The relationships between real income and the price level implicit in panel (a) are here made explicit. As the *IS* curve is shifted to the right, a higher level of income is associated with any given price level, so the curve *AD* also shifts to the right.

Although too commonly used by economists to be changed now, this name is nevertheless utterly misleading. To begin with, the curve labeled *AD* in Figure 3.1(b) is not a behavior relationship of the type we called a demand curve when carrying out the analysis embodied in Figures 1.1–1.3 above. Rather it is a locus line which shows the interaction of a number of behavior relationships as they determine (on certain assumptions about what is to be held constant, which we have already specified) those combinations of real income and price level that are compatible with equilibrium in our *IS-LM* system. Second, and more subtly, it is not even the case that the relationships embodied in that *IS-LM* system deal only with the demand side of the economy. Recall that in deriving the *IS* curve, which underlies the curve labeled *AD,* we assumed that at every point on it, aggregate demand in the economy, the sum of consumption, investment, and government expenditure was satisfied by aggregate supply. That is the meaning of deriving points on the *IS* curve from the intersection of the curves labeled $C + I + G$ with the 45° line as we did in Figure 2.2. Be all that as it may, the name *aggregate demand curve* is, as has already been noted, far too well established now among economists for us to change it, and misleading though it is, we shall label the curve whose properties we are now about to discuss *AD.*

Consider an economy characterized by the conventionally sloped *IS* and *LM* curves portrayed in Figure 3.1(a). It is clear that, in this case, for a given *LM* curve, anything that shifts the *IS* curve to the right (left) will increase (decrease) the level of income compatible with equilibrium in this economy. It will therefore shift the *AD* curve to the right (left). Also, an increase (decrease) in the nominal money supply requires a proportionally higher (lower) price

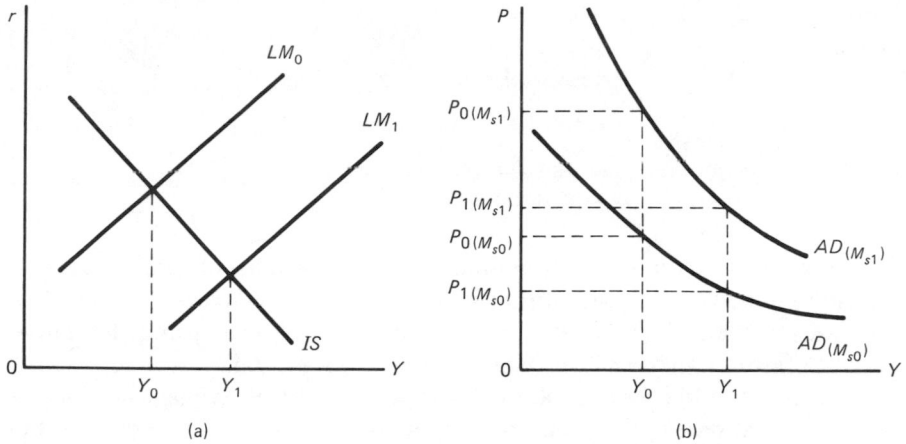

Figure 3.3 (a) The curve LM_0 is drawn first on the assumption that the money supply is M_{s0} and the price level $P_{0(M_{s0})}$ and the curve LM_1 on the assumption that the money supply is M_{s0} but the price level is at a lower level $P_{1(M_{s0})}$. For a given *IS* curve, the *AD* curve implied by these *LM* curves is drawn as $AD_{(M_{s0})}$ in panel (b). Now suppose that the nominal money supply is at some higher level M_{s1}. There is a price level $P_{0(M_{s1})}$ which exceeds $P_{0(M_{s0})}$ by the same proportion in which M_{s1} exceeds M_{s0}, and if it rules, LM_0 is the relevant *LM* curve. Thus, with this new quantity of money, Y_0 is still the equilibrium level of real income when this new higher price level rules. An exactly parallel argument holds with respect to *LM* curve LM_1. (b) The relationships between prices and real income implicit in panel (a) is here made explicit. Specifically, at each level of real income the equilibrium price level is proportionately higher the higher is the nominal money supply.

level in order to maintain a given equilibrium level of real income. Hence, an increase (decrease) in the nominal money supply shifts the *AD* curve upward (downward) by a proportional amount. These matters are illustrated in Figures 3.2(a) and (b) and 3.3(a) and (b), respectively. (*Note:* The reader's attention is explicitly drawn to the fact that the seemingly arbitrary distinction between rightward and upward shifts implicit here is not in fact arbitrary, for reasons that will soon be apparent).

Earlier we discussed how the properties of the *IS-LM* system are affected by special assumptions concerning the sensitivity of the demand for money to the rate of interest, and it should not surprise anyone to learn that these assumptions also have implications for the *AD* curve. First, if the demand for money is independent of the rate of interest, we have seen that shifts in the *IS* curve do not change the level of real income; nor do such shifts move the *AD* curve whose location in this case is determined solely by the interaction of the supply and demand for money. Second, if, in addition to being independent of the rate of interest, the demand for real balances is proportional to real income,

$$\frac{M_d}{P} = kY \tag{3.1}$$

then a simple rearrangement of this expression, combined with the requirement that the supply and demand for money be equal to one another yields us

$$\overline{M}_s = M_d = kPY \tag{3.2}$$

so that

$$PY = \frac{1}{k}\overline{M}_s \tag{3.3}$$

The term PY, however, is simply another name for the value of national income measured in units of current purchasing power, or *nominal income.* In this case nominal income is determined solely by the supply of money and the curve may be drawn as a rectangular hyperbola, as in Figure 3.4.

If we make the polar opposite assumption about the demand-for-money rate of interest relationship, namely that, at some low but positive level of the latter variable it becomes one of perfect elasticity, then the aggregate demand curve is downward sloping at "high" values of the price level, which correspond, for a given nominal money supply, to "low" quantities of real money, but becomes vertical at that level of real income (call it Y^*) corresponding to the sum of consumption, investment, and government expenditure generated at r^*, the value of the interest rate at which the demand for money becomes perfectly interest-elastic. Such an AD curve is shown in Figure 3.5. Y^*, along with the whole AD curve, may be shifted rightward by any factor that shifts the underlying IS curve to the right, but it cannot be moved by a change in the nominal money supply, which will only affect the AD curve at levels of income below Y^*, shifting it, as I have already remarked above, upward.[1]

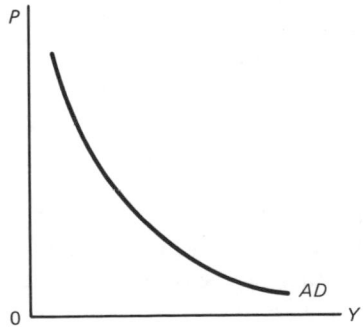

Figure 3.4 The *AD* curve is a rectangular hyperbola if the demand for real money balances is independent of the rate of interest and proportional to real income. Because, in this case, shifts of the *IS* curve do not change real income, they do not shift the *AD* curve. Shifts in the nominal money supply do shift the *AD* curve up in proportion, and because it is a property of the rectangular hyperbola that the product of the variable measured on the vertical axis and that on the horizontal is a constant, this implies that money income varies in proportion to the nominal money supply.

[1] The reader who is unsure of the relationship between the *IS-LM* apparatus and the *AD* curve will find it instructive to derive these results explicitly.

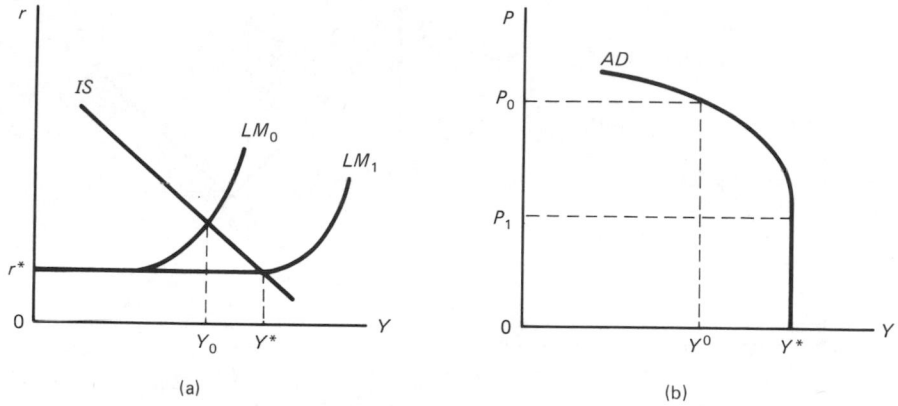

Figure 3.5 (a) With a given quantity of nominal money, the lower the price level, the further to the right does the *LM* curve lie, but with a liquidity trap at r^* the level of income cannot exceed Y^*. Thus, as the price level falls from P_0 to P_1, the level of income increases from Y_0 to Y^* but only to this latter level. (b) The relationship between the price level and real income for a given nominal quantity of money implicit in panel (a) is here made explicit. At Y^* the *AD* curve becomes vertical.

THE LONG-RUN "AGGREGATE SUPPLY" CURVE

By itself, an *AD* curve, no matter what its precise form, does not enable us to say anything about the consequences for real income and the price level of changes in the supply of money. To close the system, we need a complementary relationship, an (equally misleadingly named) *aggregate supply curve,* and it will suffice at this point to consider the so-called classical, or long-run, version of this curve. Consider an economy in which the stock of capital is constant, or at least growing so slowly that it may be treated as if constant. In this economy output will vary with labor input. With capital being constant, the relationship will display diminishing returns to labor, as is shown in Figure 3.6(a). Suppose now that perfect competition reigns throughout this economy. In that case the demand curve for labor will be given by its marginal product being equated to the real wage, and the supply of labor will also depend on the real wage. The real wage and labor input will be determined, as in Figure 3.6(b), by the intersection of these supply-and-demand curves for labor, and output may be read off the total-product-of-labor curve in Figure 3.6(a).[2]

Because the level of output in question is independent of the price level, it may be represented in the price level output space in which the curve *AD* has been drawn as the vertical line *AS*. As has been remarked already, this label is rather misleading. In order for the marginal-product-of-labor curve to be the demand curve for labor, we need to assume perfect competition, and a perfectly competitive economy is one in which, among other things, each firm can sell as much of its output as it chooses at the going price. Thus, the curve *AS* in Figure

[2] The reader who is unsure about the relationships between total product, marginal product, and the demand for a factor of production should consult an intermediate microeconomics book on these issues. See, for example, Laidler (1981, Chapter 15).

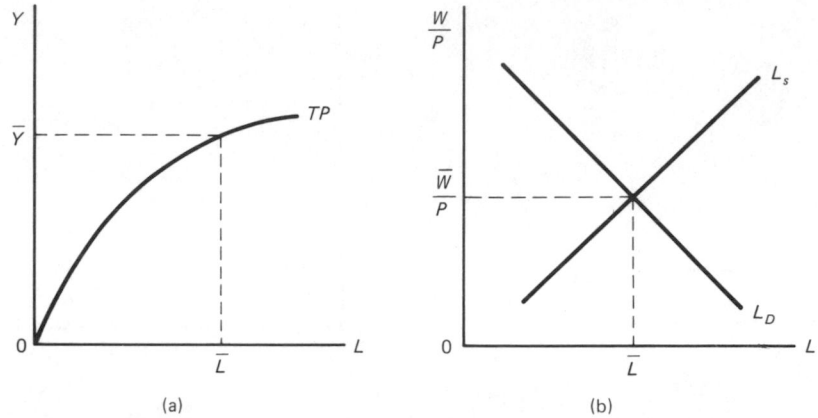

Figure 3.6 (a) *TP* is the total product curve of labor, drawn on the assumption that the capital stock is fixed. (b) L_D is the demand for labor as a function of the real wage and is the marginal product curve corresponding to the total product curve displayed in panel (a). L_s is a supply curve of labor. On the assumption of complete money wage and price flexibility, the supply and demand for labor determine equilibrium in the labor market at $(\bar{W}/P)\bar{L}$. With employment given at $\bar{L}$ we may read the equilibrium level of output $\bar{Y}$ off the vertical axis of panel (a).

3.7 is derived on the assumption that the level of aggregate demand for output in the economy is such as to enable sellers' plans to be satisfied.

Be that as it may, in Figure 3.7 the curves *AD* and *AS* are used to determine the levels of real income and prices. This vertical *AS* curve case is of particular interest to students of the demand for money because in it the level of real income in the economy is determined by factors that are quite independent of the demand supply of money. Moreover, if we carry out the experiment of changing the nominal money supply while holding all the factors underpinning both the *AS* curve and the *IS* curve constant, the reader will note that the requirement that, in equilibrium, the level of real income not change must also involve the rate of interest in remaining constant. The latter variable must take the value at which, given the consumption function and given the level of government expenditure, investment is just such as to ensure that the aggregate demand for goods and services equals the quantity produced. In this case, then,

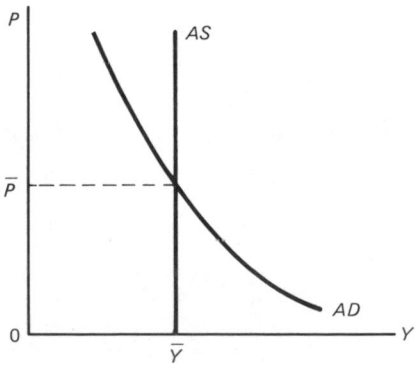

Figure 3.7 The determination of the equilibrium levels of real income and the price level by the interaction of the *AD* and *AS* curves. In the wage-price flexibility case, the curve *AS* is vertical at $\bar{Y}$ and the curve *AD* determines only the price level.

two of the three factors determining the demand for money are pinned down and only the general price level is free to move to restore equilibrium between the demand and supply of money; and so, regardless of the precise nature of the demand for money–real income relationship, or the demand for money–interest rate relationship (provided that this is not one of perfect elasticity) we may make an unambiguous prediction about the consequences of a change in the nominal money supply.[3] It will change the price level in equal proportion and will leave the values of all real variables, including the real quantity of money, unchanged. This case is known as that of *neutral money.*

No one regards the vertical *AS* curve case as relevant at all times and places, but it might not be unreasonable to think of it as describing, in a rough-and-ready way, the situation toward which an economy not continually subject to disturbances might converge over time. After all, so long as money wages and prices are to some degree flexible, and so long as market forces tend to push them down when the level of output is below that given by *AS,* which is, after all, the level of output determined by equilibrium in the labor market (of Figure 3.6), and up when aggregate demand in the economy exceeds that level, that is how the economy will move. Moveover, if we take a very long run view of an economy subject to continuous shocks, we might think of the type of equilibrium described in Figure 3.7 as characterizing the average value of output (and of other underlying real variables) about which the actual values of output and such will fluctuate over time. If we think in these terms, however, we must also remember that, with ongoing capital accumulation, and population growth, the curve *AS* will move to the right with the passage of time.

AGGREGATE SUPPLY IN THE SHORT RUN

Over "short" periods, of course, where *short* may nevertheless describe several calendar quarters, or even a few years, output as well as the general price level responds to shifts in aggregate demand, because money wages and prices are not, for one reason or another, flexible enough to keep the labor market in equilibrium and hence the economy on a long-run *AS* curve at each and every moment. There is much debate among economists as to why this is the case and what its consequences are for the behavior of output, employment, and prices over time as the economy responds to shocks. At one time it was thought that a mechanism such as we shall now describe was sufficient to capture the forces at work here, but it is now universally agreed that it deals with only part of the story at best. Nevertheless, the mechanism is worth a little attention.

Suppose we were to begin with an economy in full equilibrium on a long-run *AS* curve such as we have portrayed in Figure 3.7, and then suppose that

[3] Of course we here rule out the case in which, because of a liquidity trap, the *AD* curve becomes vertical at a level of output lower than that determined by the *AS* curve. In this case there would be no equilibrium in the macroeconomic system we are describing and prices would fall forever. Only if the *IS* curve was subject to a "wealth effect"—see Appendix A—would falling prices shift the *AD* curve to the right and eventually produce an equilibrium between *AS* and *AD.* Whether or not such a case is more than an analytical curiosity depends on whether or not the liquidity trap notion has any empirical content.

some factor, a cut in the nominal money supply, say, or a shift of the investment function, were to cause the *AD* curve to shift downward and to the left, as we show in Figure 3.8. Then suppose it were plausible to argue that initially prices remained at their historically given value of $\overline{P}_0$. If they did, we would in effect be dealing with the fixed-price version of our macromodel, which we described in detail in the previous chapter. In that model, of course, with prices fixed, output changes to maintain the system in equilibrium when factors influencing aggregate demand change. We may capture this idea in Figure 3.8 by drawing what we may call a "short-run" aggregate supply curve *as* in the form of a horizontal line at the initial equilibrium level of price $\overline{P}_0$. The initial response of the economy to our posited shift in aggregate demand is then for output to fall from $\overline{Y}$ to Y_1, with the price level remaining constant. However, as time passes, provided that there is some degree of price flexibility in the system, the price level will begin to fall. As it does, the price level and output will move back along the new *AD* curve (as the *LM* curve underlying it shifts to the right) until output returns to $\overline{Y}$ at a new lower long-run equilibrium price level $\overline{P}_1$.

The problem with the foregoing analysis is that it is just too simple and mechanical. Why should prices initially remain constant in the face of an exogenous shock? If the shock in question arises totally unexpectedly, and its effects on the economy are not discerned until after it has begun to cause output to shift, this assumption might be defensible, and there are surely shocks in the real world that fit this description. However, if the shift of the *AD* curve was the result of some kind of policy change, the change in question might well have been debated and preannounced. In that case one might expect that some economic agents at least would be prepared to meet it with price changes as soon as it occurred rather than waiting for output to change. Then the economy's initial response would involve a mixture of output and price responses. The implication of an argument such as this is that it is unlikely that one can generalize in any way about the economy's short-run response to shifts

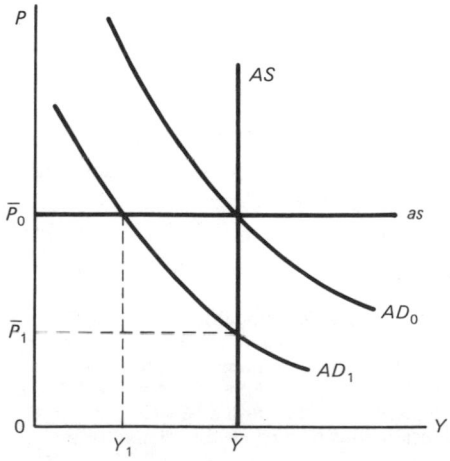

Figure 3.8 If prices are rigid in the short run, then the economy will respond to a shift of the *AD* curve from AD_0 to AD_1 by moving along the short-run horizontal *as* curve till output falls to Y_1. Subsequently, as the price level falls, the economy will move toward a new long-run equilibrium at $\overline{P}_1$ and the original level of output.

of *AD*. That response will depend on the source of the shift, the extent to which it is expected to occur, and the extent to which agents in the economy are free to respond to it by altering prices. Thus, the horizontal short-run *as* curve is at best a special case, sometimes relevant and sometimes not.

The same kind of considerations as these, which Lucas (1973, 1976) has stressed in his work, apply to our simple analysis of the time path that prices and output take after initial shock. Why should the price level fall smoothly until the new long-run equilibrium is reached? Might not the very fact of falling prices set up expectations of further price falls, which will in turn cause the rate of price fall to speed up? After a shift in *AD,* the economy is very obviously not at its old equilibrium: might agents not devote some time and trouble to investigating the source of the shock in order better to design their response to it, and will this not affect the subsequent time path of prices and output? In addition to all of this, is it not very artificial to assume that the economy is in equilibrium at full employment and at a given price level when the curve *AD* shifts? Suppose, instead, that the economy was in the midst of an ongoing inflation? How would it then respond to a fall in investment? Perhaps, instead of prices falling in absolute terms, their rate of increase would simply slow down relative to past trends.

To discuss the hows and whys of these matters any further would take us deeply into the subject matter of contemporary macroeconomic debates. Some of the issues involved in those debates will turn up later in this book, but there is simply not space here to treat them in any detail. This is a book about the demand for money, not a general treatise on macroeconomic theory, and for our present purposes the last few paragraphs yield all the lessons we require.[4] To begin with, we have seen that it is only in the long-run that we need consider nothing but the relationship between the demand for money and the price level when we try to deduce conclusions about the effects of changes in the supply of money on the economy. So long as there is any degree of price level stickiness in the economy in the short-run, factors that cause the *AD* curve to shift, not the least any changes in the money supply, will have consequences for real income and interest rates as well as the price level—or indeed instead of the price level in the extreme case of short-run price rigidity. Thus, in general we need to know about all aspects of the demand-for-money function if we are going to be able even to begin to understand the way in which the macroeconomy responds to money supply changes and such, and the simple fixed price level model set out in the preceding chapter yields important, if incomplete, insights into what is and is not of particular relevance here.

Equally important is the negative lesson that emerges from the foregoing discussion. Knowledge of the nature of the demand-for-money function is necessary for understanding the way in which the macroeconomy responds to changes in exogenous factors, not the least the supply of money, but it is not

[4] The reader who wishes to follow up these issues would do well to consult a modern macroeconomics text such as Parkin and Bade (1984) or Barro (1984). I have given my own account of the matters at issue here, albeit at a rather more advanced level in Laidler (1982, Chapter 3 and 4).

sufficient. As we have argued, the time path which the price level and real income are likely to trace out in response to any factor shifting the *AD* curve is going to depend on the state of the economy when the shock occurs, the extent to which its occurrence comes as a surprise to economic agents, not to mention the speed with which they are able to learn more about it and respond to that new knowledge after the shock has taken place. None of these matters has very much to do with the demand-for-money function, but they will nevertheless influence the way in which the arguments of that function interact over time in response to exogenous shocks: the only general conclusion we can draw from the above discussion is that the interaction in question is very likely to differ from time to time and from place to place.

QUESTIONS ABOUT THE DEMAND FOR MONEY

We are now in a position to pull together the main conclusions that may be drawn from the analysis set out in this and the preceding chapter. Let it be emphasized, though, that the conclusions in question are tentative, and that not all of them will emerge unaltered from the closer study of the theories and empirical evidence on the demand for money to which the rest of this book is devoted. One conclusion that will not change is that the significance of the demand for money stems from the fact that the variables that seem to determine it are important in their own right. The behavior of real income, interest rates, the general price level (and other factors we shall discuss later) have a vital bearing on the economic well-being of any community. Because, in the case of money, as with anything else, one or more of the variables affecting demand must change to accommodate variations in supply, the nature of the demand-for-money function is of particular interest if we wish to understand the impacts of monetary policy on the economy.

We cannot get answers to all the questions we might want to ask by looking at the demand-for-money function alone. For example, in an earlier section of this chapter we have seen that, if wages and prices are sufficiently flexible to keep the economy in equilibrium at full employment, then the effects of variations in the money supply will be concentrated on the general price level. The relevance of this result obviously turns upon characteristics of the labor market, rather than of the demand-for-money function. It does, nevertheless, suggest that knowledge of the demand-for-money function is likely to be of particular importance to anyone wishing to understand the phenomenon of *inflation,* and particularly inflation which persists for a sufficiently long period for the assumption that other factors affecting the demand for money are independent of the behavior of the supply of money to be sustainable (at least in a rough-and-ready way.) In this context, then, our analysis suggests that we should ask questions about the theoretical basis, and empirical support, for the proposition that the demand for nominal money is proportional to the general price level. We should also query the tentative suggestion that, with price and wage flexibility, all factors affecting the demand for real money are indeed determined independently of the supply of nominal money. When we do so, we shall discover that this is one instance in which our simple analysis is a little too simple.[5]

The long-run behavior of the price level is only one area for which knowledge of the demand-for-money function is particularly important. We have asserted in the preceding section of this chapter that over short periods wages and prices are sufficiently sticky that the fixed-price *IS-LM* model developed earlier is of some relevance to understanding the effects, not only of money supply changes, but also of factors shifting the *IS* curve, such as fiscal policy and fluctuations in private-sector investment. In this context the role of the rate of interest in the demand-for-money function has turned out to be of particular importance. If the demand for money is very sensitive to changes in the interest rate, then very small changes—in the limit zero—in its value are sufficient to absorb changes in the supply of money. In this case money supply changes will have little effect on real income, but real income will be particularly sensitive to disturbances emanating from the markets for goods and services as opposed to those for assets. If, on the other hand, the demand for money is insensitive to the rate of interest, we get an exactly contrary set of conclusions. Clearly, then, the theory underlying the demand for money rate of interest relationship, and empirical evidence relevant to it, are worth a good deal of attention. They will get that attention in the pages that follow.

Quite apart from the above specific issues, and we have only highlighted one or two particularly important items in the last few paragraphs, we must consider the general question of the stability over time of the demand-for-money function. All the conclusions we have derived in this chapter are based on, among other premises, the assumption that the relationship between the demand for money and the factors affecting it does not shift around unpredictably. If it does shift unpredictably, we lose our ability to derive results about the consequences of changes in the quantity of money for the variables that concern us, and we must also face the possibility that shifts in the demand-for-money function themselves are an independent source of disturbance to the macroeconomy. The theoretical reasons why we ought (or ought not) to expect the demand-for-money function to remain stable over time are therefore obviously worth attention, as is the empirical evidence on the extent to which it does or does not, in fact, remain stable. As we shall see, one of the questions we shall have to consider here is whether any shifts in the function that might be observed are the result of genuinely random and hence unpredictable factors, or rather are the result of changes in some variable or variables we ought to have included in the function but, through faulty theorizing, we omitted.

The foregoing discussion by no means exhausts the list of problems with which the rest of this book deals, but it does indicate some of the key issues that arise in analyzing the role of the demand-for-money function in a macroeconomic context, and some of the reasons why economists regard understand-

[5] As we shall discover below, the analysis underlying the relationship between the demand for money and the rate of interest also has important implications for the way in which the demand for money interacts with the inflation rate in an economy where prices are rising systematically over time.

ing the demand-for-money function to be well worth the effort. Let us now turn to a discussion of various theories about the demand for money which yield competing hypotheses about the nature of the function, leaving until Part IV the assessment of the available empirical evidence on these matters.

APPENDIX A: The Wealth Effect

As noted in Chapter 3 (p. 29, footnote 3), the wealth effect is a mechanism whereby changes in the price level shift the *IS* curve. They influence the level of aggregate demand directly, rather than by way of their effect on interest rates. The basic hypothesis about behavior underlying the mechanism is that consumption, in addition to depending on income, also depends on the real value of the stock of assets held in the economy. The greater the stock of wealth, the higher consumption. If the stock of wealth varies inversely with the price level, so will consumption.

The wealth-effect mechanism was first introduced into macroeconomics as a means of showing that, if prices are flexible downward, even when the minimum interest rate permitted by a horizontal *LM* curve is above that required for full-employment aggregate demand as given on the *IS* curve, the economy will still reach full-employment equilibrium eventually; the wealth effect will keep the *IS* curve, and hence the *AD* curve, shifting to the right so long as prices fall, and prices will fall until full employment is reached. Since its introduction in connection with this particular problem, the wealth-effect mechanism has attracted much analytic attention, and several elegant, not to mention illuminating, models of both micro- and macroeconomic behavior have been built around it, particularly by Patinkin (1965).

For the wealth effect to operate, it is necessary that the stock of real wealth vary with the price level. The real value of equity capital is clearly independent of the price level, since it is a physical stock of goods. Moreover, though individuals may issue to one another bonds denominated in units of current purchasing power, bonds whose real value changes when the price level changes, these make no difference to the overall position in the economy, since the wealth of debtors and creditors moves equally and oppositely when the price level changes. So long as there are no effects of changes in the distribution of wealth, privately issued bonds are irrelevant so far as the wealth effect is concerned. Its operation seems to require that some of the economy's assets, denominated in nominal terms, be the debt of no one in the economy. If such assets exist, a rise in the price level will make their holders worse off without making anyone else correspondingly better off by diminishing his real indebtedness. A fall in the price level will make their owners better off at the expense of no one.

It is sometimes argued that government debt, including that part of the money supply that represents the liability of the government rather than of a privately owned banking system, represents such an asset since it is owned by the private sector of the economy yet represents the debt of no one in the private sector. If we accept this argument for the moment, it will be clear that a fall in the price level will involve a rise in the real value of the government debt, a consequent rise in the value of the overall level of wealth in the economy, hence a rise in the level of consumption expenditure.

However, it is generally agreed that it is too simple to treat the full value of interest-bearing government debt as net wealth to the private sector of the economy. Interest payments on such debt have to be met by taxes levied on the private sector. If people in the private sector realize this, an increase in the real value of government debt outstanding will also involve an increase in the present value of future tax liabilities and some economists, for example Barro (1974), have argued on the basis of this insight that government debt is not to any extent net wealth to the private sector. However, there is some reason to argue that the two influences in question will not completely cancel each other out. Government securities are easily marketable assets which, moreover, can be bequeathed to one's heirs. Tax liabilities are not bequeathed specifically to one's heirs. Also, to the extent that taxes are levied on labor income—which can be regarded as a return to a nonmarketable asset called human capital—the effect of increasing the real value of government debt outstanding, and financing the increased interest payments out of taxes, is to convert some of the return to a nonmarketable asset into a return on a marketable security. If marketability enhances the value of an asset, an increase in the real value of government debt outstanding represents some increase in the community's wealth, although not by the full amount of the increase in the value of the debt.

Non-interest-bearing government debt, however, can be treated as net wealth in its full amount. This is because an increase in the real value of such debt outstanding carries with it no corresponding increase in tax liabilities. The same is true, however, of non-interest-bearing private debt, not just of public debt. Suppose a private bank holds interest-bearing securities denominated in units of current purchasing power as its assets, but that its corresponding liabilities are non-interest-bearing demand deposits. In this case a fall in the price level will increase the real value of the bank's interest income but leave the real value of its interest payments constant at zero. A fall in the price level thus enhances the profitability of the bank, hence the wealth of its owners, while the rise in the wealth of its depositors is just offset by the fall in the wealth of the bank's debtors. If instead of nominal assets the bank held equity, we would find an increase in wealth accruing to its depositors, no change in the real value of the bank's assets, and hence no change in the real liabilities of its debtors. Once more there would be an increase in the community's net wealth, but this time accruing to the bank's customers rather than to its owners.

The foregoing analysis stems from the debate that followed the publication of Pesek and Saving (1967) and draws in particular on Johnson (1969) and Laidler (1969). If it is correct, and the matter is ultimately an empirical one, it is appropriate to treat non-interest-bearing money and perhaps some, in the present state of knowledge unspecified, proportion of interest-bearing government debt as net wealth to the private sector of the economy. Hence there is certainly some interdependence between the behavior of the price level and the *IS* curve, which is not captured by the analysis set out in Chapters 2 and 3. For some macroeconomic issues—such as those dealt with by Patinkin and alluded to above—this is an important matter; but for our purposes, which involve assessing the significance of alternative formulations of the demand-for-money function for the behavior of the economy, the extra analytic simplicity gained by ignoring the wealth effect seems well worth the associated sacrifice of analytic precision.

two

THEORIES OF THE DEMAND FOR MONEY

chapter 4

A Brief Overview

METHODOLOGICAL CONSIDERATIONS

The statement that the demand for money measured in real terms depends on the level of real national income and the rate of interest is a particular hypothesis about the nature of the demand function for money. The issues raised in the final section of Chapter 3 amount to asking how good a hypothesis it is. At first sight this is a question to be answered by immediate reference to empirical evidence, for it seems reasonable to suppose that one could ask how much of the variation in the quantity of money demanded in any particular economy can be explained by variations in these variables. This can, of course, be done, but before embarking upon such an empirical study one should ask in advance what conclusions could be drawn from its results.

If it were to turn out that all the variations in the demand for money could be explained by the variables in question, it might be concluded that the theory was a perfect one. At the other extreme, if these variables turned out to explain nothing at all, the theory might be judged perfectly useless.[1] Neither of these outcomes is very likely; more probably the theory will turn out to explain 50% or 90% of the variation in the demand for money, and whether a theory that can explain 90% of the variation in the demand for money is good or bad is not a question that can be sensibly answered. It all depends on how one defines *good* and *bad.* Provided there is no difference between them in terms of scope, logical simplicity, or consistency with other economic models and such, one can say that a theory that explains 90% of the variation in the demand for money is *better* than one that explains 50%. If there are several alternative

[1] But "all the variation" implies that one has all the relevant evidence. Since such evidence is continually being generated, one never has all of it, and the notion of a theory being completely verified by the evidence is totally irrelevant to scientific procedure. Even if a theory is found that explains all available evidence perfectly, there is always the possibility that new evidence, incompatible with the theory in question, may turn up.

theories involved, one can pick the best of them on the basis of a criterion such as this, for so long as it also satisfies the other criteria mentioned above, a theory is "good" if it passes empirical tests better than some other theory and "bad" if it fails to do so. In short, to learn about economic theory by referring to empirical evidence, we need not one but several hypotheses that can be put to the test simultaneously. Only in this way can useful theoretical ideas be sorted out from those that are misleading.

The lesson here for the problem of the demand for money is that it is not possible to learn much about the empirical relevance of the proposition that the demand for real money depends stably and predictably on the level of real income and the rate of interest until the predictions that follow from this proposition are compared with those that follow from other, different, hypotheses about the variables on which the demand for money depends. As we shall see in the next few chapters, there is no shortage of alternative theories and, as we shall also see, most of what we know about the empirical nature of the demand-for-money function has been learned from tests that sought to compare the performance of such competing hypotheses. It is useful, then, to go over the various theories in some detail before considering any empirical evidence.

ALTERNATIVE THEORETICAL APPROACHES

It may strike the reader as strange that one should talk about the theory of the demand for money at all. This is not the economist's usual approach to such problems. Textbooks of microeconomics do not contain chapters with titles like "The Theory of the Demand for Refrigerators," but rather present a generalized analytic framework in terms of which the demand for any good can be treated. Though there is now a substantial body of literature that deals with the demand for money as merely a special case of the general theory of demand, it was only in the 1950s that this approach received a clear and influential statement.[2] Before then, and even now to a great extent, the demand for money was usually treated as a case apart, needing separate analysis, and persuasive reasons for doing this are not hard to find. The usual approach to demand theory is to postulate that an individual consumer receives satisfaction from the consumption of various goods, and that it is from this satisfaction, usually called *utility,* that his market demand for goods and services derives. In the case of durable goods there is an intermediate step, for the demand for a *stock* of durable goods is derived from the utility the consumer receives from the *flow* of services they provide. Usually, the nature of the utility function involved is dismissed as the business of psychology, and apart from some very general assumption about its nature involving the principle of the diminishing marginal rate of substitution between goods in consumption, it is not investigated by economists.

Now, money does not seem to fit very well into this framework. It is not physically consumed, nor does it, like other consumer durable goods, seem to

[2] Though the potential of this method was clearly identified by Hicks as long ago as 1935.

yield a flow of services that give psychological satisfaction to an individual. It does not keep food fresh as does a refrigerator, or provide entertainment as does a television set. Stocks and bonds are in the same category, but they yield their owners a cash income that may be spent on consumption goods, and money does not always do this. In some economies interest income is to be had from some assets also used as money, but the desire to hold cash cannot be explained by this fact. There are many instances of money yielding no interest and being held nevertheless. It may look, then, as if utility theory cannot be used as a direct explanation as to why money is held, so that the demand for it must be treated as a special case. Two peculiar and interrelated characteristics of money are usually emphasized in theories that set it apart from other goods. The first is that money is acceptable as a means of exchange for goods and services, and the second is that its market value is, if not always stable, then at least generally highly predictable, over short time periods at least.

These two characteristics are usually collectively called *liquidity* and are not the exclusive property of money. Other assets also possess them in varying degrees. In some cases it may be possible to convince the seller of a good to accept some other item in exchange for it; furthermore, the prices of some assets are quite predictable and fluctuate little. Thus, sellers of new automobiles are willing to accept used vehicles as trade-ins, and the existence of a well-developed used-car market makes the trade-in price of a particular vehicle at a particular time relatively easy to predict. However, unlike such assets as used cars, money is *universally* acceptable as a means of exchange, and its value in terms of goods in general is usually more predictable than that of other assets. Money is the most liquid of assets, and it is argued that there are two reasons why this leads to its being demanded.

When transactions are undertaken, it is usually necessary to have money on hand with which to make payments, but this fact alone is not a sufficient explanation of why money is held.[3] In a perfectly frictionless world, an individual would buy an income-earning asset the moment he received a payment, selling it again only the very moment he required money to make a payment on his own account. He would thus never hold money. However, the world is not frictionless; purchases and sales of assets take time and trouble and hence are not costless. Also, it is far from clear that an income-earning asset can be sold at any particular moment at the price for which it was bought. There is an element of uncertainty involved here, and, though gains are to be made by holding such assets, so are losses. Costs and losses alike can be avoided by bridging the gap between the receipt of payments and the making of expenditures by holding money rather than other assets.

Closely related to this argument is the consideration that no individual economic agent can be completely certain about when it is that he will be involved in acts of buying and selling goods and services. Thus, he can never be

[3] The requirement that payments be made in money at the time goods are purchased is an institutional arrangement sometimes referred to as a "cash in advance constraint." Such a constraint was introduced into modern monetary theory by Robert Clower (1967) and has been the basis of much theoretical work. I do not discuss this work further in this book, not because it is unimportant, but because it has yet to generate empirical studies.

quite sure that his current receipts will match his current planned expenditures at every moment. Again, this would not matter in a perfectly frictionless world but, where it is costly to exchange income-earning assets for money, it pays an individual to keep money on hand in order to acquire extra flexibility for his market activities. Because of the costs involved in buying and selling income-earning assets, because the price of such assets can be uncertain, because the timing of some market transactions is also uncertain, and because money is readily acceptable in any transaction, it comes to be held. Notions such as these form the basis of a great deal of theorizing about the demand for money.

In the last few paragraphs we have argued that money does indeed perform important services for its owners, even if such services are not of the kind that yield psychological satisfaction. Since, however, it has never proved necessary to investigate the nature of the psychological satisfaction that arises from the consumption of other goods in order to analyze the demand for them, it can well be argued that the psychological overtones with which utility theory is invested are irrelevant to it. Certain approaches to the theory of demand take this position. If one adopts such a view, the fact that the services of money are not psychological becomes irrelevant in applying utility theory to the problem of the demand for it. It becomes sufficient to postulate that money yields services to its owner, and then to analyze the determinants of the demand for money in the same way one would for any other good. Whether this is a sensible approach or not is better judged by the predictive power of the theory that emerges from it rather than by philosophical discussions of its underlying assumptions.

CONCLUDING COMMENT

Theories of the demand for money based on an application of the general theory of demand are not logically incompatible with the notion that the demand for money in fact arises from its usefulness in making transactions, or with the proposition that it is an excellent hedge against the risks inherent in holding other assets. Nor are the latter two approaches contradictory to one another. In principle they are complementary. However, theories that stress the importance of transactions lead us to emphasize the importance of variables in the demand-for-money function that differ from those indicated by theories that stress the uncertainty involved in holding other assets. An approach that deliberately avoids any analysis of motivation and simply applies generalized notions about the determination of the demand for any good to the demand for money leads to a yet different, but for obvious reasons less tightly specified, model.

These various models could be regarded as leading us toward one general theory of the demand for money, and Gilbert (1953) argued that all theories of the demand for money rest on considerations having to do with uncertainty and the passage of time; but it is methodologically convenient to treat them as alternatives and then to ask how much of the variation in the demand for money is to be explained solely by the factors that each particular hypothesis suggests are important. If it should be the case that no one set of variables dominates the demand-for-money function, one will find this out from the results of his experiments, but if one particular set of variables does dominate the scene, that will also be discovered from such a procedure, and information of this character would be of particular interest. The more one can explain with fewer variables, the simpler, and hence more manageable and easy to understand, will be the theory that emerges from such work. As a matter of method, then, rather than as a matter of strict logic, the theories presented in subsequent chapters are stated so that the differences rather than the similarities between them are emphasized. They are presented as alternatives and their complementary characteristics are downplayed. In this way, we make it easier to state clearly the issues that have been dealt with in recent empirical work.

chapter 5

The Classics, Keynes, and the Modern Quantity Theory

IRVING FISHER'S VERSION OF THE QUANTITY THEORY

One of the most complete, as well as influential, pieces of analysis based on the role of money as a means of exchange did not explicitly formulate the problem in the framework of a theory of demand, though, as we shall see, the results are readily transformed into such terms. Rather than the demand for money, the concept emphasized was the transactions velocity of circulation of money, the rate at which it passes from hand to hand. Irving Fisher, the economist most closely associated with this approach, built on ideas that had emerged from the nineteenth-century literature on monetary economics in his book *The Purchasing Power of Money* (1911).

Fisher's analysis begins with a simple identity. In every transaction there is both a buyer and a seller. Hence for the aggregate economy the value of sales must equal the value of receipts. Now the value of sales must be equal to the number of transactions conducted over any time period multiplied by the average price at which they take place. However, the value of purchases must be equal to the amount of money in circulation in the economy times the average number of times it changes hands over the same time period. Hence, where M_s is the quantity of money, V_T is the number of times it turns over, its transactions velocity of circulation, P is the price level, and T is the volume of transactions, one can write, as an identity

$$M_s V_T \equiv PT \tag{5.1}$$

Nothing follows from an identity except another identity, but it can be used as a classificatory device in the process of theory building; one can consider the four variables listed above and ask what it is that determines their values. In broad outline Fisher's answers were as follows. The quantity of money is determined independently of any of the three other variables and at any time can be taken as given. Moreover, T, the volume of transactions, can also be taken as given. In an economy that has its only long-run equilibrium at full-employment levels of income, and Fisher in company with nearly all his contemporaries held this view, it seems reasonable to assume that there is a certain fixed ratio of the volume of transactions to the level of output.[1] Fisher also treated V_T as independent of the other variables in the identity, and, although he did not regard it as being immutable over time, he did view it as taking a more or less constant equilibrium value over short time periods to which it rather quickly returned after any disturbance. Thus, the equilibrium value of the final variable P is determined by the interaction of the other three.

More specifically, if T and the equilibrium value of V_T are taken as constants, we arrive at the proposition that the equilibrium price level is determined solely by, and is proportional to, the quantity of money. These further assumptions permit us to translate our identity, the *equation of exchange,* into a version of the *quantity theory of money,* a theory of the determination of the price level, which can be written

$$\overline{M}_s\overline{V}_T = P\overline{T} \tag{5.2}$$

with the bars over V and T signifying that they are constants, and that over $\overline{M}$s signifying that it is an exogenous variable.

Though not stated as such by Fisher, the foregoing argument is equivalent to the following analysis cast in supply and demand terms. The demand for nominal money depends on the current value of the transactions to be conducted in the economy and is equal to a constant fraction of those transactions. Furthermore, the supply of nominal money is exogenously given, and in equilibrium the demand for money must be equal to its supply. This can be written

$$M_d = k_T P\overline{T} \tag{5.3}$$

$$M_d = \overline{M}_s \tag{5.4}$$

and these two equations combine to yield

$$M_s \frac{1}{k_T} = \overline{M}_s\overline{V}_T = P\overline{T} \tag{5.5}$$

where

$$\overline{V}_T \equiv \frac{1}{k_T} \tag{5.6}$$

Whether one puts this approach in terms of velocity or in terms of a demand function linking money balances to the volume of transactions in an economy, one still has to ask the question, what determines the equilibrium value of

[1] Though Fisher and his contemporaries did not use the analytic device explicitly, it is not misleading to think of them as analyzing an economy that was usually fluctuating around an equilibrium on the vertical AS curve discussed in Chapter 3 (p. 27–29).

velocity (or its inverse, the money/transactions ratio)? When it is argued that the demand for money stems from its use in the transactions-making process, it is but a short step to saying that the exact amount of money normally needed to carry out any given volume of transactions is determined by the nature of this process as it exists in any particular economy. There is an underlying analogy here with the analysis of a production process, the volume of transactions playing the role of the output and money that of an input.

Once the matter is posed this way, theorizing about the demand for money inevitably begins to concentrate on the nature of this production process. The institutional arrangements surrounding the settlement of accounts come in for study. To give one example, it appears that an economy in which the use of credit cards is widespread would require less money to carry on a given volume of business than one in which all payments must be made directly in cash. For similar reasons, the practices of businesses with regard to granting one another trade credit attracts attention. On another level, the quality of communications in an economy appears important. The fact that funds can be transmitted by telephone or telegraph should lead to a smaller requirement for money than there would be in an economy in which all messages must be sent by mail. One could list such examples as these almost without end, but enough has been said already to give the reader the flavor of this approach to the theory of the demand for money.

The important thing about this view, for our purposes, is that factors such as credit practices, communications, and so on, though they can certainly change over time, do not alter rapidly. Thus, if one thinks of them as being the principal determinants of the demand for money in an economy, it can be argued that over short time periods there is little scope for variation in the amount of money demanded relative to the volume of transactions being conducted. He would thus expect the equilibrium value of the velocity of circulation to be stable over such periods and, taking a longer view, would expect changes in velocity to be rather slow and drawn out, responding to slow institutional changes. Thus, as a good short-run approximation the equilibrium value of the transactions velocity of circulation is treated as a constant. Actual measured velocity might fluctuate around this value, but only in a random fashion as the monetary system is subjected to exogenous shocks, and not in a way that is systematically related to any endogenous variables in the system.

It is also tempting to look at the relationship between the volume of transactions and the level of national income in this way, depending as the former does on such matters as the number of stages goods go through between the raw material and the final-product stage, and the number of independent firms involved. Though vertical integration of industries can certainly take place and cut down on the volume of transactions associated with any given level of output, it is not likely to be a rapid process. Hence it can be ignored for the purposes of short-run analysis—or so it tends to be asserted in this approach to monetary theory. Similarly, the proportion of national income actually involved in market transactions can change over time as economic units become more and more specialized and hence interdependent, producing less and less for their own consumption and more and more for the market. Again, however, a change such as this is not likely to be a rapid one and can perhaps be ignored for short-run purposes. As we shall see in due course, however, such long-run changes in transactions of technology can be rather important to the understanding of the behavior of velocity over long time periods.[2]

This transactions approach to monetary theory, as far as short-run analysis is concerned, tends to lead to the hypothesis that the demand for money is a constant proportion of the level of transactions, which in turn bears a constant relationship to the level of national income. Moreover, the assumption that full employment is the only equilibrium for the economy is not an essential part of the theory. We can easily fit the above hypothesis about the demand for money into a general macroeconomic framework and ask what it implies. In terms of the fixed price level model of Chapter 2, if the demand for money depends only on the level of income and prices, we have the special case in which, because the demand for money is independent of the rate of interest, the level of real income depends solely on the size of the money supply. Moreover, if the relationship between the demand for money and real income is one of strict proportionality, then in the flexible-price model of Chapter 3 we have the case in which the money supply alone is sufficient to determine the value of nominal income, independently of how the latter variable breaks down into real income and price level components. Whether or not this particular approach to monetary theory leads to correct conclusions is a moot point, but it cannot be denied that it leads to interesting conclusions. It is thus a piece of analysis to be taken very seriously and to be tested with great care.

THE CAMBRIDGE APPROACH

Fisher's approach to monetary economics has much to recommend it. By postulating that the demand for money arises from the need of individuals to trade with one another, it links the demand for money to the volume of trade going on in an economy at any time and leads directly to a macroeconomic theory of the demand for money; it also leads to fairly precise predictions about the nature of the demand-for-money function and hence is eminently testable. None of this, however, is a logically necessary consequence of analyzing the demand for money from the point of view of the role it plays in the transactions-making process. The Cambridge approach to modeling the demand for money, as epitomized in the work of Marshall and Pigou, starts in the same place and ends with a formal statement of the demand-for-money function that looks very similar to the one that arises from Fisher's approach, but it follows a totally different path to get there, as the reader of Pigou (1917) soon discovers.

The Cambridge economists did not ask, as Fisher did, what determines the amount of money an economy needs to carry out a given volume of trans-

[2] This whole line of reasoning, however, overlooks the large and rapid fluctuations that can take place in the volume of transactions conducted in financial markets. For a discussion of long-run effects see pp. 144–145.

actions, but rather what determines the amount of money an individual agent would wish to hold given that the desire to conduct transactions makes money holding desirable at all. Their approach emphasizes the choice-making behavior of individuals and is much more akin to an application of the general theory of demand to a particular problem than it is to a special theory of the demand for money. When the problem is cast in these terms, the kinds of variables an economist is led to look at tend to be different from those to which Fisher's approach points. The framework that suggests itself here is one in which constraints and opportunity costs are the central factors, interacting with individuals' tastes. In the Cambridge approach the principal determinant of people's "taste" for money holding is the fact that it is a convenient asset to have, being universally acceptable in exchange for goods and services. The more transactions an individual has to undertake, the more cash he will want to hold and to this extent the approach is similar to Fisher's. The emphasis, however, in on *want* to hold, rather than *have* to hold; and this is the basic difference between Cambridge monetary theory and the Fisher framework.

An individual agent cannot hold all the money he wants, if only because his stock of cash balances cannot exceed his total wealth, the constraint on his money holding. Moreover, even if it were possible for a person to have all his wealth in the form of money, it is far from clear that this would be what he would desire. There are alternative ways of holding assets, and many of them offer advantages that money does not offer. Stocks and bonds yield an interest income that money does not; if the more money held, the less is the convenience to be gained from holding yet more of it, then after a point it will prove preferable to sacrifice some of this convenience in order to have some interest income. Moreover, stock and bond holding brings with it a chance for making capital gains (or losses), as indeed does money holding in times of a fluctuating price level, and anyone deciding how to allocate his wealth ought to take such matters into account before deciding on how much of it to devote to money balances.

All this is to say that in addition to depending on the volume of transactions an individual may be planning to conduct, the demand for money also varies with the level of his wealth and with the opportunity cost of holding money, the income forgone by not holding other assets. Moreover, the demand for money measured in nominal terms varies exactly in proportion to the price level. The convenience of holding money derives from its usefulness in carrying out the transactions necessary to obtain goods and services. If their prices were to increase by a certain proportion, the quantity of money an individual would have to hold in order to achieve just the same convenience as before would also have to increase by the same proportion.

We have not explicitly mentioned factors such as the availability of money substitutes for making transactions, the availability of good communications, and so on (the items stressed by the Fisher approach), but these can hardly be excluded from this scheme; in part, at least, they determine the degree to which it is convenient to hold money rather than other assets at any given time. However, these matters are given a subservient position in the

Cambridge analysis of the problem of the demand for money. This approach amounts to saying that if one looks at the problem of money holding in an economy from the point of view of individual choice-making behavior, one will consider the convenience an individual derives from money holding for the making of transactions, his wealth, the rate of interest, the expectations he holds about the future course of events, and so on, as being potentially important influences on the demand for money. It says little about the nature of the relationships one can expect to prevail among these variables, and it does not say too much about which ones are important. Rather, when formalizing their model, this group of economists, particularly Pigou, chose to simplify it by assuming that for an individual the level of wealth, the volume of transactions, and the level of income—over short periods at least—move in stable proportions to one another. They then argued that, *other things being equal,* the demand for money in nominal terms is proportional to the nominal level of income for each individual, and hence for the aggregate economy as well. Thus, they wrote the demand equation for money:

$$M_d = kPY \tag{5.7}$$

which, combined with an equilibrium condition for the money market,

$$M_d = \overline{M}_s \tag{5.4}$$

yields

$$\overline{M}_s \frac{1}{k} = \overline{M}_s V = PY \tag{5.8}$$

This looks very similar to Fisher's Equation (5.5), but V represents not the *transactions* velocity of circulation of money, referred to above as V_T, but rather its *income* velocity—not the number of times a unit of money physically turns over, but rather its rate of circulation relative to the rate of production of real income.

The Cambridge approach appears to lead to a model similar to Fisher's and seems to yield the same implications about the determination of the level of money income, but to give it this interpretation would be a mistake. Both Fisher and the Cambridge economists stated their theories on an other-things-being-equal basis. What Fisher required to be constant, the institutional framework determining the technical nature of the transactions-making process, may reasonably be expected not to change perceptibly over short periods; hence his approach may be regarded as providing a theory of the money market which implies a constant equilibrium velocity of circulation in the short run. Not so the Cambridge approach, with its emphasis on the rate of interest and expectations, because these are variables one can expect to vary significantly over quite short periods. To state the Cambridge model in a manner that makes it look like Fisher's is therefore to hide important differences between the formulations.

In terms of the macroeconomic model presented in the last chapter, some economists have suggested that Fisher has propounded a hypothesis that the rate of interest has no significant effect on the demand for money. There is room for debate about the appropriateness of interpreting Fisher in this way, but it is certainly not appropriate to attribute so definite a proposition to Marshall and Pigou. Although the formal version of the Cambridge demand-for-money function does not include an interest rate variable, it is nevertheless true that one of the main contributions of the Cambridge school to monetary theory was to call attention to the fact that such variables as the rate of interest may be important determinants of the demand for money.[3] They left it to their successors, however, to investigate their suggestions in detail.

KEYNESIAN THEORY

Keynes's (1930, 1936) development of the Cambridge approach to the problem of the demand for money now forms the basis of the treatment of the subject in macroeconomics textbooks.[4] He analyzed with more care than his predecessors the motives that lead people to hold money and was more precise on the nature of the convenience to be had from its possession. As we have seen, the peculiar characteristic of money as an asset, emphasized by Fisher and the Cambridge school alike, was that money, alone among assets, is universally acceptable as a means of exchange. Keynes too listed the "transactions motive" as an important—but by no means the only—factor underlying the demand for money. He postulated that the level of transactions conducted by an individual, and also by the aggregate of individuals, bears a stable relationship to the level of income, and hence that the "transactions demand" for money depends on the level of income.

Keynes confined the use of the term *transactions motive* to describing the necessity of holding cash to bridge the gap between receipts and planned regular payments. For those classes of payments that cannot be considered regular and planned, such as paying unexpected bills, making purchases at unexpectedly favorable prices, and meeting sudden emergencies caused perhaps by accidents or ill health, he also suggested that people find it prudent to hold some cash in case they are not able to realize other assets quickly enough to be of use to them. This he called the *precautionary motive* for holding money and suggested that the demand for money arising from it also depends, by and large, on the level of income.

Keynes himself did not regard the demand for money arising from the transactions motive and the precautionary motive as being in any sense techni-

[3] Thus, though Equations (5.7) and (5.8) are formally identical to Equations (3.1)–(3.3), they are to be interpreted differently in this context. Here the symbol k should *not* be taken as denoting a parameter that remains constant over time.

[4] The distinction between the Cambridge approach and the work of Keynes is a somewhat arbitrary one. Keynes was a Cambridge economist and *A Tract on Monetary Reform* (Keynes, 1923) is completely within the tradition of Marshall and Pigou. What we are here calling the Keynesian approach to the theory of the demand for money was well developed in the *Treatise on Money* (1930), but it is only in *The General Theory of Employment, Interest, and Money* (Keynes, 1936) that its full macroeconomic implications are worked out.

cally fixed in its relationship to the level of income. He was quite clear that the convenience to be had from holding cash for these purposes can be traded off against the return from holding other assets and made the transactions and precautionary demands for money functions of the rate of interest. However, he did not stress the role of the rate of interest in this part of his analysis, and many of his popularizers ignored it altogether, not because the rate of interest is not important in Keynes's analysis, but because its chief importance is to be found in the role it plays in determining the "speculative demand" for money.[5] Marshall and Pigou had suggested that uncertainty about the future was a factor influencing the demand for money: Keynes's analysis of the speculative motive represents an attempt to formalize one aspect of this suggestion and to draw conclusions from it. Rather than talk of uncertainty in general, the field is narrowed to uncertainty about one economic variable—the future level of the rate of interest—in the following manner.

A bond is an asset that carries with it the promise to pay its owner a certain income per annum, fixed in money terms, and the decision to buy a bond is a decision to buy a claim to such a future stream of income. How much any individual agent is willing to pay for a bond, hence the market value of that bond, depends critically on the rate of interest because the prospective purchaser will wish to earn at least the going rate of interest on that portion of his wealth he is holding in the form of bonds. Thus, if the rate of interest is 5%, he will be willing to pay up to, but no more than, $100 for a bond that offers an income of $5 per annum in perpetuity. If the rate of interest is 10%, however, no one will be willing to pay more than $50 for the same bond.

It follows, then, from the very nature of bonds that changes in the rate of interest involve changes in their price; a rise in the interest rate means that their market value falls, and a fall in the interest rate means that it rises. Changes in the rate of interest thus involve capital gains and losses for bond holders. However, these same changes in the rate of interest do not involve any change in the value of money. If we consider the choice between holding money and bonds, it should be clear that, in addition to offering the attraction of an interest income—which money does not always offer—bonds, when the rate of interest is expected to fall, also offer to their owners the possibility of making capital gains. In such circumstances they are particularly attractive to hold; but when the rate of interest is expected to rise, the situation is quite the opposite, for then capital losses face the bond holder. It follows that when the rate of interest is expected to fall, the demand for money is relatively low, since people hold bonds in anticipation of capital gains; when it is expected to rise, however, the demand for money is greater, as people seek to avoid making capital losses on holding bonds. This is all well and good, but the theory as stated thus far

[5] The distinction between the demand for transactions and precautionary balances, determined chiefly by the level of income, and that for speculative balances, determined by the rate of interest, is often referred to as the distinction between the demand for *active* and *idle* balances. Since all money is at each moment being held by someone, this terminology is not too helpful empirically, and we do not use it in this book.

lacks a variable to tell us when the rate of interest is expected to change and in what direction. Keynes's solution to this problem was to consider the current level of the rate of interest.

He argued that, at any time, there is a value, or perhaps a range of values, of the rate of interest that can be regarded as normal, so that when the rate is above this normal range, there is a tendency for people to expect it to fall, and, when it is below this range, to expect it to rise. In this view, any individual agent at any particular moment either expects the rate to fall, in which case he anticipates capital gains as well as interest income from holding bonds and will definitely hold bonds, or he expects the rate to rise, in which case he anticipates capital losses on bonds. So long as these expected capital losses are not enough to offset the interest income from bond holding, the agent will continue to keep all his available wealth in bonds.[6] However, if the capital losses in question are expected to be large enough more than to offset his interest earnings, the agent will hold nothing but money. There is a third possibility, namely that expected capital losses just offset his interest earnings so that the overall anticipated yield from bond holding is zero. In the special case where bonds are perpetuities, so that capital value changes are inversely proportional to changes in the rate of interest, this occurs when the expected rate of change in the rate of interest is equal to the current level of the rate of interest; in such circumstances the agent is indifferent as to what proportion of his wealth is held in money.

For an individual agent with given and precise expectations about the future value of the interest rate, the speculative demand for money is a discontinuous function of its current level. There is a given value of the current rate above which the expected yield on bond holding is positive, below which the yield in question is negative, and at which it is zero. These yields in turn involve (1) a zero speculative demand for money, (2) a speculative demand for money equal to the individual's available wealth, and (3) any demand for money between these two extremes. For the aggregate economy, however, it is postulated that, given the normal range of the interest rate, different people have different expectations about its rate of change toward their own precise estimate of its future value. The lower the current rate, the more rapidly people will expect it to rise, hence the more individuals will want to hold all their resources in money; by similar reasoning, the higher the rate, the smaller the aggregate demand for speculative balances. Provided that the money and bond holdings of each agent are insignificant relative to the totals for the economy, and provided that there is some diversity of opinion about the expected rate of change of the rate of interest at any moment, the aggregate speculative demand-for-money function becomes a smooth and negative function of the current level of the rate of interest.

The simplest form of the total Keynesian demand-for-money function makes transactions and precautionary balances functions of the level of income

[6] The adjective *available* should remind the reader that some of the individual's wealth will be devoted to holding transactions and precautionary balances.

and speculative balances a function of the current rate of interest and the level of wealth, the latter variable being included because the foregoing argument about the speculative demand for money is cast in terms of the proportion of its total assets the economy will seek to hold in cash. Moreover, these two relationships are thought of as being additive. We obtain, then, as the demand function for money, with W representing real wealth,

$$M_d = [kY + l(r)W]P \tag{5.9}$$

The first term within the brackets represents transactions and precautionary balances, and the second term represents speculative balances.[7] If we confine the analysis to short periods of time over which the level of wealth does not vary, this variable can simply be ignored and we are left with an equation for the demand for money similar to that used in Chapters 2 and 3.

The equation is similar, but not identical, for the parts of Keynes's analysis of particular interest for the behavior of the macromodel developed there concern the speculative demand for money and suggest that it cannot be treated as a simple, stable, approximately linear, negative relationship with respect to the rate of interest. Let us look at this more closely. For the individual the choice is to hold his wealth either in money or bonds, depending on what he expects to happen to the rate of interest; smoothness in the aggregate relationship between the demand for money and the rate of interest arises from the fact that different individuals have different expectations about the future rate of change of the rate of interest at given levels of this variable. The lower the rate of interest, the more rapidly it will be expected to rise and the more people will hold money rather than bonds.

It is a short step from this to argue that at some low level of the rate of interest everyone in the economy will expect the rate to rise rapidly enough to make them either unwilling to hold bonds, preferring money instead, or indifferent between bonds and money. At this point the demand for money in the aggregate becomes perfectly elastic with respect to the rate of interest. The latter variable can fall no further, and any increases in the quantity of money will simply be absorbed without any fall in interest rates. This is the doctrine of the *liquidity trap,* which argues that the interest elasticity of the demand for money can, at low levels of the rate of interest, take the value infinity. As we

[7] The parentheses around the term r in this equation indicate that l denotes a functional relationship rather than a linear parameter. The relationship in question is of course to be regarded as a negative one, but, as we shall see below, the whole point of Keynes's analysis of the speculative demand for money is to suggest that the relationship between the speculative demand for money and the rate of interest cannot be treated as well approximated by a stable, linear relationship. The fact that the whole expression is multiplied by P, the price level, indicates that this theory, like the preceding ones, is a theory of the demand for real money. It therefore implies that, other things being equal, the demand for nominal money is proportional to the price level. Note, however, that the "other things being equal" here include the level of real wealth. A change in the price level can cause this to change if a person holds some of his wealth in instruments denominated in nominal terms. Thus, to say that the demand for nominal balances is proportional to the price level is not the same as saying that a change in the price level will lead to a proportional change in the demand for nominal balances. This is true only if everything else is left unaffected by the change in the price level.

saw in Part I, this hypothesis implies that when such circumstances arise monetary policy is quite without effect, fiscal policy being the only means of economic control. Even though Keynes himself was sceptical about its practical significance, it is clearly a doctrine to be compared carefully with the empirical evidence.

Although the liquidity-trap doctrine is the most striking of the implications to be derived from Keynes's work on the subject of the demand for money, it is not the only one that is important in the context of the model described in Part I of this book. His analysis of the speculative demand for money rests on the proposition that at any moment there is a value, or range of values, of the rate of interest that people regard as normal. Nothing in the analysis suggests that this normal range of the rate of interest is constant over time, but the amount of money demanded for speculative purposes depends on the current level of the rate of interest relative to this normal level. This model implies, then, that the relationship between the demand for money and the rate of interest will be unstable over time, shifting around as what is regarded as a normal range for the rate of interest changes. If this hypothesis is true, then all of the conclusions drawn in Part I, which hinged on stability of the relationship between the demand for real money, real income, and the interest rate, are misleading. Obviously this hypothesis about the demand-for-money function is well worth investigating.

Keynes's analysis of the demand-for-money function arrives at conclusions completely opposite to those of Fisher. The latter implicitly has the demand for money insensitive to the rate of interest and stably related to the volume of transactions (hence of income) in the short run, this relationship changing only slowly over long periods as the institutional framework surrounding market activity changes. Keynes, though in agreement about the stability of the transactions demand for money, by following the Cambridge tradition and treating the problem of the demand for money as one of choice-making behavior, found reason to argue that the demand for money in total might be dominated by speculative behavior to such a degree as to make predictions about it based on transactions motives alone quite misleading in their implications about the role of money in the macroeconomy.

FRIEDMAN AND THE MODERN QUANTITY THEORY

Keynes's work on the demand for money represents a development of one line of the earlier Cambridge theory, inasmuch as it is based on a much closer analysis of the motives that prompt people to hold money than appears in the work of Marshall and Pigou. However, the view that the demand for money should be treated not as a special matter but rather as a particular application of the general theory of demand is never far in the background in the Cambridge tradition. A body of theory, often referred to as the *modern quantity theory,* which receives its most comprehensive statement in the work of Milton Friedman (1956), brings this aspect of Marshall and Pigou's work to the forefront and makes the general theory of demand the explicit starting point of the analysis.[8] Friedman's work in the demand for money draws attention away from the motives that prompt the holding of money and—taking for granted the fact that people do hold money—carefully analyzes the factors that determine *how much* money people want to hold under various circumstances. He thus treats money in exactly the same way an economist would treat any durable good, were he asked to construct a model of the demand for it, and in doing so formulates a demand function whose form is dictated by the ultimate aim of testing its predictions against empirical evidence.

Friedman begins by postulating that money, like any other asset, yields a flow of services to the agent who holds it. Apart from noting that these services derive from the fact that money is a "temporary abode of purchasing power," there is no detailed analysis of the motives that are satisfied by them. All that is said about these services is that the more money held, the less valuable relative to the services of other assets those flowing from money become. This is but a particular application of the general principle of the diminishing marginal rate of substitution between goods in consumption. As with any other application of demand theory to a special case, the bulk of the effort is put into closely analyzing the nature of the budget constraint and picking out relevant variables to measure the opportunity cost of holding money. That wealth is the appropriate constraint on asset holding, and therefore on the demand for money, should go without saying, as it should that the rates of return to be earned by holding assets other than money are the relevant opportunity costs. This much is evident from the work of Marshall and Pigou, but they do not provide a careful working out of the specific definition of wealth to be used in analyzing the demand for money on an empirical level, or a precise listing of the relevant alternative rates of return to be considered. It is here that Friedman's key contributions lie. Let us take up the wealth concept first.

One role played by the budget constraint in demand theory is to define the maximum amount that can be bought of whatever good is being studied, or, in the case of an asset, the maximum amount of it that can be held. If an individual agent were to dispose of all his assets, durable goods, bonds, and the like, he could certainly acquire and hold money instead, and this stock of assets is what we usually would refer to as his wealth. However, in a world in which there are no restrictions on what can be bought or sold, wealth thus defined does not impose a maximum bound on the amount of money an agent can hold. If he has labor income, there is no reason why he cannot sell a claim to this income stream and devote the proceeds of this sale to money holding as well. Bonds are nothing more than a claim to future interest income and stocks a claim on the future income from some piece of capital equipment. There is not that much *economic* difference between trade in these assets and trade in future labor income, and this suggests that the concept of wealth should in-

[8] The emphasis here should be on "modern" rather than "quantity" theory, because Friedman's analysis bears little resemblance to that of the traditional quantity theory. Some commentators, for example, Patinkin (1969), have suggested that Friedman's analysis is best regarded as an extension of that of Keynes. However, Friedman's empirical views are, as we shall see, very different from those of Keynes, no matter what may be the similarities of their theoretical ideas.

clude the present value of labor income or, as it has come to be called, human wealth. Analytic precision certainly suggests that this is a sensible course to take. There are, however, practical arguments that suggest that, as far as empirical analysis is concerned, there is an important distinction to be made between human and nonhuman wealth.

Nonhuman wealth can be bought and sold, and there can be substitution almost without limit within this class of wealth. In the absence of slavery, the scope for substitution between human and nonhuman wealth in the portfolio is limited. There is some scope, however; an individual is always at liberty to sell nonhuman assets and spend the proceeds on further education to improve his earning power or, conversely, to neglect his education and accumulate nonhuman wealth instead. The possibilities for such substitution between human and nonhuman wealth are nevertheless limited, and in the context of the demand for money the question arises whether or not nonhuman wealth alone is a better measure of the constraint on the holding of it than is total wealth. Friedman's theoretical approach is to postulate that an inclusive definition of wealth should be employed but that, in recognition of the problems raised by the lack of a market in human wealth, the ratio of human to nonhuman wealth should also be considered a subsidiary variable in the demand for money function. However, no one to my knowledge has made use of this latter variable in any empirical study, though in recognition of the problem that caused Friedman to suggest its use, some economists have preferred to employ a narrower, more conventional nonhuman definition of wealth. As we shall see below, nothing of fundamental importance seems to hinge on this matter.

The opportunity cost of holding money is the income to be earned from holding bonds, equity (in the sense of durable goods yielding a service income to their owners as well as corporate stock), and, if one includes human wealth in the constraint, the return on it also. The principle of the diminishing marginal rate of substitution between money and other assets ensures that if the return on any of these other assets rises the demand for money will fall. The return on these other assets has two components. First, the interest (or service) income yielded by them must be considered, but so also must the way in which their market prices are expected to vary, for a forgone capital gain (or loss) is every bit as much a part of the opportunity cost of holding money as is forgone interest. As explained earlier, the price of income-earning assets varies inversely with the market rate of interest, so that the expected percentage rate of change of this rate of interest can be used to measure the expected percentage rate of capital gain and loss from holding other assets. The percentage rate of change of the rate of interest is of course opposite in sign to the rate of capital gain (or loss) it is here being used to measure. It must be subtracted from the rate of interest itself to obtain the expected yield on the relevant asset, this yield being what is forgone if money rather than the asset in question is held.[9]

[9] This is of course the same variable that underlies the Keynesian speculative demand for money, but this does not make Friedman's views the same as Keynes's. The essentially Keynesian step is to relate the expected rate of change of the interest rate to its current level, and Friedman does not do this.

Though we have talked about rates of return on various assets as separate variables, it should be obvious that a change in one rate of return will also lead to a change in all the others. If the rate of return on bonds rises, for example, they will become more attractive to hold, so that people will try to exchange other assets such as equities for them, thus bidding up their price and bidding down the price of equities, continuing to do so until the rates of return on various assets are brought back into an equilibrium relationship. If the rates of return on various assets move together, we can greatly simplify the demand-for-money function by picking one representative rate and letting it stand for all the others in the function. Which rate fulfills this role best is an empirical matter, but for the moment let us simply call it "the rate of interest" and include it, as well as its rate of change, in the demand function for money, leaving the question of finding its empirical analog until later.

If the rate of return on holding money were constant, we could leave matters here, but if the price level can vary, this is not the case. If the price level rises, the real value of money holdings, denominated as they are in nominal terms, falls, and vice versa. Rising or falling price levels provide a return to money holding, which in the former case is negative and in the latter case positive. The expected percentage rate of change of the price level must then be interpreted as an expected own rate of return to money holding. Other things being equal, the higher the expected rate of return to holding money, the more of it will be held, and the lower it is, the less will be held. Thus the expected rate of inflation is a potentially important variable in the demand-for-money function.

Since money is held for the services it provides its owners, and since these services arise from its being an "abode of purchasing power," it follows that the demand function for money we have been discussing is one that determines the demand for money measured in units of constant purchasing power. It is a demand function for real money balances and, if we wish to convert it into a demand function for nominal balances, it must be multiplied through by the price level. Thus Friedman's model of the demand for money can be written as follows, where M_d is the demand for money in nominal terms, r is the rate of interest, W is wealth, h is the ratio of human to nonhuman wealth, P is the price level, and all time derivatives denote expected rates of change:

$$M_d = f\left(W, r - \frac{1}{r}\frac{dr}{dt}, \frac{1}{P}\frac{dP}{dt}, h\right)P \tag{5.10}$$

with the following restrictions being put on the relationships between the variables in question:

$$\frac{\delta M_d}{\delta\,[r - (1/r)\,(dr/dt)\,]} < 0 \tag{5.11}$$

(Other things being equal, the higher the yield on other assets, the smaller the demand for money.)

$$\frac{\delta M_d}{\delta\,[\,(1/P)\,(dP/dt)\,]} < 0 \tag{5.12}$$

(Other things being equal, the higher the rate of change of prices, the smaller the demand for money.)

$$\frac{\delta M_d}{\delta P} = f\left(W, r - \frac{1}{r}\frac{dr}{dt}, \frac{1}{P}\frac{dP}{dt}, h\right) \tag{5.13}$$

(Other things being equal, the higher the level of prices, the proportionately higher the demand for money.) So long as money is a "normal" as opposed to an inferior good, we also have

$$\frac{\delta M_d}{\delta W} > 0 \tag{5.14}$$

(Other things being equal, the higher the level of wealth, the greater the demand for money.)[10]

This theory identifies certain variables as being potentially important determinants of the demand for money and also (with the exception of h) specifies the sign of the relationship which the demand for money can be expected to bear toward them. It does not, however, say anything about how large or important any of these relationships are, leaving these matters open to empirical investigation. One cannot say more about this approach to the problem of the demand for money without reference to empirical evidence. We do not expect conventional demand theory to tell us much about the relative importance of various factors affecting the demand for other consumer durables, and there is no reason why it should tell us more about the demand for money.

In light of the analytic method Friedman adopts, theory has done its job if it states the problem in such a way as to sort out what empirical questions can usefully be asked. Once this has been done, it remains to carry out the empirical work that will enable one to find out whether the relationships between the demand for money and the variables listed above are important and whether or not they are stable over time. Since wealth—possibly defined in a novel way—rather than income appears in this particular function, and since the rate of interest is but one of several other variables, not least the expected rate of inflation, listed as being of potential importance, this model, worked out as it is from the first principles of demand theory, suggests that the demand-for-money function used in the model presented in Chapters 2 and 3 may be quite a poor approximation of reality. The answers to the empirical questions posed by this approach, then, are clearly worth having.

[10] The variable h is not discussed here, not only because it is not used in any of the empirical work we shall describe but also because it is far from clear from Friedman's analysis what sign its derivative should take.

chapter 6

Further Developments in the Keynesian Approach to the Theory of the Demand for Money

INTRODUCTORY COMMENT

In the preceding chapter we dealt with theories of the demand for money that were on the whole designed with macroeconomic application in mind. They were either explicitly macroeconomic in their formulation, as was Fisher's work, or, as with Friedman's approach, they discussed the problem in terms of the behavior of a typical individual, implicitly assuming that what is true for such an individual is also true of the aggregate economy. Not all theories of the demand for money are like this. Recent work extending the Keynesian analysis of transactions, precautionary, and speculative motives for holding money yields implications for individual behavior that are not so readily applied to the aggregate economy by way of simple analogy. Nevertheless, this work draws our attention to certain factors involved in the decision to hold money that we might otherwise have overlooked; for this reason alone it is worth discussing.

THE TRANSACTIONS MOTIVE

Theoretical work on the transactions demand for money due to both Baumol (1952) and Tobin (1956) seeks to put this analysis on a more rigorous footing and to draw more precise implications about the variables that determine this segment of the demand for money than Keynes's analysis did.[1] If one wishes to obtain precise conclusions from a model, he must usually make precise assumptions. Those we make here yield the simplest version of Baumol's model. This model enables us to illustrate the most important insights of this body of work without leading us into the mathematical complexities that more elaborate

[1] Baumol and Tobin worked independently on this problem, coming to very similar conclusions about it. Of the two, Baumol took a slightly simpler approach to the problem, and it is his analysis that is followed here. A geometric exposition of the model can be found in Johnson (1963).

versions of the approach produce. Let us consider the behavior of an individual agent, be it a firm or a household, and assume that he receives an income payment once per time period, say per month.[2] Suppose that this agent must spread out his purchases over time, and for the sake of simplicity in the analysis also suppose that the whole of his receipts are spent at a constant rate over the period. Then, at every moment except the final instant at the end of the month when the last item of expenditure is made, the transactor finds himself holding some assets, the as yet unspent portion of his income. His problem is how to hold these assets, given that there exist interest-yielding bonds that can be owned as well as cash, and given that there is a fixed cost involved in exchanging bonds for cash.

Clearly the agent will try to arrange things so that he minimizes his costs over the period. This problem can be solved in the following way. Let T be the real value of the agent's income, which is also equal to the real value of the volume of transactions he carries out; r the rate of interest per period, which is assumed constant over the period; b the real cost of turning bonds into cash (what Baumol calls the "brokerage fee"); and K the real value of bonds turned into cash every time such a transfer takes place. The costs incurred by the agent have two components. First, every time he sells bonds, he must pay a brokerage fee, and since he spends all his income and sells bonds in equal lots of size K, the outlay in brokerage fees is equal to $b(T/K)$. At the same time, if money is held instead of bonds, interest is forgone, and this too must obviously be treated as a cost. Since expenditure is a constant flow, the agent's average money holding over the period is $K/2$, that is, half the amount of his receipts from a sale of bonds. This, multiplied by the rate of interest per period, gives the opportunity cost of holding money.

The total cost of making transactions, where γ is the cost, can then be written

$$\gamma = b\frac{T}{K} + r\frac{K}{2} \tag{6.1}$$

To find the value of K that minimizes this cost we need only take the derivative of Equation (6.1) with respect to K, set it equal to zero, and solve for K. This gives

$$\frac{\delta\gamma}{\delta K} = \frac{-bT}{K^2} + \frac{r}{2} = 0 \tag{6.2}$$

so that

$$K = \sqrt{\frac{2bT}{r}} \tag{6.3}$$

[2] The actual time period involved is of little importance, for it follows from the analysis presented below that the level of cash balances demanded for a given level of income per annum is independent of the frequency of payment except in certain, very special, cases. See footnote 3 on page 61.

Since, as noted above, money holdings over the period have an average value of $K/2$, the demand-for-money equation that emerges from this analysis is

$$\frac{M_d}{P} = \frac{K}{2} = \frac{1}{2}\sqrt{\frac{2bT}{r}} \tag{6.4}$$

That is, the demand for transactions balances measured in real terms is proportional to the square root of the volume of transactions and inversely proportional to the square root of the rate of interest.[3] This can be rewritten as

$$M_d = \frac{1}{2}\sqrt{\frac{2bT}{r}}\,P = \alpha b^{0.5}T^{0.5}r^{-0.5}P \tag{6.5}$$

where

$$\alpha \equiv \frac{1}{2}\sqrt{2}$$

The reader will note that in deriving this "square-root rule" nothing was said about the utility of holding money for transactions purposes or about trading off such utility against interest income. One of the strong attractions of Baumol's approach to the demand for money is that it does not appear to find such notions necessary. All that is needed is that money be the means of exchange in the economy and that there be a cost involved in transforming interest-earning assets into money, that there be a brokerage fee. If one substitutes zero for b in Equation (6.4), the expression will clearly reduce to zero, telling us that if no cost were involved in selling bonds there would be no demand for money, even in an economy in which it is the only means of exchange. Without the brokerage fee it would pay to synchronize bond sales perfectly with purchases of goods, so that money would not be held except at the instant at which it passes through the hands of the person selling bonds and buying goods.

The brokerage fee is then the vital variable, and it is important to interpret it carefully. To think of its analog in the real world as being literally a fee charged by a bond dealer for selling assets for a client is misleading, for this puts too narrow an interpretation on what it represents. The role it plays in the

[3] Some readers may note that this is but a particular application of a well-known general approach to the problem of inventory management. It should be noted that it follows from Equation (6.4) that a lengthening of the income period, which involves an increase in T for a given level of annual income, will involve an equiproportional increase in r, leaving the demand for money unchanged. Also, note that if the size of b is sufficiently great that the agent never finds that it pays to hold bonds, and if the payment period then lengthens, the agent's money holding will vary. The reader may also note that, although Equation (6.4) looks like a continuous function, there is in fact a problem of interpretation here. It is derived from a model that assumes that the size of the average cash withdrawal times the number of withdrawals is exactly equal to T, the volume of transactions. This assumption puts discrete limits on the value K can take. For example, the maximum value K can take is to be equal to T. If we set r equal to zero in Equation (6.4) and solve for K, we would think that a withdrawal of infinite size might result. I am indebted to Alvin Marty for drawing my attention to this problem.

model is that of any cost involved in selling income-earning assets; this could just as well be the time and trouble taken by an individual agent to sell an asset himself as anything else. To put matters on a very simple level, if it takes time and causes wear and tear to one's shoes to walk around the corner to a savings bank to obtain cash for a deposit there, one is incurring a brokerage fee in doing so just as much as if he were paying someone to sell government bonds for him in an organized securities market. This simple example underlies frequent references the reader may well encounter in the monetary economics literature to the "shoeleather costs" of transacting. When the brokerage-fee concept is interpreted in this very general way, suspicions that it is unrealistic to treat its value as being independent of the value of the transfer made, rather than being related to its size, should diminish. In any case, if we add a component to the brokerage fee that varies with the size of the cash withdrawal so that each withdrawal involves a cost of $b + cK$, this will simply add a term $cK(T/K) = cT$ to Equation (6.1) and will have no effect on the optimal size of K.

The brokerage fee is not necessarily the same for all individuals or constant over time for any one individual. It arises from the time taken to transform income-earning assets into cash, and its value will vary with the value of time to the individual concerned. Time not spent on financial transactions can be spent earning income, and so the wage rate of the individual can be regarded as a determinant of the brokerage fee involved in his financial transactions. The higher the wage rate he could be earning, the more it costs him to spend a given amount of time transforming income-earning assets into cash. This is a point of some importance because it suggests that if this theory of the demand for money is of empirical relevance we ought to find that the level of wage rates has an influence on the quantity of money demanded in addition to that of the volume of transactions (or of the level of income standing as a proxy for the volume of transactions).[4]

Income payments in the real world are usually made in terms of cash rather than bonds, and there may be costs involved in acquiring bonds in exchange for money at the beginning of each period. So long as this cost does not vary with the size of the bond purchase, it does not affect anything. Where g is the fixed cost of acquiring bonds in exchange for cash, Equation (6.1) becomes

$$\gamma = b\frac{T}{K} + r\frac{K}{2} + g \tag{6.6}$$

Since g does not vary with the size or frequency of cash withdrawals, the optimal values of these variables are independent of it, except in the case where the cost of acquiring bonds is so high as to persuade the individual agent to

[4] The relationship between the brokerage fee and the level of wages developed here was not set out by Baumol and Tobin in their original articles. Here we are applying an insight developed by Thomas Saving (1971) in the context of an analysis of the precautionary demand for money. Joel Fried (1973) and Edi Karni (1974), drawing on a suggestion of Barro and Santomero (1972), independently applied the idea to the transactions demand for money.

keep all his assets in cash if he is initially paid in cash. Usually, however, even when modified in this way, the model continues to predict that the demand for money will increase in less than proportion to the volume of transactions, that is, that there are economies of scale in money holding for the individual.[5]

This prediction has two potentially important implications for macroeconomics. The first is that for the aggregate economy the demand for money depends on the distribution of income as well as on its level. If we assume, as we have before, that the volume of transactions conducted in an economy is in a fixed ratio to the level of national income, it will be apparent that the more a given amount of income is concentrated in a few hands, the lower will be the demand for money for a given level of aggregate income. This is simply because the economies of scale in money holding discussed above accrue to the individual agent, so that one agent carrying out a given volume of transactions will hold less cash than two agents carrying out half that volume each. If the distribution of income varies, so will the demand for money. This is not to say that the earlier transaction-based models we have considered necessarily rule this matter out. However, in discussing them it has been implicitly assumed that they lead to a demand function for money for an individual that is not only proportional to his income but is also much like that of any other individual. Such assumptions permit the distribution of income to be ignored in formulating an aggregate function, but the Baumol-Tobin model forces us to question this practice.

The second noteworthy implication of there being economies of scale in money holding is that with a given distribution of income any increase or decrease in the supply of money will have a greater short-run effect on the level of real income than it would if the demand for money were proportional to the level of income. At a given interest rate and price level a doubling of the quantity of money in the proportional case requires a doubling of the level of income to absorb it. Under the simple square-root rule, a quadrupling of real income will be needed. In the long run, however, holding real transaction volume and the real value of the brokerage fee constant, the price level will move

[5] The reader should note that in the aggregate it is impossible for everyone to receive one income payment per period and spend it continuously. Somebody must be acquiring continuous receipts and making lump-sum expenditures once per period. It is easy to show that, provided there is a brokerage fee for the exchange of cash for bonds, this type of individual's demand for money will also be proportional to the square root of the volume of transactions and inversely proportional to the rate of interest per period. This point is analyzed by Baumol (1952). Of course, once individuals are in a position to choose their own pattern of payments and receipts, it is far from clear that their activities will result in a simple reciprocal pattern of continuous outflows matched by lump-sum inflows. Certain theoretical aspects of this problem are investigated by Clower and Howitt (1978).

The reader should also note that to add a variable component to the brokerage fee adds a term in the level of transactions to the resulting demand-for-money function and, as Brunner and Meltzer (1967) have shown, the individual's elasticity of demand for money with respect to the volume of transactions ceases to be a constant 0.5 in this case, but becomes a variable that approaches a lower limit of 0.5 as the volume of transactions becomes small and an upper limit of 1.0 as it becomes large. How large the volume of transactions has to become before the economies of scale in money holding that this model predicts become unimportant is an empirical question, and in any event much effort has been put into seeking empirical evidence of such economies.

in proportion to the money supply, as in other models. Both the nominal value of transactions and the nominal value of the brokerage fee vary in proportion to the price level, producing a proportional relationship between the demand for money and the price level, as shown in Equation (6.5).

The foregoing implications then give us good reason for taking this theory of the demand for money seriously. They suggest that not only may a linear demand-for-money function be a misleading simpliciation but also that a function that includes only the level of income and the rate of interest may not be completely enough specified to allow it to form part of a model expected to yield accurate predictions about any actual economy. In particular, this approach to the transactions demand for money suggests that both the level of wages and the distribution of income are factors whose influence on the demand for money are worth looking into.

THE PRECAUTIONARY MOTIVE

The transactions demand for money exists even when an individual's pattern of income receipts and expenditures is given to him and known with perfect certainty. In contrast, the precautionary demand for money stems from uncertainty about the timing of cash inflows and outflows. In recent years several economists have developed formal models to deal with issues that arise in this context. The following represents an attempt to present the key features of this analysis in as simple a form as possible.[6]

Consider the behavior of an individual whose income matches his expenditure, not on a period-by-period—let us say month-by-month—basis, but on average over a number of months. In any particular month there may arise an excess or a shortfall of income over expenditure. If there is an excess, it is added to his wealth, but a shortfall must be made good within the month by decreasing his wealth. As in the Baumol model of the transactions demand for money, the individual can hold his wealth in the form of money or in terms of interest-earning bonds. He decides at the beginning of the month how to allocate his wealth holding over the month between bonds and money. In doing so, he bears in mind that money can be used to meet any shortfall of income from expenditure without cost, but if bonds have to be sold during the month to obtain cash, a lump-sum brokerage fee whose size is independent of the value of the bonds sold is incurred.[7]

[6] The genesis of this line of work in recent literature is to be found in Patinkin (1965, Chapter 5). Much of the subsequent literature is surveyed by Orr (1970), but the reader's attention is also directed to papers by Whalen (1966), Gray and Parkin (1973), and Goldman (1974). Note, however, that the basic work on these matters was that of Edgeworth (1888). Although worked out independently by the author in an attempt to simplify the model of Gray and Parkin (1973), the following analysis is similar in all its essentials to that of Weinrobe (1972).

[7] This assumption of a lump-sum brokerage fee is made partly to maintain an affinity between this analysis and that of the transactions motive carried out above, but it also makes a crucial contribution to the simplicity of the argument set out here. The relationship between the probability distribution of discrepancies between payments and receipts and the demand-for-money function becomes considerably more complex if a component is introduced into the brokerage fee whose size varies with the magnitude of a bond sale. We take this point up again below.

Clearly, a key ingredient in his decision must be an estimate of the frequency with which cash shortfalls of particular sizes are likely to occur, and it is assumed that the individual has knowledge of this. Though he does not know in which month shortfalls of any particular size will occur, he does know the proportion of months in which they will occur or, to put the same matter another way, he knows the probability distribution of such shortfalls. Figure 6-1 shows one particular form such a distribution could take. It portrays a normal distribution. The horizontal axis measures the difference between cash outflows and inflows in any month, and the vertical axis measures the proportion of months in which, on average, a discrepancy between expenditure and outlays of a particular size will occur.

Our normal distribution is drawn symmetrically about zero, and the following assumptions are implicit in its shape. First, equality between expenditure and receipts is a more frequent occurrence than any specific positive or negative discrepancy. Second, the larger the size of a particular discrepancy, the less frequently it occurs. Third, an excess of expenditure over receipts of any given size occurs just as frequently as an excess of receipts over expenditure of the same amount; such discrepancies cancel out on the average, and our initial assumption of long-run equality between expenditure and receipts is thus satisfied. Nothing crucial hinges on the precise shape we have assumed for this distribution, although it is important that at some stage the frequency with which a particular discrepancy arises falls with the size of the discrepancy in question. It will now be shown that, given our assumptions, a demand-for-money function can be derived directly from the segment of the curve that lies to the right of zero in Figure 6.1.

Consider an individual agent who enters each month holding an amount of money equal to M (in dollars). In those months in which his income falls short of his expenditure by less than M, he has no need to sell bonds and incur a brokerage fee, but in all other months he will incur such a fee. The proportion of months in which he incurs a brokerage fee times the brokerage fee gives his average monthly outlay for such costs. Where $C(M)$ is the average brokerage-fee outlay associated with holding M of precautionary balances, and $p(S > M)$

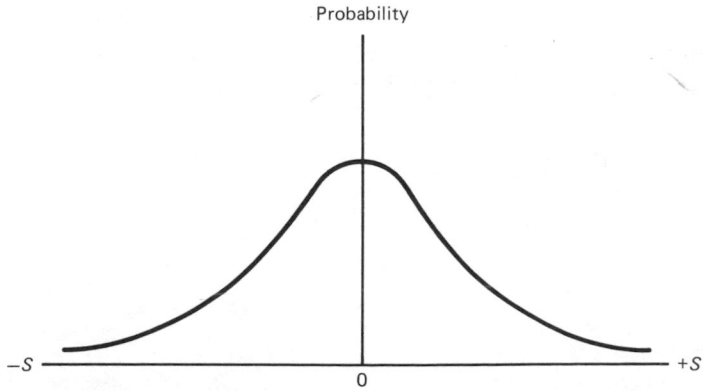

Figure 6.1 The probability distribution of the shortfall (S) of receipts from expenditure.

is the proportion of months in which, or the probability that, the shortfall of income below expenditure will exceed M, we can write, where b is the brokerage fee,

$$C(M) = p(S > M)b \tag{6.7}$$

Now suppose that the agent adds \$1 to his money holdings. We now write

$$C(M + I) = p(S > M + 1)b \tag{6.8}$$

Clearly, the amount that adding \$1 to his money holdings saves him in brokerage fees is obtained by subtracting the second expression from the first, and this yields

$$C(M) - C(M + 1) = p(M + 1 > S > M)b \tag{6.9}$$

Or, in words, adding an extra dollar to his money holdings saves an individual, on average per month, the brokerage fee times the proportion of months in which the amount of cash he needs to make good an excess of expenditure over income falls between M and $M + 1$.

This saving in brokerage fees is not, however, obtained without cost. An extra dollar held in precautionary balances is a dollar not held in bonds. If the rate of interest per period (*not* per annum, but per month in this example) is r (percent), it costs our individual \$1 $\times$ r = r cents to obtain the savings in brokerage fees we have just discussed. On the assumption that the rate of interest is constant over the month and independent of the number of bonds the agent holds, the marginal cost of adding to precautionary balances is constant at r cents per dollar. The individual agent seeking to minimize the costs of dealing with an uncertain pattern of payments and receipts will add cash to his precautionary balances until the saving in brokerage fees obtained by yielding an extra dollar falls to a level at which it just offsets the interest thereby forgone.

Figure 6.2 puts the above reasoning in geometric terms. On the vertical axis we measure both the marginal cost per dollar, in terms of interest forgone, of adding an extra dollar to precautionary balances and the marginal saving in brokerage fees obtained by so doing. Given a constant rate of interest, the marginal cost curve is simply the horizontal line r, while the curve relating marginal savings in brokerage fees to the amount of cash held is derived from the right-hand segment of the probability distribution drawn in Figure 6.1.

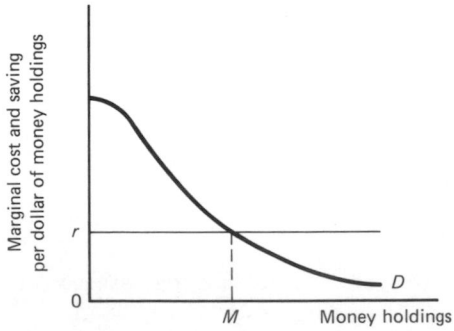

Figure 6.2 The demand curve for precautionary balances.

As we have seen, to find the saving obtained by adding the $(M + 1)$th dollar to money holdings, we multiply the probability of having a shortfall of receipts from outlays of just $M + 1$ dollars by the brokerage fee, and similarly for any other value of money holdings. Thus, the curve labeled D in Figure 6.2 is simply the right-hand side of the probability distribution depicted in Figure 6.1 with the probability variable on the vertical axis multiplied by the constant brokerage fee b. The point at which this curve crosses the horizontal line r obviously gives us the level of precautionary balances at which the marginal benefits obtained in terms of saved brokerage fees just equal the marginal costs incurred. Hence it tells us what quantity of precautionary balances will be held. In short, the curve labeled D is the demand curve for precautionary balances.[8]

We are now in a position to see what factors this analysis of the precautionary motive suggests we should find influencing the quantity of money demanded. Their effects are depicted in Figure 6.3. First consider the rate of

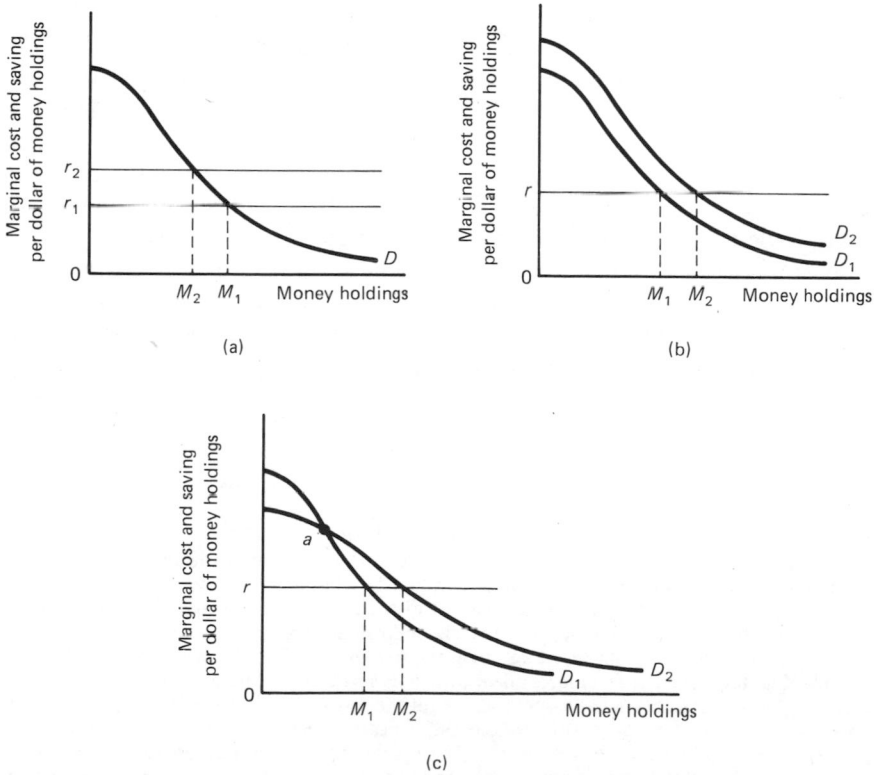

Figure 6.3 (a) The effect of an increase in the interest rate on the precautionary demand for money. (b) The effect of an increase in the brokerage fee on the precautionary demand for money. (c) The effect of an increase in income and expenditure on the precautionary demand for money.

[8] It should now be clear to the reader why it was remarked above that, although nothing critical hinges on the normality of the probability distribution portrayed in Figure 6.1, it is important that at some point, as we move to the right, it begins to slope downward.

interest. An increase in the rate of interest obviously increases the marginal cost of holding money from r_1 to r_2 and causes a shift along the demand-for-money function from M_1 to M_2 [panel (a)]. The demand for money also varies with the brokerage fee. If this increases, the marginal savings from holding any given level of precautionary balances will increase in proportion to the change in question, hence the demand-for-money function will shift upward as the brokerage fee increases [panel (b)]. If, as we did earlier, we interpret this fee as referring to the time and trouble involved in exchanging bonds for money, and recognize what the level of real-wage rates tells us about the opportunities forgone in devoting time and trouble to such activity, we have another argument suggesting that the real-wage rate should be a variable in the demand-for-money function.

The analyses carried out above all took the level of real income and expenditure as given. In general, we can assume that the higher the overall level of real income and expenditure, the greater the chance of the shortfall of receipts over expenditure exceeding any given value in any period. The precise extent of this tendency cannot be deduced unless we are much more specific than we have been about the nature of the processes that cause the patterns of cash inflows and outflows to be uncertain and about the nature of the interdependence, if any, of the timing of cash inflows and outflows. To carry out such an analysis in any detail is beyond the technical scope of this book.[9] However, if an increase in income is, as it usually will be, associated with an increase in the dispersion of the distribution of the discrepancy between payments and receipts depicted in Figure 6.1, it will result in the demand-for-money function pivoting about some point such as *a*, as depicted in Figure 6.3(c). This is because, if the probability of relatively large discrepancies occurring is increased, it must be at the expense of the probability of relatively small discrepancies falling. The sum of the probabilities attached to all possible discrepancies must always, by definition, equal unity.

[9] The following example gives the outline of such analysis. Suppose the individual's monthly volume of expenditures is a random variable described by a normal distribution, and that his monthly receipts can be characterized by a similar distribution. Then, provided that in any month the values of receipts and expenditures are independent of one another, the mean of the distribution of the difference between expenditures and receipts is simply the difference between the mean of the two separate distributions. Given our assumption that, on average, expenditures and receipts balance, this difference will be zero. The variance of the distribution of expenditures minus receipts is the sum of the variances of the two independent distributions, and its standard deviation is the square root of this variance. Now suppose that the individual's volume of transactions doubles in such a way that, after this doubling, we can treat the new distribution of expenditures as if it were the result of adding together two independent distributions of expenditures with equal means and variances. Make an exactly similar assumption about the way in which the distribution of receipts changes, and then the new distribution of the difference between expenditures and receipts will have a zero mean and a variance twice that of the original distribution. But this implies that when the volume of expenditures and receipts doubles in this way, the standard deviation of the distribution will increase in proportion to the square root of 2. Hence we have derived the result that, other things being equal, the level of precautionary balances that will result in a given probability of having to make a cash withdrawal will vary in proportion to the square root of the volume of transactions. This result will hold only if there is strict independence of the distributions of payments and receipts. Any tendency for payments and receipts to be inversely correlated month by month will reduce the extent of such economies of scale in money holding, and a tendency toward a positive correlation between them will accentuate it.

The implication of this argument about the effect of an increase in the average volume of payments and receipts on the demand-for-money function is straightforward. The lower is the rate of interest, and hence the higher are money holdings initially, the greater will be the positive effect on the demand for precautionary balances associated with an increase in income and expenditure. At very high interest rates, above *a* in Figure 6.3(c), the demand for money will actually fall as income and expenditure increase. This rather odd result—for which, it should be added at once, there is no empirical support—begins to vanish from the analysis when a variable component, depending on the size of the cash withdrawal, is added to the brokerage fee. A formal analysis of the reason for this is far beyond the technical scope of this book. Suffice it to say that it arises from the fact that as the dispersion of the distribution we are discussing increases the implied increase in the probability of making a large, *hence expensive,* withdrawal increases. The effect of larger withdrawals being more expensive is to give an extra incentive to increase money holding, an incentive which is absent from the fixed-brokerage-fee model in which the cost of all withdrawals, regardless of size, is the same.

Finally, note that, like every other theory of the demand for money we have discussed and shall discuss, this is a theory of the demand for real balances. It implies that the demand for nominal balances varies in proportion to the price level. If the average price at which each transaction takes place were to double, this would amount to no more than doubling the size of the units in terms of which payments, receipts, and the brokerage fee are measured and would thus result in a doubling of the nominal quantity of money demanded.

THE SPECULATIVE MOTIVE

As we saw in the previous chapter, the really novel aspect of Keynes's approach to the demand for money lay not so much in his treatment of the transactions and precautionary motives for holding cash as in his analysis of the speculative motive. It is hardly surprising, then, that this aspect of his thought has been worked on further and considerably refined. The speculative motive for holding money arises because, unlike most other financial assets, the capital value of money does not vary with changes in the interest rate and because there is uncertainty about the manner in which the interest rate will change in the future. Keynes suggested that, as far as the choice between holding bonds and money is concerned, each individual acts as if he is certain about what is going to happen to the interest rate and hence holds either bonds or money depending on his expectations. It was only by suggesting that different people, at any time, have different expectations about the rate of change of the interest rate that, in the aggregate, Keynes achieved a smooth relationship between the speculative demand for money and the rate of interest.

Subsequent work on this problem, due chiefly to Tobin (1958), has concentrated on producing a more sophisticated analysis of the behavior of the individual agent.[10] This is obviously necessary, since even quite casual observation shows that one does not find individual wealth holders owning either nothing but money or nothing but bonds, or "nothing but" any other single asset one could name. Rather, people hold diversified portfolios, a mixture of assets. If agents really did behave as if they were certain about the future, they would hold only the asset they expected to yield the highest return. The holding of diversified portfolios thus needs explaining. The theory described—though it is here confined to dealing with the problem of diversification between money and bonds—is capable of quite general application to this problem.

The key to the analysis is a relatively simple proposition about the typical agent's tastes: he treats wealth as a "good" and risk as a "bad," something that reduces the satisfaction derived from wealth. To give a concrete example, it is postulated that the agent prefers, say, $100 offered to him with certainty to a fifty-fifty chance of receiving either $50 or $150. In both cases the expected gain is $100: in the first case the sum is guaranteed and, in the second, if the offer is accepted many times, on half the occasions $50 will be forthcoming and on the other half $150, making $100 on average. However, in the second case there is a risk attached to the outcome, and this is thought of as reducing the desirability of this alternative. If the risk were larger—say the possible sums were $25 and $175—the alternative would be even less desirable.[11]

[10] The analysis that follows is not a straight exposition of Tobin's article. In particular it differs in making utility a function of expected wealth and risk rather than a function of the expected rate of return on a portfolio and risk. The latter procedure involves an assumption that the composition of a portfolio is independent of its size, that the wealth elasticity of the demand for money and bonds is unity; this assumption rules out the theoretically interesting possibility of a perverse relationship between the demand for money and the rate of interest dealt with below. Tobin's original paper is not altogether clear on this matter, and I am indebted to Peter Diamond for first drawing my attention to some of the problems involved.

[11] The notion of a trade-off between risk and return in fact follows from the assumption that the marginal utility of wealth falls as wealth increases. Consider the accompanying diagram, where wealth (W) is measured on the horizontal axis and utility (U) is measured cardinally on the vertical axis. $100 with certainty yields a utility of $U(100)$, while a fifty-fifty chance of $150 or $50 yields a fifty-fifty chance of $U(150)$ or $U(50)$, and the average utility expected here is obviously less than $U(100)$ because $50 in excess of $100 represents less of a gain than $50 subtracted from $100 represents a loss. This is because the marginal utility of wealth is diminishing. Clearly, a similar argument would show that a fifty-fifty chance of $25 or $175 would yield even less utility. This analysis becomes more complex as continuous distributions are attached to potential outcomes of situations but, provided the distributions in question are normal, it is possible to treat utility as a function of expected wealth and the standard deviation of the distribution about this expected value, the latter variable measuring risk.

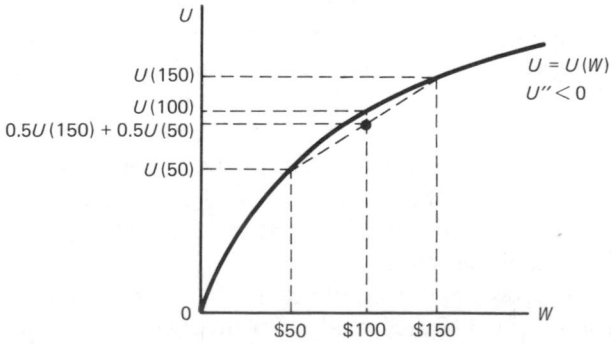

Utility as a function of wealth.

Now let us see how this quite simple and appealing notion can be applied to the problem of the speculative demand for money. Consider an individual agent who receives his income once per period and who saves. He must have some way of holding his savings between periods, so let the assets available to him be money and bonds. If we assume the price level to be constant, there is no question of money either earning a return for, or imposing any risk on, the person who holds it. However, since bonds pay interest and are subject to fluctuations in price, they yield income—albeit an uncertain one. This income has two components: the interest payments accruing to the bond holder, an amount we take as certain, and capital gains and losses which must be predicted. For the sake of simplicity, in the analysis that follows we assume that the agent, when he assesses the probabilities of making capital gains and losses on bonds, does so in such a way as to make the expected value of such gains and losses zero, so that the expected value of the yield on holding bonds becomes just equal to the market rate of interest.[12] However, there is a risk attached to the return to be had from holding bonds, which can be measured by the standard deviation, a common measure of dispersion, of the probability distribution in terms of which the individual describes his expectations about the future price of bonds.[13]

Now the problem confronting the individual agent at the end of a period is to allocate his savings, whose amount it is assumed has already been decided, between bonds and money so as to maximize the utility he expects to derive from them. Holding more bonds increases the expected interest income to be earned on his savings and this increases the wealth he expects to have in the next period. To this extent it tends to increase his utility. However, it also increases the dispersion of the possible values his wealth will take in the next period.[14] Since risk reduces the agent's utility, the introduction of extra bonds into the portfolio involves trading off extra expected wealth in the next period against extra risk. A diagram or two will help to make this clear and will enable us to carry the analysis further.

In Figure 6.4 expected wealth in the next period w is measured on the vertical axis and risk on the horizontal axis. The curves I_0, I_1, and so on, are *indifference curves* whose interpretation is familiar. Each curve represents a locus of combinations of expected wealth and risk between which the individ-

[12] This assumption is not a necessary one. One may have a positive or negative expected value of capital gains and losses without basically altering the analysis. However, to take this approach complicates things, for the slope of the budget constraint in the figures that follow is no longer given by the interest rate in such a case, but rather by the interest rate plus the expected rate of capital gain. Unless one can relate the latter variable to the interest rate, perhaps in the way Keynes did, the relationship between the demand for money and the interest rate produced by this theory becomes obscure.

[13] The use of the standard deviation of this distribution is not arbitrary but is in fact dictated by the utility theory that underlies this model. On this matter the skeptic can consult Tobin (1958).

[14] In the model discussed here, holding more bonds means bearing more risk. It is not difficult to think of a model in which it is money that is the risky asset. For example, if the bonds in question are redeemable at a given value in real terms in the next period, and if the price level in the next period is uncertain, it is money holding that involves risk. However, in a model such as this, an individual will still hold a diversified portfolio and the demand for money will still vary with the rate of interest. Matthews (1963) deals with several aspects of this type of problem.

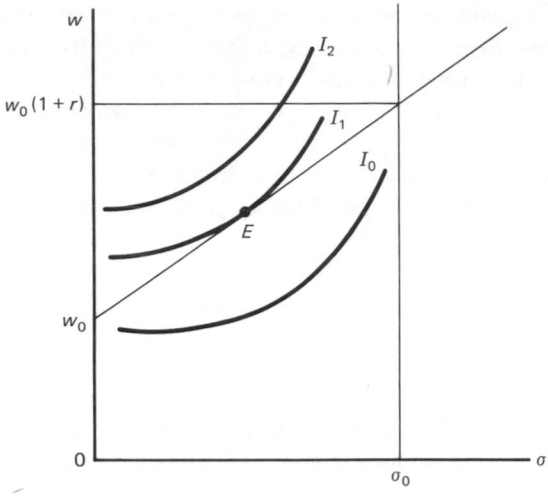

Figure 6.4 The individual agent's choice of how to allocate his wealth between money and bonds involves trading off expected wealth against risk.

ual agent is indifferent. Each curve slopes upward to the right as a result of the assumption that expected wealth is a "good," something that adds to utility, and risk is a "bad," something that detracts from it. It follows from this assumption that if his wealth is increased the individual will be better off unless risk is also increased to hold him at the same level of satisfaction as before. For the same reason, the indifference curves are to be interpreted as reflecting higher levels of utility as one moves upward and to the left. More wealth with no extra risk attached, or less risk with no compensating decrease in wealth, makes the individual agent better off. The curves are convex downward because it is posited that the more wealth owned, the less some extra wealth will mean to the agent, and hence the smaller the increase in risk he will be willing to bear to increase his expected wealth further.

The line $w_0 - w_0(1 + r)$ is the budget constraint, the line that shows the combinations of risk and expected wealth the individual can actually choose among in arranging his portfolio. If he chooses to hold all his wealth in the form of money, he will earn no return on it, but neither will he face any risk. Hence the budget constraint passes through the point w_0, which measures the amount of wealth he initially begins with and the amount he will end up with if he holds it all in the form of money. Similarly, if he chooses to hold all his wealth in bonds, his expected wealth in this circumstance will be equal to $w_0(1 + r)$, where r is the rate of interest and σ_0 is the maximum risk the wealth holder can bear, that which he faces when all his assets are held in the form of bonds. If all bonds are assumed to be the same in terms of the interest they offer and the risk that holding them carries with it, any point along $w_0 - w_0(1 + r)$ is available to the wealth holder; he can mix money and bonds in his portfolio, and the more of the latter he holds the proportionately more return he can expect to earn, while the risk he is taking also increases in proportion to the bond content of his portfolio.

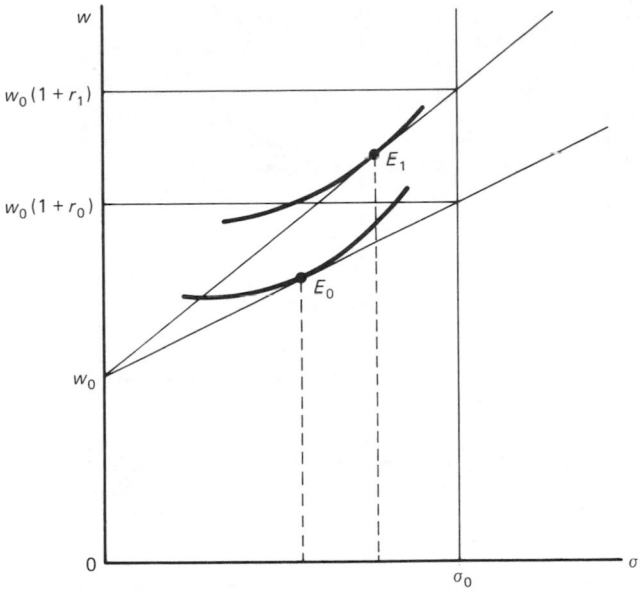

Figure 6.5 The agent's response to a higher rate of interest.

Now the wealth holding agent's problem is to obtain the maximum amount of utility from his portfolio, given the rate of interest and given the riskiness attached to holding bonds. His aim is to reach the highest indifference curve available to him, and this is clearly at the point E where the budget constraint is just tangent to indifference curve I_1. At this point he will be holding a portfolio consisting partly of money and partly of bonds. This analysis then succeeds in explaining asset diversification in portfolios, but its use extends beyond this because one can use it to derive a relationship between the market rate of interest and the demand for money.

Consider Figure 6.5, which is essentially the same as Figure 6.4. If the market rate of interest is r_1 rather than r_0, and the riskiness of bonds is the same, the slope of the budget constraint obviously is steeper. Instead of being in equilibrium at E_0 the wealth holder will settle at E_1, which in Figure 6.5 is to the right of and above E_0. Thus, he will be earning more return and bearing more risk. However, though the rate of interest is different in the two situations, the riskiness of bonds is not, so the conclusion that more risk is being borne implies at once that more bonds are being held at a higher rate of interest. That is, the higher the rate of interest, the smaller the demand for money. From this analysis it is possible to derive for the individual a speculative demand curve for money that is continuous and downward-sloping, unlike the Keynesian approach, which yields a smooth relationship only in the aggregate.

However, the relationship does not *have* to be downward sloping because its nature depends on the indifference curves from which it is derived. It is quite possible to draw these so that at a higher rate of interest less risk is taken (that is, more money is held) or indeed so that just the same amount of money is

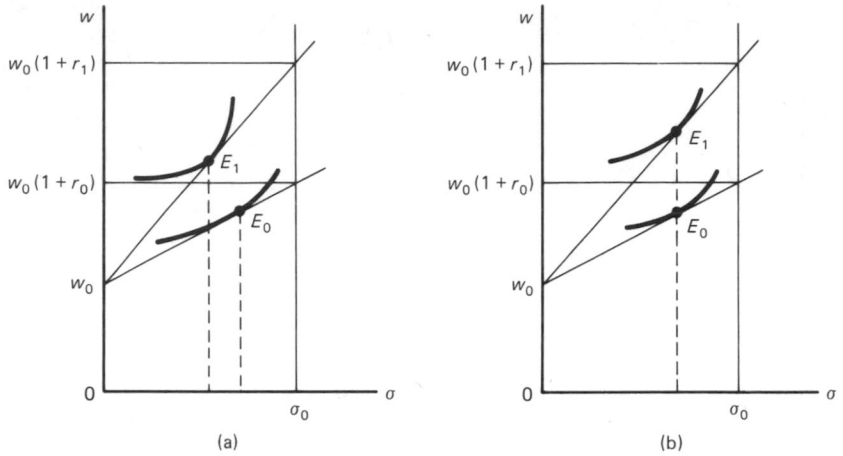

Figure 6.6 (a) An indifference map that yields a higher demand for money at higher rates of interest. (b) An indifference map that yields the same demand for money at different rates of interest.

held; these possibilities are shown in Figure 6.6. The nature of the demand-for-money function derived from this analysis depends on the nature of the indifference map underlying it and becomes an empirical matter rather than one of theory. This should not perturb the reader unduly, for such conclusions often emerge in economics.[15]

This is no more than a case of the substitution effect and the income effect (it may be better to call it the *wealth effect* here) potentially working in opposite directions. Consider Figure 6.7, which reproduces Figure 6.5. The movement from E_0 to E_1 can be regarded as partly a movement around an indifference curve and partly a movement to a higher one. The substitution effect $E_0 - E_2$ clearly leads to less money being held at a higher rate of interest, but the wealth effect from $E_2 - E_1$ could go either way. However, so long as an increase in wealth leads people to desire to hold more bonds, the wealth effect of a higher rate of interest will reinforce the substitution effect and lead to more bonds, and hence less money, being held. Since this seems so reasonable a postulate about the nature of the relationship between the level of wealth and the demand for bonds, the possibility of a perverse relationship between the demand for money and the rate of interest seems to be virtually ruled out.

It should be stressed here that we are dealing with the relationship between the demand for money and the rate of interest of an individual who has a given amount of wealth to allocate between money and bonds at each value of the interest rate. This is not necessarily the same relationship as that between the demand for money and the rate of interest when the rate of interest

[15] The possibility of a "backward-bending" supply curve of labor is a famous example of this and, indeed, if the reader will but substitute income for w on the vertical axis of Figure 6.4, and hours worked for σ on the horizontal axis; and interpret the intercept of the budget constraint as being nonlabor income and its slope as being equal to the wage rate, he will find that he has exactly the model that can yield this implication.

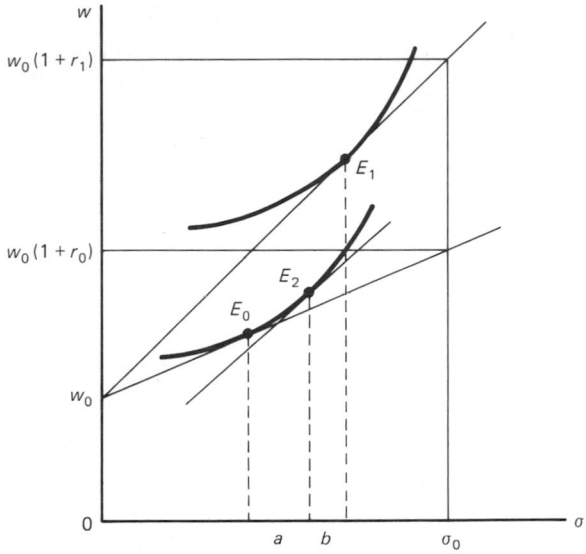

Figure 6.7 The distance *a* represents a substitution effect, *b* the wealth effect, and $a + b$ the total effect of the rate of interest being r_1 rather than r_0.

changes. Changes in the rate of interest leave wealth unaltered only for individuals who are not holding bonds when the rate changes. For those who are holding bonds, a rise in the rate involves a fall in their wealth, and vice versa. So long as the demand for money changes in the same direction as wealth, so long as money has a positive wealth elasticity of demand, these effects will reinforce the already analyzed tendency of the relationship between the demand for money and the rate of interest to be negative.

The effect of changes in the riskiness of bonds on the demand for money should also be discussed. In terms of our diagrams, an increase in the riskiness of bonds involves a shift to the right of σ_0, so that the budget constraint becomes more shallow at a given rate of interest. This is shown in Figure 6.8, where it is clear that greater riskiness of bonds has an effect in every way equivalent to a lower interest rate, increasing the quantity of money demanded. Similarly, a decrease in the riskiness of bonds causes the demand for money to decrease. Interest makes bonds attractive to hold, and riskiness detracts from their desirability. A rise in the interest rate and a decrease in risk are alternative ways of making bonds more attractive to hold, and so it is hardly surprising that they work in equivalent ways.

We have here, then, a theory of the speculative demand for money by an individual, which suggests that it depends on the individual's wealth, the rate of interest (which in this theory stands for the expected yield on holding bonds over some period), and the standard deviation of the probability distribution the individual attributes to possible rates of capital gain and loss on bonds—the risk attached to holding them. Though nothing is explicitly said about the price level here, it should be clear that because the utility function underlying this analysis makes utility a function of real wealth we again have a function in

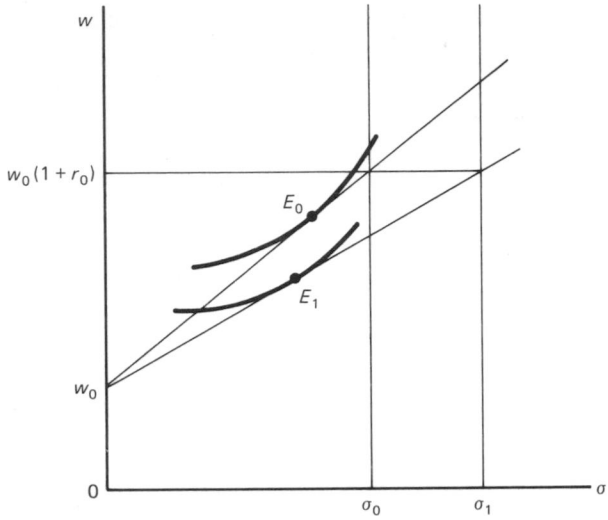

Figure 6.8 The effect of an increase in the riskiness of bonds causes a movement from E_0 to E_1.

which, other things being equal, the demand for money measured in nominal terms is proportional to the price level.[16] The key characteristic of this theory, as we have presented it, is that it deals with the allocation of wealth between two assets, the return on one being certain and the return on the other being subject to risk. The reader should also note that there is nothing about the *zero* rate of return on money that is essential to the results generated. It is its *certainty* that matters. If money were to bear a positive, but still certain, rate of return r_m, the only difference this would make to the above analysis would be to shift the intercept of the budget constraint with the vertical axis of our diagrams up from w_0 to some point $w_0(1 + r_m)$. As we shall see in the next chapter (p. 83), the possibility of money bearing interest is an important point to consider when deciding how to test hypotheses having to do with the speculative demand for money.

This is, in any event, a model of individual behavior and concerns only part of the individual agent's overall demand for money. We cannot claim that it directly tells us much about the nature of the aggregate demand-for-money function. However, inasmuch as it is a theory that explains the holding of diversified portfolios by individuals, there can be little doubt that if speculative motives are important in the aggregate, they are probably better analyzed in terms of a model such as this than in terms of Keynes's approach. The latter does not allow for individual portfolio diversification. Even so, this approach does get us a little further forward in formulating hypotheses about the nature of the economy's aggregate demand-for-money function. It suggests that some

[16] But remember that saying the demand for money is proportional to the price level (other things being equal) is not the same as saying that a change in the price level will necessarily lead to a proportional change in the demand for money. The "other things" may not remain equal. (See Chapter 5, footnote 7, p. 53.)

measure of the economy's assessment of the riskiness of assets other than money may be worth including in that function.

CONCLUSIONS

Each of the three approaches to the analysis of the demand for money dealt with in this chapter is cast in terms of individual behavior, and each of them deals with only one aspect of an agent's demand for money. They do not therefore directly yield predictions about the nature of the economy's aggregate demand-for-money function, the relationship on which this book is focused. Nevertheless, if these models do not tell us directly about the aggregate demand-for-money function, they do give us several hints about its possible nature. Thus: if economies of scale exist in individual demand functions they may also exist in the aggregate, while distributional effects may be important; if brokerage fees influence individual behavior, and these involve costs measured in terms of time and trouble, it may be that the aggregate demand for money varies with the level of real wages ruling in the economy; and if the riskiness of bonds influences individual behavior, it may be that such a factor is also important in the aggregate. Therefore, quite apart from being interesting pieces of analysis in their own right, these recent extensions of Keynesian theorizing about the nature of the demand-for-money function also raise interesting questions about aggregate behavior that are worthy of empirical investigation.

three

DATA PROBLEMS AND ECONOMETRIC ISSUES

chapter 7

Measuring the Variables of the Demand-for-Money Function

INTRODUCTORY COMMENT

In our theoretical discussions we have talked about money, the rate of interest, wealth, and the like, as if it were quite clear what these words referred to. The reader has no doubt some rough idea of what is meant by each of these terms, an idea that suffices for understanding of the logic of the theories. However, if empirical tests are to be carried out, a precise definition must be given for each term so that data can be gathered, and clearly specified empirical hypotheses, based on various models of the demand for money, can be formulated.

THE MEASUREMENT OF MONEY

Consider first the problem of finding an empirical measure of money. There is no sharp distinction in the real world between money and other assets, but rather a spectrum of assets, some more like one's rough idea of money than others. Theories based on the transactions motive emphasize the proposition that a demand for money exists because, unlike other assets, money is a means of exchange. They are theories of the demand for assets which are readily acceptable and transferable in everyday transactions, and the money concept to which they apply was, until the early 1970s, rather easily defined at least in the context of the U.S. economy; there were but two assets that clearly had such a characteristic. These were currency and demand deposits at commercial banks. The sum of these assets available to the public at that time was widely agreed to constitute the relevant measure of the money stock as far as theories of the transactions demand for money were concerned. Matters have become a little more complicated in the last decade. In the early 1970s, beginning in New England, there were introduced "NOW" accounts, transferable by check like demand deposits but unlike them bearing explicit interest, albeit at a regulated rate. In 1981 such accounts became available on a nationwide basis and are believed by many to belong in a definition of money used to test transactions demand theories against recent data. However, such accounts are more expensive to transfer than demand deposits, and it is possible to argue plausibly that they do not really constitute "transaction balances" in the same sense as do demand deposits.

Each economy raises its own problems in measuring "means of exchange." For example, in the British economy currency and current accounts at commercial banks might be regarded as generally acceptable and readily available means of exchange. But the availability of automatic overdrafts to bank customers has led some to argue that unused overdraft limits also constitute "money" in a meaningful sense. Or again, in Canada certain classes of deposits at trust companies (institutions somewhat similar to savings and loan associations) and certain classes of time deposits at chartered banks have long been transferable by check. In these cases the charges levied for making transfers by check are sometimes sufficiently high as to deter people from using such assets as if they were the equivalent of ordinary checking accounts, and so it is far from obvious a priori whether or not it is appropriate to treat all such assets as equally efficient means of exchange. Moreover, as with the United States, the situation in Canada began to change in the 1970s and has continued to so as the commercial banks introduced new types of interest-bearing low-cost checkable deposits, notably, in 1981, accounts paying interest on a daily basis; these new assets probably do belong in a definition of money that is relevant to testing theories about transactions demand.

All in all there is little, if anything, that one can say about the issues involved in measuring the money stock relevant to transactions demand theories that is generally true of all times and places. In some economics it is clear which assets are means of exchange and which are not, but not in all, as the above examples show; nor do the dividing lines between means of exchange and other assets stay put over time in any particular economy. The boundary shifts as the financial system evolves, and the most that one can say in general is that the economist seeking to test transaction demand theories needs to be sensitive to the institutional framework of the economy generating his data.[1]

Not all theories of the demand for money are based on the transactions motive. As a result, even if the borderline between means of exchange and other assets was clearcut, it would be hard to settle on an appropriate and generally acceptable definition of money on a priori grounds. Theories of the speculative demand for money downplay its characteristic as a means of exchange and emphasize instead the fact that it is an asset whose capital value does not vary with the rate of interest. In the United States currency and demand deposits, and these days NOW accounts, have this characteristic to be

[1] The problem of the continuity of the meaning of a money supply series is one that is particularly amenable to solution by the construction of an index number series to measure money. See pp. 84–85 for a brief account of recent work on this matter.

sure, but they are not the only assets that possess it. Time deposits at commercial banks, deposits at mutual savings banks, and savings and loan association shares are, in this sense, just as much "money" in the United States as are their equivalents in other economies. Moreover such assets yield an interest income to their holders at a rate higher than that borne by checkable deposits and currency. The extent to which checkable deposits bear interest varies from time to time and place to place, but it would be hard to find a case of their bearing interest at a rate equal to, let alone higher than, that available on noncheckable deposits.

Currency—except very occasionally in the past in the case of notes issued by privately owned banks—is an asset that bears no interest at all. Despite this, individuals hold currency, not to mention low- or zero-interest checkable deposits, in significant amounts, and the speculative motive for holding money can be of little relevance as far as the demand for such "narrow money" is concerned. It is more likely to play a role in determining the demand for assets such as noncheckable time deposits and perhaps savings and loan association shares. Hence its importance can best be tested in the context of the demand for money defined over a broader spectrum of assets than currency and checkable deposits.

Theories based on the precautionary motive are no better at yielding a clearcut guide as how best to define money for empirical purposes. There is no doubt that currency and demand deposits may be held for precautionary reasons. However, in the context of the United States it can be argued that the costs of transferring funds from, say, a money market mutual fund or a time deposit to a demand deposit when they are needed to cover an unexpected cash outflow are small relative to those involved in converting, say, certificates of deposit or savings and loan association shares into a demand deposit. If this argument is correct, it will follow that money market mutual funds and time deposits can reasonably be included in a definition of money to which the theory of the precautionary demand for money is relevant but that the other above-mentioned assets should be excluded. At the very least, the existence of such an argument prevents such a possibility from being ruled out a priori.

Theories of the demand for money which rest simply on the proposition that money yields a flow of unspecified services to its owners raise similar problems. Every asset yields services to its owner, and in defining one set of assets as being money and another as not being money, one is really arguing that the services yielded by the various assets in the first category are sufficiently similar to one another as to make it possible to treat them as if they were all one asset, and sufficiently different from those yielded by other assets to disqualify the latter from being put in the same category. It is the asset holder's decision, rather than that of the economist studying his behavior, that determines which assets are close substitutes for one another and which are not. The only way to find out what asset holders think is to study their behavior; in the context of this more general approach to the problem of the demand for money, the correct definition of money becomes an empirical matter, at least within rather broad boundaries laid down by one's "rough idea" of what money is.[2]

In the light of the foregoing arguments, it is hardly surprising that several definitions of money have been employed in the course of testing theories of the demand for money. As far as the United States economy is concerned, the bulk of the work carried out down to the mid-1970s confined the definition of money to currency plus demand deposits at commercial banks, "old M_1," as it is now called or currency plus demand deposits plus time deposits at commercial banks, "old M_2." There was a good reason for so limiting the definition of money, for in addition to clarifying the theory of the demand for money per se, these empirical tests were supposed to throw light on the scope of economic policy, particularly monetary policy. One wished, then, to know about the role played in the economy by assets whose volume could be controlled by the monetary authorities, and these assets were currency in circulation and the liabilities of commercial banks. It was thus not unreasonable to concentrate on these assets to the exclusion of others. As we have already noted, however, from the 1970s onward, developments in the banking system began to undermine the relevance of these simple notions of what constituted narrow and broad money. In particular, NOW accounts have come to be included in the narrow-money concept ("new M_1") while the broader concept ("new M_2") has had to be extended to include such assets as, for example, shares in money market mutual funds and money market certificates issued by commercial banks. The process of financial innovation which has required these adjustments is an ongoing one, and ideas about the "appropriate" definition of money in the U.S. economy will undoubtedly continue to change in the future as they have in the recent past.

One novel approach to the problem of measuring money currently under investigation involves the construction of index numbers to measure the quantity of money. Instead of simply adding up what are, after all, heterogenous assets on a dollar-for-dollar basis, it is argued that those assets that are more readily and cheaply transferred should be given more weight in measuring the aggregate money stock than those that are less liquid. One type of index number that has been used, notably by W. Barnett (1980) for the United States, to generate aggregate money supply indices is the so-called Divisia Index whereby each type of asset to be included in the total money supply is weighted by the difference between the rate of return it earns and some representative market

[2] The notion that the question of the correct way to measure money for purposes of carrying out empirical work on the demand for money and related problems is itself an empirical issue is set out and defended in Laidler (1969) and Friedman and Schwartz (1970, Part 1). For a criticism of this approach to the problem, see Mason (1976), who argues with considerable justice that this approach carries with it a grave danger of leading one into circular arguments—the definition of money that enables a theory to work well is chosen as appropriate and then evidence generated using it is cited as supporting the theory in terms of which the data were selected in the first place. This danger undoubtedly exists in principal, but as we shall see in Chapters 10 and 11, there seems to be enough results concerning the demand-for-money function that do not depend on the precise variable chosen to measure money that Mason's objection may not be a fatal one.

rate of interest. The argument underlying this procedure is that the greater is this difference, the greater must be the "liquidity services" the asset in question yields to its holder, and hence the more is it "money."

The difficulty here is that the difference between rates of return in question measures, at best, liquidity on the margin rather than the average liquidity of a particular asset. If one were to picture a perfectly competitive banking system in which all types of bank liabilities bore interest at the market rate, the Divisia Index would yield the peculiar result that the money stock was equal to zero.[3] This is a theoretically extreme example, not likely to be encountered in practice, and it may well be that in current circumstances the Divisia Index is a reasonably good one to employ. However, this example does, at least, warn us that the use of this index is not theoretically satisfactory in all circumstances and that experiments with other types of index are worthwhile. A promising line of enquiry here uses turnover rates on different classes of assets as weights, the idea being that the more frequently an asset is transferred, the more useful do agents find it as "money." [See P. A. Spindt (1983).]

Far more work has been done on the demand for money in the U.S. economy than in any other, but many other countries have been studied with less thoroughness. To discusss the details of definitions of money used in studies of these other countries would require us to deal with their individual financial systems to an extent that would be quite inappropriate in a book such as this. Suffice it to say that, as far as possible, people working on countries other than the United States have tried to utilize definitions of money roughly corresponding to those used in studying U.S. data. It should also be noted that because financial innovation over the last decade or so has not been confined to the United States, people working in other countries too have found it necessary to adjust their notions of how to measure money in order to accommodate such changes. In a number of cases [for example, S. Namba (1983) for Japan, Cockerline and Murray (1981) for Canada] experiments with Divisia Index numbers have also been carried out.

One final point concerning the measurement of money should be made. As we have stressed again and again in the first two parts of this book, the demand for money is a demand for *real* balances. The concepts of the money stock we have been discussing here are measured in nominal terms. To get to a measure of real money from nominal money, it is necessary to divide by an appropriate price index. The selection of the latter variable is relatively uncontroversial. It is generally accepted that a broadly based index such as, in the

[3] The problems involved here stem from certain fundamental issues in monetary theory that are beyond the scope of this book, though they are touched on in Appendix A (Chapter 3). The basic point is that in an economy that uses token as opposed to commodity money, the marginal cost of producing real balances is essentially zero. Under competitive conditions real balances become a free good to the economy, and all the very difficult questions that arise in general about accounting for the services provided by free goods in measuring income, wealth, and economic welfare are relevant to the case of money. The reader who wants to follow up this issue is referred to Friedman (1969) and Johnson (1969), two of the fundamental papers on the matter. Fried and Huwitt (1983) discuss closely related issues.

case of the United States, a gross or net national product deflator is an appropriate choice, but sometimes a consumer price index is used, particularly for those countries where national product deflators are either unreliable or unavailable. By and large, one measure of a broad spectrum of prices moves in harmony with another, and little seems to hinge on such a choice in most cases. Sometimes, though, price indices are distorted by being heavily weighted with officially set prices, particularly in countries where governments seek to control inflation by direct price controls, and this can raise problems in particular instances.

As we shall see in due course, many important empirical results concerning the demand for money are rather insensitive to the precise way in which money is measured and how that measurement evolves over time. However, "many" is not "all," and we shall have to return to some of the issues raised above, particularly those having to do with financial innovation, when we discuss the outcome of empirical work. For the moment it will suffice for the reader to be aware that the problem of measuring money in the real world, in a way that corresponds to the concepts underlying theoretical work on the demand for money, raises real problems for those intent on empirically testing rival hypotheses about the nature of the function.

INCOME AND WEALTH

The independent variables in the demand-for-money function fall into three groups. First, there are what we shall call the *scale* variables in the relationship, wealth and income; second, there are the *opportunity cost* variables, the yields on assets other than money, and the yield on money itself, including the expected rate of inflation; finally, there are the *other* variables that particular approaches to the theory of the demand for money suggest may be relevant, the level of wages, the riskiness of bonds, and so on. We shall now discuss the scale variables.

The level of income is often thought of as standing as a proxy for the volume of transactions in the economy and hence has played an important role in empirical tests of transactions-based theories of the demand for money. It is also important because it is one of the principal arguments in the demand-for-money function utilized in the macroeconomic model presented in Part I. The measurement of this variable presents little problem because, although gross national product and net national product series have been used to measure it, as well as gross domestic product series in some cases, these variables move rather closely together over time and no important difference in results is obtained by using one or the other.

The empirical measurement of wealth is not so straightforward. For Britain it is possible to construct a series on financial wealth and Khusro (1952) and Grice and Bennett (1984) have used such a series in studies of the demand for money in that country. However, this is a very narrow wealth concept, and only for the United States do data exist that permit the construction of long time series for various broad measures of the aggregate level of nonhuman wealth, real as well as financial, owned by the private sector of the economy. An important problem here concerns how much consolidation there should be of disaggregated wealth data in producing an aggregate figure. For example, if households own firms, as they do, and one thinks of households' wealth as the constraint on households' money holding, and firms' wealth as the constraint on firms' money holding, should one, in aggregating the two to obtain the constraint upon the combined money holding of firms and households, ignore the fact that firms' wealth is in fact included in households' wealth, being the value of the stock households own? Should one simply add the two wealth figures together, or should one remove all elements of double counting from the aggregate wealth of the two sectors and treat the value of household wealth alone as constraining the money holding of households and firms combined?

There is no straight theoretical answer to this question, but empirical work by Meltzer (1963) seemed to show that the results achieved are not importantly influenced by the degree of such consolidation in the wealth data used, at least within the private sector. Therefore, he measured wealth as the consolidated net worth of the private sector, including that sector's ownership of government debt. Meltzer's evidence also suggested, however, that to treat the government as "owned" by the private sector, and hence to add government assets rather than government debt to the assets of the private sector, made a difference in the results achieved. As has been explained earlier (Appendix A, Chapter 3) to treat government debt as net wealth ignores the possibility that the private sector regards the future tax liabilities inherent in the necessity that the government pay interest on its debt as decreasing its net worth. Meltzer's preferred way of measuring wealth is, therefore, open to criticism inasmuch as it ignores this possibility.

Sufficiently detailed data on nonhuman wealth measured over a time span long enough to be useful do not exist for economies other than the United States, so it is only for the latter economy that demand for money functions using direct broad measures of nonhuman wealth have been fitted. Even in the context of work in the United States most economists have been deterred from using this variable, both by the conceptual problems involved in measuring the "correct" aggregate variable just discussed, but also by Friedman's arguments discussed earlier (Chapter 5, pp 55–56) to the effect that an even more inclusive wealth concept, embodying the value of human as well as nonhuman capital, should be used when measuring the constraint on money holding. Of course, to measure this more inclusive concept of wealth presents formidable difficulties of its own, and virtually all attempts to come to grips with them have started from the simple idea that wealth is the discounted present value of expected future income. So long as the rate of discount used can be regarded as constant, wealth varies in exactly the same fashion as expected income. If expected income rises by 10%, so will wealth; if it falls, so will wealth, and so on. One is interested in studying the relationship between *variations* in the level of wealth and *variations* in the demand for money and, because this is the case, it is not important whether wealth is measured directly or whether *expected* or, as it is often called, *permanent income* is used as a proxy for this variable. It is to the discussion of this variable that we now turn.

EXPECTED INCOME

No problem in economics has received more attention recently than that of expectation formation on the part of economic agents, but for close to two decades it seemed that a remarkably simple approach to modeling the relationship between the actual behavior of a variable and expectations about its future behavior would suffice to produce satisfactory empirical results, and much of the empirical work on the demand for money we shall discuss below has employed it. This approach involves applying what is interchangeably known as the *error learning* or *adaptive expectations* hypothesis to data on the actual values of whatever variable agents are thought to be forming expectations about.

Let us call the variable in question X, and let the subscripts t, $t - 1$, and so on, refer to the periods during which its value is actually being observed. Let X^e be the value X is expected to take in the future, and let the subscripts t, $t - 1$, and so on, refer to the periods during which the expectation in question is held. It is obvious that we can write the change that takes place in the value X is expected to take, the extent to which expectations adapt, between two periods, as $X^e_t - X^e_{t-1}$. The error-learning hypothesis postulates that this change is proportional to the difference between the expectation about the value of X_t held in the period $t - 1$ and the value X_t actually ends up taking, that is, to the amount by which the initially held expectation turns out to be in error. Thus with λ a positive fraction we can write the error-learning hypothesis as

$$X^e_t - X^e_{t-1} = \lambda(X_t - X^e_{t-1}) \tag{7.1}$$

Elementary rearrangement of this expression gives

$$X^e_t = \lambda X_t + (1 - \lambda)X^e_{t-1} \tag{7.2}$$

and from this, by continuous back-substitution, it follows that

$$X^e_t = \lambda X_t + \lambda(1 - \lambda)X_{t-1} + \lambda(1 - \lambda)^2 X_{t-2} + \cdots + \lambda(1 - \lambda)^n X_{t-n} \cdots \tag{7.3}$$

In short, the error-learning hypothesis implies that the expected future value of a variable can be measured by taking an exponentially weighted average of current and past values of that variable, the very simple assumption underlying this procedure being nothing more than that, in trying to assess the future, people take past experience into account—and take more notice of the recent past than of more distant times.

The error-learning hypothesis seems plausible enough in a rough-and-ready sort of way, and expected income, measured by applying a formula such as Equation (7.3) to data on real national income, has often been used as a scale variable in demand-for-money functions in tests designed to investigate the role of a broadly defined notion of wealth in the relationship. Even so, to say that this approach is plausible stops a long way short of saying that it is the best that can be done. Work dealing with the so-called *rational expectations* notion which builds on the seminal contribution of J. F. Muth (1961) starts from this simple observation.[4] To see what is involved, suppose that an economic agent did indeed start out using the error-learning hypothesis to form expectations of his own income, but suppose he found that this practice was leading him into systematic forecasting errors of some sort. For example, suppose he discovered that he was usually overpredicting his income at times when it was falling and underpredicting it at times when it was rising (as he usually would if his income followed a cyclical time path). A rational maximizing agent, as economists always suppose the subjects of their analysis to be, would notice that he was making systematic errors and would modify the way in which he used information on current and past income in forming his expectations about its future course until he had eliminated them. He would then no longer be forming his expectations by applying Equation (7.3) to the relevant series, but he would be forming them in a way that was "rational" in the sense that any errors he made would be random over time; anything other than a random pattern of errors would eventually be recognized and allowed for in the expectations formula he used.

If we take this line of reasoning seriously, it still might lead us to the proposition that the agent will form his expectations about income (or any other variable for that matter) by applying some sort of averaging process to current and past values of the variable in question, but that process will not in general be the simple special case of exponentially declining weights described in Equation (7.3). Just what the averaging process will be in any particular case must depend on the way in which the variable about which expectations are being formed moves over time. There is no general formula to describe it. What a statistician would call an "optimal time-series forecast" of income has not been used explicitly to measure permanent income in any empirical study of the demand for money of which I am aware, but such techniques have been applied in work on the consumption function recently and presumably will be used in the demand-for-money area in due course.[5] However, the general idea that the demand for money might respond with a more complex lag pattern to the behavior of real income than one which can be captured in exponentially declining weights has been incorporated in a number of studies, as we shall see. Letting the data find the appropriate weights to apply to current and lagged values of income (at least within certain bounds) might be interpreted as com-

[4] The rational expectations idea has of course been more widely applied in models of inflation than in the context of the demand for money per se. In particular, it has been used by Lucas (for example, 1974) and Barro (for example, 1977, 1978) to get to grips with some of the issues concerning the interaction of aggregate supply and demand in the short run which were raised in Chapter 3, pp 29–32.

[5] For a particularly thorough application of the rational expectations notion to the analysis of consumption-permanent income relationships, see Flavin (1981).

ing quite close to the idea of measuring permanent income as an optimal time series forecast of income, and a good deal of empirical work does just that.

One can carry the rational expectations notion a good deal further than the foregoing discussion does, of course, because there is no good reason why a maximizing agent should use only information about the past behavior of the variable he is trying to forecast. Rather, he might be expected to make use of all information that seems to him to be relevant to his forecast. If we set aside the considerable practical problems of the costs of data acquisition and processing, this observation may be translated into the proposition that in forecasting the future value of any variable an economic agent will act as if he was using a complete econometric model of the system generating that variable, a system of which, as often as not, his own behavior will be a part. This version of the rational expectations notion has had a considerable impact in the area of economic theory in the last 10 years or so, but for obvious reasons it is extremely difficult to implement empirically.[6]

The implications of the foregoing discussion for the measurement of alternative scale variables for the demand-for-money function are easily summarized, although somewhat disheartening. At least one very influential theory of the demand for money suggests that a rather inclusive notion of wealth is the appropriate scale variable to utilize, and although direct measurement of such a variable has always been recognized as virtually impossible, it looked for a while as though this problem could be circumvented by replacing wealth with the "expected" or "permanent" stream of income it yields, a variable that could in turn be measured for the aggregate economy quite easily by applying the error-learning idea to data on current and past values of real national income. Although this simple procedure has been widely used, and as we shall see, with considerable success as well, the notion of "rational" expectations casts considerable doubt on its validity. Until the results generated from this earlier work have been further investigated using new techniques that pay explicit attention to the rational expectations notion, they must be treated with skepticism and interpreted with great care, as must those of studies which postulate a distributed-lag relationship between the demand for money and real income and permit the data to determine the lag pattern.

RETURNS ON ALTERNATIVE ASSETS

Now let us turn to the problem of measuring the opportunity cost variables that might be included in the demand-for-money function. Consider first the question of choosing an appropriate variable to measure the yield to be earned on holding assets other than money. In practice, the availability of data limits the choice to one or two series, particularly when long time periods are to be studied. Thus, for the United States, though there are several available candidates when only post–World War II data are to be studied, notably for example

[6] The technique has been much used in the analysis of expected inflation: See, for example, Barro (1977, 1978).

the yields on 3 month treasury bills, or on savings and loan association shares, the series used for studies on longer periods have usually been either the yield on 20-year corporate bonds or that on 4–6-month commercial paper. They are the yields to be earned on instruments having 20 years (or 4–6 months) to run to redemption, yield being defined as the ratio to its current market price of the average income per annum to be earned from holding to maturity the instrument in question. This yield thus includes any change in the price of the asset that must take place to bring its current price into equality with its redemption price.

As it happens, the two series in question move quite closely together over time, and, for the purpose of testing for the presence of a rate of interest variable in the demand-for-money function one is probably as good as the other. However, the choice here has sometimes been regarded as contentious, and there are reasonable a priori arguments as to why either one is the appropriate selection. On the one hand, it is argued that the long rate is better because it is more representative of the average rate of return on capital in the economy at any time, and hence is a better indicator of the general opportunity cost of holding money than is the yield on short-run commercial debts. On the other hand, it is argued that the latter instruments, because of their short maturity, are closer substitutes for money than longer bonds, so that the yield on them is particularly relevant among the alternatives that are forgone by holding cash. There is merit in both these arguments, but they ignore the fact that much work has been done on the problem of the term structure of interest rates, the interrelationship of yields on assets of varying maturity.

The most satisfactory theory of the term structure appears to be one that rests on the proposition that (with suitable adjustment for risk) expected holding-period yields on assets of various maturities tend to be equalized by the market. The yield expected to be earned over any week, say, by owning 20-year bonds, tends to be brought into equality with that to be earned on instruments of all other maturities. This expected holding-period yield, of course, includes capital gains and losses made over the period. Now if this is the case—and if the planned holding period of money and bonds is a short one, in the sense that decisions to hold money or bonds do not bind the one who decides to do so irrevocably for long time periods—then expected yields on various assets over a short holding period are the relevant opportunity costs of holding money and, if the aforementioned theory of the term structure is correct, this yield on any one asset will (once again with suitable adjustment for risk) be more or less equal to that on any other. The yield on 4- to 6-month commercial paper is therefore more likely to be a good measure of short holding-period yields on assets other than money, and hence of the relevant opportunity cost of holding money, than is the yield to maturity on 20-year bonds.[7] Whether it is or not is

[7] The reader who wishes to pursue this matter further should start with Michaelson (1973). He should also note that the yield to maturity on a short instrument will not be a perfect proxy for the relevant holding period yield on a long one. The latter is likely to be higher to compensate agents for holding a riskier, or less "liquid," asset. On this, see Fried and Howitt (1983) who argue that the level of the "liquidity premium" involved here is likely to rise and fall with the general level of interest rates.

ultimately an empirical question and in fact both rates of interest have been used in various tests.

The foregoing discussion has made the point that the period over which money holding is planned is a short one, so that a short rate of interest probably provides an appropriate measure of the opportunity cost of holding money. Nevertheless, it has been pointed out by Laidler (1971 pp. 129–130), Karni (1972), and Friedman (1977) that the holding period for money is itself chosen by agents, so that, in principle, the whole term structure of interest rates is relevant to measuring the opportunity cost of holding money at any moment. Heller and Khan (1979) have attempted to implement this idea by, for each observation, running the regression of yield on term to maturity and term to maturity squared and then using the coefficients thus obtained as measures of the level and maturity structure of interest rates. Though they obtained reasonable results, their methods have not been followed up by others, perhaps because, as we have already noted, results on the role of the opportunity cost of money holding on the demand for money are not all that sensitive to the precise measure chosen.

One implication of the foregoing arguments is that even if the holding period of money is short, there nevertheless exist assets on which the rate of return over that short holding period is subject to little uncertainty. This in turn suggests that theories of the speculative demand for money have little scope for application in practice because of the existence of such assets, and that the liquidity-trap hypothesis may better be conceived of as dealing with the behavior of long-term relative to short-term interest rates than with the behavior of the rate of return on assets other than money relative to the rate of return on money itself. Nevertheless, the issue raised here is an empirical one. Even a little uncertainty about the holding-period yields on other assets may be enough to give speculative elements an important role in determining the demand for money, particularly broadly defined money.

Rates of return on bills and bonds are not the only opportunity cost variables that have been used in demand for money studies. We have already mentioned the rate of return on financial intermediaries' liabilities, and it should be noted that Hamburger (1966, 1977b) has argued that physical assets might also be good substitutes for money; hence he has used as an opportunity cost variable the rate of return on equities as measured by the ratio of dividend yield to price (and hence exclusive of capital gains and losses). This variable measures the real return on physical capital, and in inflationary situations needs to be supplemented by some opportunity cost variable incorporating an inflation rate variable, and in fact Hamburger's work has always involved the use of such an extra variable. (Just what it should be is discussed below pp. 94–96). Finally, it should be noted that Hamburger (1977a) was also one of the first to realize that when modeling the demand for money in open economies the rate of return to be earned on foreign securities is worth considering as an opportunity cost variable. He applied this idea to the cases of Britain and Germany, arguing that foreign interest rates might influence the demand for money in those countries; other writers, for example Poloz (1981), have more recently investigated the role of U.S. interest rates in influencing the demand for money in Canada.

THE OWN RATE OF RETURN ON MONEY

Though much of the theoretical work dealt with in Part II treated money as an asset bearing a zero rate of return, such an assumption is hardly empirically accurate. In the United States NOW accounts, time deposits and such, and their equivalents in other countries explicitly bear interest; and variations in the rate of return they yield ought to influence the demand for money defined broadly enough to include them. Though in many economies cartel arrangements among the banks—sometimes sanctioned by government regulation—have resulted in demand deposits bearing no explicit interest, this is not universally the case. It was only in 1933 that it became illegal for banks in the United States to pay interest on their demand deposits. Moreover, we have already seen (p. 84) that interest-bearing checkable accounts have been reintroduced in recent years, while in Canada interest-bearing deposits on which checks can be drawn have long been available. In any event, if explicit interest is not paid to depositors, banks can still evade cartel arrangements by making indirect payments to their customers. Setting service charges at a level below the cost of operating an account, making loans to depositors at preferential interest rates, giving free advice on business and tax problems, to say nothing of more obvious promotional schemes offering free gifts, are among the methods available to banks for making payments to depositors without explicitly calling those payments interest. Thus, it is an error to suppose that even narrowly defined money does not pay a return to those who hold it, and variations in such a return ought to lead to variations in the quantity of money demanded.

Despite the foregoing arguments, the great majority of the empirical studies dealt with below have treated money, whether broadly or narrowly defined, as bearing interest at a zero rate, or at least at an unvarying rate, which can therefore be ignored. Some workers, however, have been more careful and have included explicit measures of the own rate of return on money in their studies. A key problem here is how to measure the rate of interest actually paid on demand deposits, and two broad approaches have been taken to this issue. First, it was assumed, for example by Feige (1964) and Lee (1967), that banks vary the interest rate they pay to their customers only by varying the charges they levy for servicing checking accounts. Thus it is argued that variations in the ratio of the total value of service charges to the volume of demand deposits can be treated as being inversely correlated with the rate of interest on demand deposits and hence can be used as a proxy for that variable. Barro and Santomero (1972) refined this approach and used data from a survey of commercial banks for the period 1950–1968 to discover how remitted service charges actually varied with the size of the deposit held and in this way derived a measure of the rate of interest on demand deposits.

An alternative approach is that of Klein (1974a, b) who takes as his starting point the hypothesis that banks manage to avoid completely any cartel arrangements and do in fact pay, albeit by covert means, what he terms a competitive rate of return to their customers. Klein calculates the competitive rate of return on demand deposits in the following way. The main cost any institution bears in having a demand deposit outstanding rather than some nonmoney liability is the interest it forgoes on the proportion of its newly acquired assets that must be held in non-interest-bearing reserves against that liability. If demand deposits were truly non-interest-bearing, and no other marginal costs were involved, the return to be made by having an extra dollar's worth of deposits outstanding would be the interest earned on the non-reserve fraction of that dollar which the bank could invest in interest-earning securities. Thus, if the market rate of interest were 5%, and the reserve ratio to be held against demand deposits 20%, a bank that did not pay any interest on demand deposits could earn a rate of return of 4% on every dollar deposited with it. Klein's basic postulate is that competition forces the bank to pass this marginal profit on to its depositors. Hence, in our simple example demand deposits would bear interest, covertly paid, at the rate of 4%.

Klein's actual computations are more complex than this simple example because they allow for other implicit costs and subsidies inherent in U.S. banking regulations, but they follow the broad outlines just set out. He applies a similar procedure to computing the competitive rate of return on time deposits also, for although these bear explicit interest, the rate at which it is paid is also subject to cartel arrangements and regulations. He then computes the own rate of return on narrow money as a weighted average of the zero rate borne by currency and his estimate of the competitive rate on demand deposits. When dealing with broad money, the competitive rate on time deposits is included in a similar average.

Klein's measure of the own rate of return on demand deposits *assumes* that banks pay their customers a competitive rate of return on demand deposits and is open to criticism for making this assumption. Certainly, the Barro-Santomero results suggest that the rates paid by banks were below the competitive level at the time of their study. Later work by Startz (1979) based on a direct study of banks' expenses comes to the same conclusions. Two further unpublished studies are cited by Judd and Scadding (1982b), [Axilrod et al. (1979) and Becker and Bental (undated)] as also suggesting that Klein's estimates of the own rate of return on demand deposits are too high. Thus Klein's work on this issue, ingenious though it is, needs to be interpreted with care.

THE EXPECTED INFLATION RATE

The final opportunity cost variable we should discuss is the expected rate of inflation. Here, as with expected (or permanent) income, the adaptive-expectations hypothesis was widely used in early studies, notably by Cagan (1956) who used it to generate a series for the expected rate of inflation in a pioneering study of the demand for money in hyperinflations. Thus, the expected inflation rate has frequently been measured as an exponentially weighted average of current and past values of the actual inflation rate. The error-learning hypothesis is, of course, just as open to criticism based on the "rational expectations" idea when applied to measuring expected inflation as when applied to measuring expected income. How good an approximation it provides to the expectations that would be formed by a rational maximizing agent depends very much on the nature of the time path followed by the inflation rate at a particular time and place, and although in the case of Cagan's study the approximation in question turned out to be a good one, this cannot be the case in general.[8]

As in the context of measuring permanent income, so the practice of letting the data find the weights to be attached to current and past rates of inflation, instead of imposing exponentially declining weights, as adopted by, for example, Shapiro (1973), goes some way to meeting these difficulties. Furthermore, particularly in studies of the influence of expectations about inflation on the so-called inflation-unemployment trade-off, some workers (for example, Barro 1977, 1978) have carried the rational expectations idea further still. It has been argued that because in a fully employed economy the price level moves in proportion to the money supply, the expected rate of growth of the money supply, generated from a model of the underlying processes governing money creation, can be used to measure the expected inflation rate. Perhaps it can, but the proportional relationship between money and prices underlying this practice arises only in long-run equilibrium in an economy in which among other things the demand-for-money function is stable over time. A measure of the expected inflation rate, which presupposes the stability of the demand-for-money function, is not ideally suited for use in tests designed to investigate that stability.

For some times and places there exist data on inflation expectations generated by opinion surveys of one sort or another, and these have occasionally been used, for example by Goldfeld (1973), in demand-for-money studies.[9] However, the operation of market mechanisms provides us with a simple indirect way of coping with the role of expectations about inflation in the demand-for-money function, at least for advanced economies with well-developed and competitive capital markets. Assets, such as 20-year bonds and 4–6-month commercial paper, whose rates of return are widely used in demand-for-money studies as opportunity cost variables are, like money, nominal assets whose real value depreciates with inflation. Thus, when inflation is expected, the public is reluctant to hold them unless the rate of return they bear is adjusted upward to compensate for the expected erosion of real-capital value brought about by inflation. The higher the expected rate of inflation, the greater such an adjustment must be; but this is to argue that variations in the expected rate of inflation will be reflected in variations in these rates of return. To include the rate of return in a nominal asset in the demand-for-money

[8] See Mussa (1975) for an analysis of the conditions under which adaptive expectations are rational.

[9] Survey data often produce qualitative data on expectations rather than quantitative evidence. They tell us whether people expect inflation to be higher or lower, but not by how much. See Carlson and Parkin (1975) for a pioneering attempt at extracting quantitative information about expectations from such qualitative evidence.

function is thus to include a measure of the expected inflation rate therein. Moreover, the measure in question is produced by market forces, and its reliability does not depend on any particular hypothesis about how inflation expectations are formed. No matter how agents form their expectations about inflation, their market activities will ensure that variations in the rate of return on nominal assets will reflect variations in those expectations.

The foregoing reasoning takes us a long way toward solving the problems of finding an appropriate measure of the expected inflation rate to use in demand-for-money studies, but it does not take us all the way. To begin with, only if asset markets were free of all distorting influences, not least those stemming from the fact that the nominal returns agents earn from asset holding are subject to taxes, would we expect fluctuations in nominal interest rates to reflect perfectly fluctuations in inflation expectations. As it is, for economies such as the United States, though the relationship is probably close enough to be useful, it is far from perfect. Moreover, not all economies have well-developed asset markets that generate reliable data on nominal interest rates. In some cases markets do not exist, and in others, though they exist, they are so strictly regulated that the data they generate on interest rates are quite misleading. In such cases other expedients to measure expected inflation might be available. For example, when Frenkel (1977) came to investigate the Weimar hyperinflation (one of those included in Cagan's pioneering study), he noted that foreign exchange was a relevant alternative asset to domestic money and measured the opportunity cost of holding money by the forward premium in the foreign exchange market, arguing that this premium measured directly the expected rate of inflation. Here again, however, we do not always have data on foreign exchange rates, so Frenkel's solution to measuring expected inflation cannot be universally applied.

In short, there are many instances, particularly when less developed countries are studied, in which the problem of measuring expected inflation cannot be circumvented by resorting to the use of indirect measures such as we have just been discussing. In such cases there is no universally applicable solution to the problem of measuring expected inflation and an important aspect of judging any study of the influence of expected inflation on the demand for money must be an assessment of the adequacy of the measure of expected inflation used.

OTHER VARIABLES IN THE FUNCTION

Relatively little needs to be said about the other variables that may, according to one or another of the theories discussed in Part II, play a role in the demand-for-money function. The real-wage rate, which theories that put a brokerage fee into the demand-for-money function suggest might be relevant, has been used in four studies: Dutton and Gramm (1973) Karni (1974) Diewert (1974) and Phlips (1978). The first of these used an economywide average real-wage rate variable, while the second used average hourly earnings. One study [Slovin and Sushka (1983)] has incorporated a measure of the riskiness of bonds, and a series that measures variations in the inflation rate has been developed recently by Klein (1975). Inasmuch as such variations may reduce the predictability of the value of money, Klein's measure can be regarded as capturing fluctuations in the liquidity of money, and he has used it as a variable in an empirical study of the demand for money in the United States (Klein, 1977), as has Laidler (1980). The distribution of income has not been directly incorporated into empirical work on the demand for money as yet. However, at least two studies, by Bordo and Jonung (1981) for five countries (The United States, Canada, The United Kingdom, Sweden, and Norway) and Klovland (1983) for Norway, have tried to investigate the effects of long-run institutional change on the demand for money along lines suggested by Fisher's analysis (see p. 46 above). They have used, for obvious enough reasons, such variables as the proportion of the labor force employed outside of agriculture, the ratio of population to bank offices, the ratio of currency to the total money stock, and the ratio of nonbank financial assets to total financial assets to measure the degrees of monetization and financial development of the economies they studied.

CONCLUDING COMMENT

As we have now seen, giving empirical content to the theoretical notions that form the bases of the theories of the demand for money discussed in Part II of this book is far from straightforward, and by no means all of the problems that arise here have satisfactory and universally applicable solutions. More detailed discussion of the issues this raises is best carried on in the context of specific studies. Before we can turn to these, however, we need to say something about some of the econometric problems that arise in the context of studies of the demand for money. These form the subject matter of the next chapter.

chapter 8

Some Econometric Issues

INTRODUCTORY COMMENTS

We are mainly interested in the demand for money because we are concerned about the way in which the quantity of nominal money in circulation in an economy interacts with other factors to influence the behavior of interest rates, real income, employment, and the price level. We are concerned with the aggregate demand-for-money function, and in the previous chapter we have discussed some of the issues involved in measuring the variables used in empirical studies of that function. Virtually all of the tests of various hypotheses about the relationship we shall discuss have applied least squares regression and correlation analysis to time series of observations on subsets of the variables in question. Such analysis provides a well-known method of fitting functional relationships to data, and it is not necessary here to enter into a discussion of its technical details. Nevertheless, the application of such techniques does raise certain questions of which the reader must be conscious if he is to interpret the empirical work we shall soon discuss with an appropriately critical attitude.

THE IDENTIFICATION PROBLEM

Any theory of the demand for money leads to propositions about the nature of the relationship between the quantity of money agents in the economy want to hold and the variables that underly that decision, the variables in question typically being some real income or wealth measure representing the scale variable in the function, some interest rate or rates measuring the opportunity cost of holding money, and of course the price level if we are dealing with the demand for nominal money. The first thing to note here is that we cannot in fact be sure that we ever actually observe the quantity of nominal money demanded. What we see is the quantity of money in circulation, and it is only by assuming that this money is all willingly held that we can treat it as measuring the dependent variable of our function. Moreover, though it may be true that variations in real income, the price level, and some representative interest rate lead to variations in the nominal quantity of money demanded, it is also true that variations in the nominal quantity of money supplied (among other variables) lead to variations in income, the price level, and the rate of interest. When we are confronted by time series data on these variables, it is far from obvious that the relationships among them which can be given quantitative content do indeed reflect the structure of the demand-for-money function rather than the combined influences of all the other behavior relationships that make up the structure of the economy. It is far from clear, that is to say, that the demand-for-money function can be *identified.*

To see better what is involved here, it is helpful to set aside the complications of dealing with a complete macroeconomic model and to consider instead the way in which the identification problem arises in the context of the simple supply-and-demand apparatus with which we began Part I of this book. In Figure 8.1, therefore, we show the demand for some good X as a negative function of its own price and the supply function as a positive function of that price. Let the problem be to measure the relationship between the demand for X and its price from observations generated in this market. As can be seen from Figure 8.2, this will be possible if the supply function shifts while the demand function remains stable [panel (a)]. In this case all observed values lie on the demand curve. If only the demand function shifts, the supply curve will be observed [panel (b)], while if both functions shift, a situation such as that shown in panel (c) will arise and we will obtain a scatter of observations that lie between the demand curve and the supply curve, telling us nothing about either, though we can still use regression analysis to fit a function such as the line FF to them. In fitting such a curve, however, it is clear that we do not obtain a measure of the relationship between the demand for X and its price.[1]

Of course, econometricians have worked on means of overcoming the problems we are illustrating, and the outlines of a satisfactory solution to them are easily enough grasped in the context of the simple supply-and-demand

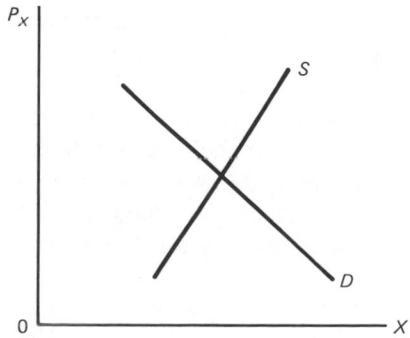

Figure 8.1 The supply and demand for X.

[1] The classic article on identification of supply and demand curves is Working (1927, reprinted 1953) and is still worth reading.

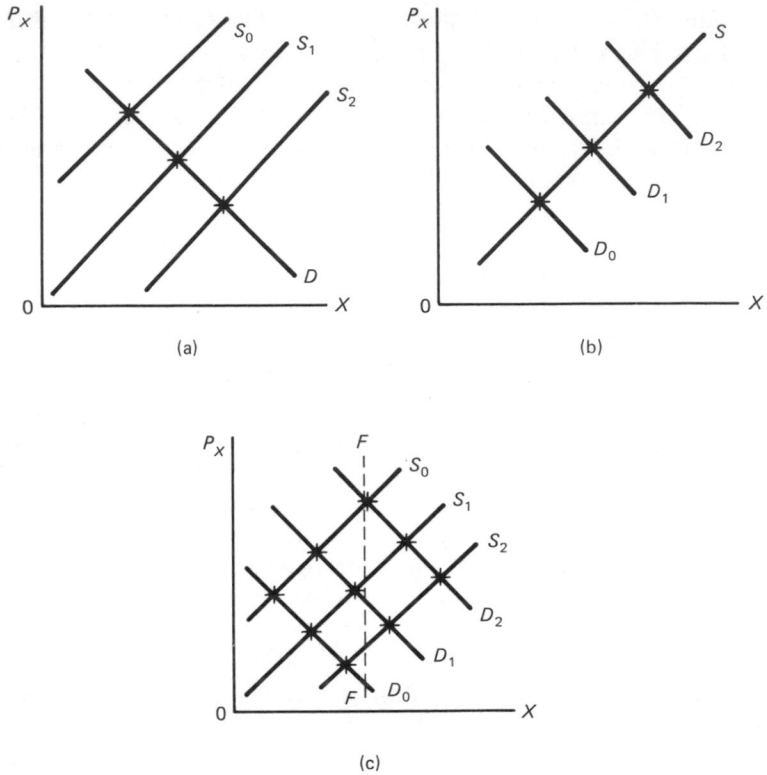

Figure 8.2 (a) Only the supply curve shifts, ensuring that all observations (marked with crosses) lie on the demand curve. (b) Only the demand curve shifts, so that observations outline the supply curve. (c) Both curves shift, yielding a set of observations that, if regression analysis is applied to them, will produce a curve such as *FF*, which is neither a supply function nor a demand function. *X* is the dependent variable.

apparatus used in Figure 8.2. To begin with, if the demand curve for X does shift around, that can be allowed for by including those factors causing it to shift as extra exogenous variables in the demand function to be fitted. Then, so long as at least one of the variables causing the supply curve of X to shift does not appear in its demand function, so long as at least some of the shifts in the supply function of X are *independent* of any shifts of the demand function, it has been shown that it is indeed possible to identify the relationship between the demand for X and its price. In these circumstances the use of regression analysis to estimate a relationship between the quantity of X traded, its own price, and the other variables affecting the demand for X will yield estimates of the parameters of the demand function for X, including that linking quantity demanded to price.[2]

The important point here is that to ensure that he can identify the demand curve for X, the person studying it must know about certain properties of

[2] The reader well versed in econometrics will realize that, strictly speaking, for the above conclusion to be true, the demand curve must be just identified—it must be possible to derive one, and only one, value for each of its parameters. If it is overidentified, other techniques whose details need not concern us here must be applied.

the entire supply-and-demand system generating his observations. In particular, he must know which exogenous factors cause his supply and demand curves to shift and whether or not they vary independently of one another. If we apply these principles to the matter of estimating a demand-for-money function, their implications are reasonably clear. Suppose that we believe the demand for nominal balances to depend on the level of real income, the price level, and a representative interest rate and their supply to depend on that same interest rate and the stock of base money available in the economy. Then, if fluctuations in the stock of base money are independent of fluctuations in real income and prices or of any other variable, including random factors that might cause the demand for money to vary, the parameters of the demand function will be identified. If the latter condition does not hold, then they would not be.

As the reader will see in due course, some workers have paid attention to the identification problem when studying the demand for money, but, as Cooley and Leroy (1981) have argued, even where the problem has been addressed, efforts to ensure that conditions under which the demand-for-money function is identified do in fact hold have been rather perfunctory. In the example given above, as they point out, any tendency for the monetary authorities to accommodate shifts in the demand for money with base money changes would undermine identifiability. In any event, far too often the whole identification problem has been ignored. The fact that parameter estimates obtained for the demand function when the problem has been ignored tend to be very much like those generated in studies where it has been explicitly addressed certainly suggest that this issue may not be a critical one, but Cooley and Leroy are nevertheless right in arguing that this fact stops far short of demonstrating conclusively that this is the case.

Another approach to the identification problem as it arises in the context of the demand-for-money function is worth some comment. Suppose we chose to fit the relationship in real rather than nominal terms, treating the quantity of real money as the dependent variable. In an economy in which the price level fluctuates endogenously, there is no separate supply function for real balances. In this case we have but a single equation to worry about and hence need not concern ourselves with the identification problem as we have just discussed it. Provided we are willing to take it for granted that the demand for real balances is independent of the price level, rather than asking that this property of the function be tested; and crucially, provided we are willing to argue that all factors affecting the demand for real balances are determined elsewhere in the system, independently of the demand function, we are able to identify the other parameters of the relationship.[3] This does not mean, however, that all our troubles are over.

[3] This latter condition, theoretically speaking at least, will hold if the economy generating our data is operating at full employment. Such an economy is described in the flexible-price vertical aggregate supply curve analysis presented in Chapter 3 (pp 27–28), and it is argued there that the supply and demand for money determine only the price level, with real income and interest rates being determined elsewhere in the system.

SIMULTANEITY

Once it is pointed out that the price level and therefore the quantity of real money are endogenous variables, it is hard to ignore the fact that so, usually, are real income and interest rates. The endogeneity of the variables on the right-hand side of our demand-for-money function, whether it be formulated in nominal or real terms, raises a set of issues for least squares regression analysis to which econometricians refer by the term *simultaneity* or *simultaneous equations bias.*

Even if all of our data were measured with perfect accuracy, and if the arguments of our demand-for-money function were capable of explaining every scrap of variation in the quantity of money demanded, the identification problem would still arise. This problem is not peculiar to the application of regression analysis, which takes it for granted that some residual fluctuations of the dependent variable of the relationship being studied are unexplained and should be attributed to an *error term.* The additional problem of simultaneous equations bias of least squares arises in the presence of such error terms. To be specific, when variables endogenous to the economic system turn up as explanatory variables on the right-hand side of the demand-for-money function, the simultaneity problem arises because these variables in their turn are determined elsewhere in the system and because their determination too is subject to residual error.

If the economic system as a whole is from time to time subject to random shocks, these might be expected to cause simultaneous random fluctuations in all endogenous variables of the system. These random fluctuations will be correlated with one another, not because there is any question of the relevant fluctuation in one endogenous variable causing a fluctuation in another, but simply because they have a common cause elsewhere in the system. When one performs the regression of real-money-balances on, say, real income and the rate of interest, one is of course treating all variations in one endogenous variable as being the result of those in two other such variables. To the extent that the system to which these variables belong is subject to the kind of common shocks we have just discussed, the quantitative estimates we obtain of the parameters of the function will, if we ignore their presence, be biased by the influence of errors common to the three variables but having their cause elsewhere in the system.

The most common way in which economists cope with this problem is to remove the offending errors from the right-hand side variables of the demand-for-money function.[4] This may be accomplished, at least in principle, by performing the regression of each of these variables on variables that are truly exogenous to the economic system and using their predicted values from such a regression to replace their actual values on the right-hand side of the demand-for-money function. In principle, this technique, known as "two-stage least squares," and other variations on it deal adequately with the problem of simul-

[4] Though it is the most commonly used method, it is not the only one, by any means. See, for example, Johnston (1972, Chapter 13) for a concise account of this and other approaches.

taneous equations bias of least squares, but in practice they are only effective to the extent that the choice of "truly exogenous" variables—often referred to as *instruments*—is appropriate. To call a variable exogenous does not make it so.

Two-stage least squares has been used quite frequently when demand-for-money functions have been fitted, but in many cases this does not seem to have made very much difference to the results obtained. This might be because in the context of the demand for money simultaneous equations bias is not a major problem, or it could be that, as Cooley and Leroy (1981) have suggested, an inappropriate choice of instruments has left the two-stage least squares estimates of the function just as biased as those obtained by simpler methods. For reasons that will become apparent in due course, I am inclined to think that Cooley and Leroy are unduly pessimistic about this matter, just as they are about the extent to which the identification problem may be solved in practice, but this is nevertheless an issue the reader must bear in mind as he makes up his own mind about the quality of existing evidence on the demand-for-money function.

THE PERIOD AND FREQUENCY OF OBSERVATIONS

At first sight it might seem that the length of time for which we have observations on variables to be used in tests of the demand-for-money function, and the frequency with which those observations occur, has little to do with econometric issues per se. However, this is not the case. To begin with, the extent to which a particular set of data might suffer from the kind of errors that lead to simultaneous equations bias can be related to the length of the time period it covers and to the time interval over which individual observations are averaged. Also, as we shall see in a moment, there is a whole set of econometric issues having to do with the appropriate treatment of time lags in the demand-for-money function that arise in this context too.

The availability and quality of data with which demand-for-money functions may be tested vary very much from country to country. For some countries, for example, the United States, Britain, Canada, Italy, Norway, and Sweden, data series going back well into the nineteenth century exist. As might be expected, the further back one goes, the patchier are the sources from which such series can be constructed, and long consistent runs of data exist at best for annual observations of the relevant variables. For more recent times, particularly since World War II, relevant data are available on a quarterly basis for many countries, and some series are available for monthly, weekly, or in some cases even daily observations. However, it is the least frequently observed variable that determines the frequency of observations used in any particular study, and the lack of real-income data for any period shorter than a quarter means that most studies of the demand-for-money function have used quarterly or annual data. Some investigators, notably Friedman and Schwartz (1982), taking advantage of the extremely long period for which U.S. and United Kingdom data are available have opted for an even higher degree of time aggregation in their work, using observations averaged over business cycle phases (upswings and downswings) lasting on average 2 years or more, Friedman (1959) even used data averaged over whole cycles.

Studies based on long runs of data reaching back into the beginning of this century or even earlier are, relatively speaking, immune to the problems of least squares simultaneous equations bias discussed in the previous section of this chapter. Such bias arises because observations of the endogenous variables to be included on the right-hand side of the demand-for-money function are contaminated with random fluctuations that will influence parameter estimates if they are ignored. The extent of such bias depends on how important a contribution such fluctuations make to the overall variability of these right-hand side variables. If that contribution is small, then so will be the resulting bias, and vice versa. The variability of real income (or wealth) over long time periods is dominated by the effects of secular growth, and random fluctuations due to exogenous shocks hitting the economic system necessarily contribute a relatively small amount to that variation; but as the period of observations shortens, it becomes more and more difficult to make this claim. There must therefore be a presumption that studies using long periods of data are less likely to be contaminated by simultaneous equations bias than those conducted for relatively brief periods of time.

Now the above argument rests on the fact of the secular growth of income and wealth, and the reader will have noted that it cannot be applied to the interest rate variables that one might want to include in the demand-for-money function. Nevertheless, long periods of data permit a relatively high degree of time aggregation to be used, and this too helps with the simultaneity problem. The more one averages a variable over time, the more do random fluctuations in it tend to cancel out. If a series observed monthly is averaged to produce quarterly observations, the consequences of short-term random shocks whose effects persist for only a few weeks are purged from the data and the resulting series is smoother than the monthly one. Averaging up to annual observations has a further smoothing effect, and so on. In short, there is a presumption that studies using annual data are less subject to simultaneous equations bias than those using quarterly data, and that those using cycle phase average data are even less suspect in this regard.

Using data with a rather high degree of time aggregation also helps us with the problem of measuring expectational variables. The difference between the average actual value of a variable and the average value agents expected it to take over the relevant period obviously shrinks as we move from quarterly to annual to cycle phase data, and Friedman and Schwartz (1982), for example, use the actual rate of inflation to measure the expected rate over cycle phases. Also, using a theorem from growth theory, they use the rate of growth of real income to measure the real rate of return on capital, so that for them the opportunity cost of holding money is given by the rate of growth of nominal income, which is, of course, the sum of the real growth and inflation rates.

However, using data with a high degree of time aggregation has its costs. The number of observations in any time series is obviously reduced by aggregation. Moreover, though unwanted random error is averaged out of the data, so might other variations, which though short-term might well be systematic and could potentially throw extra light on the nature of the demand-for-money function. One will never discover how serious a matter this is without actual experiments. Thus, there are excellent reasons why, despite the extra problems it generates, students of the demand for money have carried out much of their work using quarterly data.

ADJUSTMENT COSTS AND THE SHORT-RUN DEMAND-FOR-MONEY FUNCTION

As ought already to be apparent from Part II of this book, theories of the demand for money do not usually attempt to make predictions about how much cash the individual agent, or even the economy as a whole, will be holding at each and every moment. Money is, among other things, a means of exchange, and any economic agent engaged in market activity will plan to have his cash balances fluctuate over time as a result of the unsynchronized nature of his receipts and payments. Theories of the transactions and precautionary demands for money are explicitly based on just this consideration, while more general approaches, such as Friedman's, in treating money as a "temporary abode of purchasing power" also acknowledge it.[5]

The "demand for money" that our theories seek to explain is for a *target level* of money holding that agents seek to achieve *on average over time* and not at each and every moment. For cycle phase average data for a whole economy such as Friedman and Schwartz (1982) use, this might not matter very much. By the time money holdings have been added up over agents to obtain a figure for the whole economy, and then added up again over time, departures of individual cash holdings from their desired levels at any particular moment will, as like as not, have been averaged out of the data. But suppose we stopped at annual data, or quarterly data? Could we then make the same claim? Most researchers using annual data, and virtually all of them using quarterly data, have concluded that such a claim should not be made, and though the methods they have used to deal with the resulting problems have often been far from satisfactory, as we shall see in due course, an understanding of those methods is vital to an appreciation of what we have and have not learned from their empirical work on the demand for money.

The commonest of the methods in question involves the notion of "adjustment costs," and in order to understand it in the context of empirical work on the demand-for-money function, the reader should note first that many studies of the demand-for-money function postulate that the demand for real balances takes a constant elasticity form

$$\frac{M_t}{P_t} = kX_t^{\beta_1}\gamma_t^{\beta_2}E_t \tag{8.1}$$

[5] Economists taking this approach to monetary economics often refer to money as a "shock absorber" or a "buffer stock." See Laidler (1984) for a discussion of the issues raised by this approach.

where X is some scale variable, r is the interest rate, and E is an error term. The reader should also note that if we rewrite this relationship in logarithms, using lowercase boldface italic letters for logs, it reduces to a convenient linear form particularly suitable for estimation by way of regression analysis.[6] Where $\beta_0 = \log k$, we have

$$(\boldsymbol{m} - \boldsymbol{p})_t^* = \beta_0 + \beta_1 \boldsymbol{x}_t + \beta_2 \boldsymbol{r}_t + \boldsymbol{e}_t \tag{8.2}$$

I have attached an asterisk (*) to the dependent variable of this relationship to indicate that it denotes the target, or long-run, value of real balances determined by the right-hand side of the equation. Suppose that Equation (8.2) referred to the demand for money of an individual agent, and suppose that we allowed for the possibility that the agent's money holding might from time to time depart from its target value. We might argue then that the agent would encounter costs of two kinds. First, because he is away from his target money holdings, he is enjoying less benefits from money holding than he otherwise would, and second, if he adjusts his money holdings over time to move back toward the target, he will also encounter costs involved in making the necessary trades.[7] For reasons that will become apparent in an instant, suppose that both of these costs may be described in quadradic functions so that their total $\boldsymbol{K}$ is

$$\boldsymbol{K} = \alpha[(\boldsymbol{m} - \boldsymbol{p})_t^* - (\boldsymbol{m} - \boldsymbol{p})_t]^2 + \alpha_2[(\boldsymbol{m} - \boldsymbol{p})_t - (\boldsymbol{m} - \boldsymbol{p})_{t-1}]^2 \tag{8.3}$$

Of course a maximizing agent will attempt to control the path taken by his money holding over time so that these costs are at a minimum, and what this implies for his behavior may be discovered by taking the derivative of $\boldsymbol{K}$ with respect to $\boldsymbol{m}_t - \boldsymbol{p}_t$, the variable under the agent's control, and setting it equal to zero. Because of the quadratic form of Equation (8.3), to do this yields the convenient linear expression

$$(\boldsymbol{m} - \boldsymbol{p})_t - (\boldsymbol{m} - \boldsymbol{p})_{t-1} = \frac{\alpha_1}{\alpha_1 + \alpha_2}[(\boldsymbol{m} - \boldsymbol{p})_t^* - (\boldsymbol{m} - \boldsymbol{p})_{t-1}] \tag{8.4}$$

If we define $\beta_3 \equiv \dfrac{\alpha_1}{\alpha_1 + \alpha_2}$ and then substitute the right-hand side of Equation (8.2) for $(\boldsymbol{m}_t - \boldsymbol{p}_t)^*$ in (8.4) we end up with

$$(\boldsymbol{m} - \boldsymbol{p})_t = \beta_3\beta_0 + \beta_3\beta_1\boldsymbol{x}_t + \beta_3\beta_2\boldsymbol{r}_t + (1 - \beta_3)(\boldsymbol{m} - \boldsymbol{p})_{t-1} + \beta_3\boldsymbol{e}_t \tag{8.5}$$

[6] The β's are clearly elasticities in Equation (8.1). Consider β_2. It follows from (8.1) that

$$\frac{\delta(M_t/P_t)}{\delta r_t} = kX_t^{\beta_1}\beta_2 r_t^{\beta_2 - 1}$$

so that

$$\frac{\delta(M_t/P_t)}{M_t/\mathrm{P_t}} = \beta_2\frac{\delta r}{r_t}$$

[7] The reader who is familiar with the empirical literature on the demand for investment goods and consumer durables will recognize these arguments. They were explicitly borrowed from this source by economists working on the demand for money in the 1960s. See, for example, Chow (1966).

The addition of a lagged value of the dependent variable to our log linear demand-for-money function appears to solve the problem of agents not always being at their long-run target money holdings. Moreover, if we estimate the parameters of this so-called short-run relationship, we may recover those of the original long-run function by dividing the former by one minus the coefficient of the lagged dependent variable. This adjustment cost formulation of the short-run demand-for-money function has been widely used in empirical work on the demand-for-money function, and the results it has generated have often seemed to be satisfactory. However, this does not alter the fact that the interpretation of results based on it is fraught with difficulty. The analysis from which we derived it seems plausible enough if we swallow the rather arbitrary quadratic form of Equation (8.3), but closer inspection reveals that this plausibility is superficial indeed. The problems here are both econometric and economic.

PROBLEMS WITH THE LAGGED DEPENDENT VARIABLE

Consider the error term e in Equations (8.2) and (8.5), which is there to capture the effects of all factors, systematic and random, which affect the demand for money but are not explicitly included as independent variables in our function. If this error term moves completely randomly over time, then (provided that none of the other problems we shall discuss in due course are relevant) an ordinary regression equation like (8.5) fitted by least squares to time series data would yield unbiased estimates of the parameters of the long-run demand-for-money function and of the adjustment parameter underlying the short-run relationship. However, if there is any systematic component to the error term, caused perhaps by the influence of some omitted variable on the demand for money which itself moves systematically over time, then we have a problem.

A simple example will illustrate the difficulty here. Suppose that e depends on its own once-lagged value, that its behavior displays *first-order autoregression,* and write, with u_t a serially uncorrelated random variable having a zero mean

$$e_t = \rho e_{t-1} + u_t \tag{8.6}$$

Then write the long-run demand function . . . $\beta_0 + \beta_1 x_t + \beta_2 r_t$ as $f(Z)$ to save space. Substitute the right-hand side of this expression into Equation (8.5) in order to get

$$(m - p)_t = \beta_3 f(Z) + (1 - \beta_3)(m - p)_{t-1} + \beta_3 \rho e_{t-1} + \beta_3 u_t \tag{8.5'}$$

Basic regression analysis is premised on the assumption that the error term displays no autoregression. If such analysis was applied to estimating Equation (8.5) when (8.5′) was the true expression, then the influence of e_{t-1} on the demand for money would be attributed to the variable $(m - p)_{t-1}$. e_{t-1} is of course already a component of this variable so that, if ρ is positive, the resulting estimate of $1 - \beta_3$ will be biased upward, adjustment will appear to be slower than it really is, and our estimates of the long-run parameters of the demand-for-money function will also be biased upward; and vice versa.

This problem is not insoluble. Techniques for allowing for autocorrelation in the residuals of regression equations of both the first and higher orders do nowadays exist. Nevertheless, in the context of time series work on the demand for money, particularly with quarterly data, autocorrelated residuals are both a common and an important phenomenon. Thus, empirical estimates of short-run demand-for-money functions based on expressions like Equation (8.5) cannot always be taken at face value. Apart from anything else, the relevant estimation techniques have only been developed relatively recently and were not available to people working in the 1960s when much pioneering work on the demand for money was done.

The adjustment cost hypothesis is not the only means of introducing a lagged dependent variable into the demand-for-money function. If the appropriate scale variable in the relationship was permanent income, and if it was decided to proxy this variable by applying the error-learning hypothesis (see Chapter 7, p. 88) to the logarithms of current income, which would amount to postulating that agents revised their expectations of income according to the ratio of the actual value of income to the previous expectation of its value, we would have, for the long-run demand-for-money function

$$(\boldsymbol{m} - \boldsymbol{p})_t = \beta_0 + \beta_1 \boldsymbol{y}_t^p + \beta_2 \boldsymbol{r}_t + \boldsymbol{e}_t \tag{8.7}$$

with the log of expected income $\boldsymbol{y}_t^p$ being given by

$$\boldsymbol{y}_t^p = \lambda \boldsymbol{y}_t + (1 - \lambda)\boldsymbol{y}_{t-1}^p \tag{8.8}$$

If the reader will carry out the so-called Koyck transformation on the above expression, by substituting Equation (8.8) into (8.7), then subtracting from the resulting expression Equation (8.7) multiplied through by $1 - \lambda$ and lagged one period, he will get[8]

$$\begin{aligned}(\boldsymbol{m} - \boldsymbol{p})_t = {} & \lambda\beta_0 + \lambda\beta_1 \boldsymbol{y}_t + \beta_2 \boldsymbol{r}_t - (1 - \lambda)\beta_2 \boldsymbol{r}_{t-1} + \\ & (1 - \lambda)(\boldsymbol{m} - \boldsymbol{p})_{t-1} + \boldsymbol{e}_t - (1 - \lambda)\boldsymbol{e}_{t-1}\end{aligned} \tag{8.9}$$

To be sure, this is not the same expression as Equation (8.5) would yield if we used current real income as the scale variable in the long-run demand function, but it is sufficiently like it that, if (8.9) was in fact the true model of the demand-for-money function, then any one who fitted (8.5) would obtain rather good results, and vice versa.[9] He might also be misled into believing that adjustment lags were an important factor in the demand-for-money function, when in fact they were not. It is possible to attempt to distinguish between these expectations and adjustment cost approaches to introducing a lagged dependent variable into the demand-for-money function. It is also possible to

[8] This widely used manipulation is named after L. M. Koyck, the Dutch econometrician who discovered it. See Koyck (1954).

[9] The truth of this assertion is not logically necessary. Rather it follows from the empirical fact that the rate of interest is a highly serially correlated variable, so that to omit its lagged value from an equation containing its current value results in the explanatory power, if any, of the lagged variable being attributed by the regression to the current value. Note that the argument above amounts to saying that lags in the empirical relationship might derive from problems of measuring the arguments in the long run function. Goodfriend (1985) analyses a much more general version of this argument.

treat adjustment lags and expectation lags as complementary phenomena and to allow them both to appear in the function by substituting y^p for X in Equation (8.5) and then appying the Koyck transformation to the resulting expression. As we shall see in Chapter 11 (p. 140), some people working on the demand for money have indeed pursued this line of enquiry, so the lesson of the foregoing argument is not that the adjustment lag hypothesis is untestable in principle. Rather it is that empirical demand-for-money functions utilizing lagged dependent variables must be interpreted with great care since they do not necessarily reflect the workings of adjustment mechanisms.

As was remarked earlier, the adjustment cost model of the short-run demand for money raises problems having to do with economic theory as well as econometric estimation. The reader will recall that models of the transactions and precautionary demand for money, such as were discussed in Chapter 5, postulate that agents face transactions costs in adjusting their money holdings in order to derive what in the context of the present discussion is properly called the long-run demand function. The costs discussed there were lump sum in nature, but it was pointed out that it was possible to extend the relevant models to incorporate variable costs, albeit at the expense of a considerable increase in their analytic complexity. There is no need to go into such analysis explicitly to make the following important point: it is awkward to postulate as do, for example, Santomero and Seater (1981), at least implicitly, one kind of adjustment cost to derive the long-run demand-for-money function, and then, having done that, to postulate another kind to justify the introduction of a lagged dependent variable into the relationship for purposes of empirical work; if it is thought that both kinds of costs are important, then as Milbourne et. al (1983) argue, both need to be introduced simultaneously at the beginning of the analysis in order to derive valid results. Studies of the demand for money that claim to be testing transactions demand for money models, but which rely on lagged dependent variables introduced on adjustment cost grounds in order to obtain satisfactory empirical results, are thus highly suspect.

The dependent variable of Equation (8.2) is the log of real balances. That is appropriate enough, since all of our theories of the demand for money tell us that the demand for money is indeed a demand for real balances. However, when we apply the adjustment cost argument to that equation, we end up with Equation (8.5), which tells us that economic agents will adjust their real balances slowly over time in response to changes in the scale variable of the demand-for-money function (real expected income say) and the rate of interest. As far as the individual agent is concerned, the price level is at least as much an exogenous variable as are expected real income and the interest rate, and to attain a given level of *real balances,* the agent must take the price level as given to him and beyond his control and vary his holdings of *nominal balances.*

This is important because Equation (8.5) implies that, when the price level changes, nominal balances adjust instantaneously to keep real balances constant. It is not obvious that agents' adjustment to price level changes should be instantaneous when their adjustment to changes in other variables is slow, and some economists have concluded that Equations (8.3) and (8.4) are inappropriate as applications of the adjustment cost idea to the demand for money, arguing that they should be cast in terms of nominal rather than real balances. If that is done, instead of Equation (8.4) we have

$$m_t - m_{t-1} = \frac{\alpha_1}{\alpha_1 + \alpha_2}(m_t^* - m_{t-1}) \equiv \beta_3(m_t^* - m_{t-1}) \qquad (8.4')$$

and Equation (8.5) becomes, again writing the long-run function as $f(Z)$ to save space,

$$(m - p)_t = \beta_3 f(Z) + (1 - \beta_3)(m_{t-1} - p_t) + \beta_3 e_t \qquad (8.5'')$$

This expression differs from (8.5) only in having the current rather than lagged value of the log of the price level on the right-hand side. Given that the price level is a highly autocorrelated variable, particularly in quarterly data, it is a fair generalization to say that if the "real adjustment" version of the short-run demand-for-money function we discussed earlier performs well, then so will this "nominal adjustment" version. However, the two forms are not the same; it is possible in principle to distinguish between them; and the underlying economics of the two versions of the function do differ. Once more, we have a reason for taking great care about interpreting the results of demand-for-money studies that use lagged values of the dependent variable as right-hand-side variables.

THE INDIVIDUAL EXPERIMENT AND THE MARKET EXPERIMENT

While reading through the last few pages, the reader may have been struck by the fact that, although our arguments about adjustment costs were cast in terms of the behavior of the individual agent, the empirical applications to which we have referred concerned the aggregate demand-for-money function. It is a common enough practice in economics to construct a model of the behavior of a representative agent in an individual experiment and then to argue that in the market experiment the economy as a whole acts "as if" it was simply a scaled-up version of that individual agent. However, that does not make it safe to do so, because what is true of the individual is not always true of the aggregate of individuals acting together. It is always possible to commit fallacies of composition when going from propositions about individuals to propositions about the whole economy, and the following important fallacy of composition permeates the foregoing discussion, as we shall now see.[10]

[10] Care in distinguishing between individual and market experiments is, of course, a distinguishing feature of Patinkin's (1965) analysis. The following arguments are developed at greater length in Laidler (1982, Chapter 2).

The variable under the control of the individual agent is nominal balances, and he varies these in order to attain a desired level of real balances. This consideration underlay our derivation of the "nominal adjustment" short-run function (8.5″). However, throughout the analysis of the economy as a whole set out in Part I of this book, we treated the nominal quantity of money as an exogenous variable determined on the supply side of the market. If we take that analysis seriously as a framework for discussing the interaction of the quantity of money and other variables in the economy, then however plausible arguments about nominal adjustment may be at the level of the individual agent, they are, quite unequivocally, logical nonsense when applied at the level of the economy as a whole. Nominal money cannot simultaneously be a variable that is exogenous to the arguments of the aggregate demand-for-money function and a variable that responds endogenously to variations in them.

As we saw in Part I, equilibrium between the supply and demand for money in the flexible price version of our macroeconomic model is maintained by having the price level vary. When a flexible price economy is pushed off its long-run demand-for-money function, it moves back to equilibrium by way of the influence of price level changes on the stock of real balances. If the price level is perfectly flexible, such adjustment is instantaneous, and only a long-run aggregate demand-for-money function is observable. However, if prices move less than instantaneously, we would observe the economy moving slowly to equilibrium over time by way of price level changes influencing the quantity of real balances. On this basis, some economists have argued that, for the economy as a whole, the real adjustment version [Equation (8.5)] of the demand-for-money function is appropriately specified, in effect being a price level adjustment equation. Their argument will not quite do however.

To begin with, the distinction between the short-run and long-run demand-for-money functions arises from costs encountered by the individual economic agent when attempts are made to alter money holdings, not from the existence of some degree of price level stickiness at the level of the economy as a whole. Such stickiness is a consequence of the way in which the economy responds to exogenous shocks, not least in the supply of nominal money, and to interpret Equation (8.5) as an appropriately specified price level adjustment equation, we would have to argue that it is possible to capture in one simple parameter β_3 the entire transmission mechanism whereby the price level responds to discrepancies between the supply and demand for nominal money. This might be possible, though it seems implausible to say the least. If we are suspicious of this one parameter, however, then of course we must be suspicious of all other parameters estimated using a real adjustment equation like (8.5).

Even if it were possible to argue that the transmission mechanism of monetary policy was satisfactorily captured in one parameter, the real adjustment version of the short-run demand-for-money function would only be appropriately specified for experiments in which the nominal quantity of money is held constant over time and all disturbances to which the economy must react arise among the arguments of the demand-for-money function. To see this, consider the following simple example. Suppose that, where p^* is the long-run equilibrium value of the price level, we were to write

$$m_t = f(Z_t) + p_t^* + e_t \tag{8.10}$$

so that

$$p_t^* = m_t - f(Z_t) - e_t \tag{8.11}$$

Suppose also that the actual price level moves toward its long-run equilibrium value slowly according to

$$p_t - p_{t-1} = \beta_3(p_t^* - p_{t-1}) \tag{8.12}$$

Then, simple substitution and manipulation yields

$$m_t - p_t = \beta_3 f(Z_t) + (1 - \beta_3)(m_t - p_{t-1}) + \beta_3 e_t \tag{8.5'''}$$

which is only the same as (8.5) if m is constant over time. If the nominal money supply does vary exogenously in the data being studied, for that reason alone (8.5) is misspecified, even if the transmission mechanism is appropriately captured in one parameter β_3.

It may reasonably be pointed out that the assumption of an exogenous nominal money supply is an extreme one, and that in real-world economies, the nominal money supply does respond endogenously to changes in the variables underlying the demand for money. Such endogeneity can, for example, arise from the monetary authorities' attempting to maintain some control over the level of interest rates by increasing nominal money when market forces are tending to drive them up, and vice versa. It can also arise through the balance of payments when the authorities are trying to control the level of the foreign exchange rate. In such cases it might make sense to postulate that the nominal money supply adjusts slowly to changes in the demand for it, but this does not make the nominal adjustment version (8.5″) of the short-run demand-for-money function an appropriate form to use. One cannot use the existence of time lags in the *supply-of-money* function to justify including a lagged dependent variable in what purports to be a *demand-for-money* function. As we have already seen, whenever supply-and-demand functions interact to produce data for us, we must be concerned about the identification problem, and the above argument amounts to saying that it is not clear that the structure of the demand function is properly identified in an equation like (8.5) or (8.5″).

It is only relatively recently that economists have become fully aware of the problems discussed in the preceding few paragraphs, and much of the literature dealing with empirical work on the demand-for-money function, particularly that using quarterly data, either ignores them altogether or treats them in a rather perfunctory manner.[11] However, some workers have addressed the

[11] As is often the case, however, full awareness of a set of issues has come with a rather long time lag after they were raised. Important elements of the foregoing arguments are to be found in Walters (1965), Starleaf (1970), Tucker (1971), Ackerlof (1973), Artis and Lewis (1976), Jonson (1976a, b), and Lewis (1978). More recently they have been developed by Knoester (1979), Laidler (1980, 1982), Carr and Darby (1981), Goodhart (1982), Coats (1982), Judd and Scadding (1982a) and Kanniainen and Tarkka (1983).

issues head on. One group, mainly associated with Dr. Clifford Wymer, has taken the view that the appropriate way to get to grips with (among other problems) the adjustment of cash holdings to their target value is to construct an explicit model of that adjustment process and to estimate it as a complete system. Another group, associated mainly with Dr. David Hendry, argues that specifying such a complete system is so difficult that a purely statistical approach to the problem is preferable.[12]

Wymer's procedure involves, first, specifying a complete macroeconomic model in which the transmission mechanism for monetary policy is highlighted and, second, estimating the parameters of the long-run demand-for-money function simultaneously with all the other parameters of the model, including those that purport to capture the process whereby not just the demand for money, but all other endogenous variables, move over time toward their equilibrium values. This procedure is complex and requires a great deal of effort on the part of its users. It is not surprising, therefore, that it has more often been used by those whose main interest is in any case in building complete macroeconomic models of particular economies, rather than by those more concerned with studying just one of the components of such a model, namely the demand-for-money function. Also, this technique is vulnerable to the criticism that any error made in specifying one component of the system can, in principle at least, undermine the reliability not just of estimates of that component, but of the rest of the model as well.

Dr. Hendry and his associates argue that adjustment processes of any kind produce autocorrelation of various orders in economic time series data, and hence that, even if their economics is not understood, their effects can still be allowed for in empirical work by applying elaborate statistical techniques to remove all traces of autocorrelation from the error terms of equations fitted to time series data. This amounts to arguing that the parameters of a long-run demand-for-money function such as (8.2) may be identified and estimated without bias provided that the appropriate techniques are used in estimation to purge the data of the effects of adjustment processes. Though Hendry's approach is not vulnerable to the same criticisms as is Wymer's, it is not problem free. The reliability of the statistical techniques it uses is greatly enhanced by applying them to long runs of data, perhaps running into the hundreds of observations, and such long runs are not always available for data relevant to testing the demand-for-money function. Also, it may be argued that in dealing with adjustment problems by purely statistical means the approach involves its users in abdicating responsibility for finding and testing economic explanations of the way in which economies move over time.[13]

[12] Jonson (1976a) uses Wymer's techniques, as do Jonson, Moses, and Wymer (1976). Hendry and Mizon (1978) is a readily accessible example of Hendry's approach as applied to the demand-for-money function.

[13] Hendry's techniques are at the opposite pole to those of Friedman and Schwartz (1982) who, as we have noted, in effect deal with adjustment problems by aggregating their data up over time until the effects of adjustment phenomena are averaged out of their observations. It is not surprising therefore that Hendry is highly critical of their work. See Hendry and Ericsson (1983).

CONCLUDING COMMENTS

By now the reader will be wondering whether any satisfactory empirical study of the demand for money—or of any other relationship for that matter—is possible. There is indeed an important, but narrow, sense in which such scepticism is justified. It is impossible to think of a single study of the demand-for-money function in which all of the difficulties discussed above are simultaneously dealt with. However, as we shall see in due course, we do not have to rely on any one piece of work when trying to answer questions about the demand for money. There have, by now, been literally hundreds of empirical studies of the relationship. Each one of them, taken in isolation, is open to criticism for neglecting some econometric problem or another, but, taken together, the body of work now available to us has faced up to all the problems we have discussed in this chapter (and to others that space has not permitted us to discuss). When a particular result on the nature of the demand-for-money function comes through in a number of studies, conducted by different techniques, on different bodies of data, it seems reasonable to believe that the result in question tells us something about the empirical characteristics of that function, and that the result ought not to be explained away as a statistical quirk caused by neglect of the identification problem, simultaneity, autocorrelated residuals, or of anything else.

Moreover, the problems we have discussed in this chapter, though always important in principle, may not always be important in practice. If one maintains, rather than tests, the hypothesis that the demand for nominal money is proportional to the price level, the demand-for-real-money function is more likely to be identified. If one takes long runs of data, dominated by large secular movements in variables, the chances of simultaneity being a problem are much reduced, as they are if data are highly aggregated over time. The addition of a lagged dependent variable to the demand function when shorter time periods and lower degrees of time aggregation are being used, together with some attention to autocorrelation in the error term of the equation to be fitted, does not guarantee success in filtering out the effects of short-run adjustments in the economy on demand-for-money relationships, but it may nevertheless be good enough in some circumstances. Such procedures cannot always be counted on to provide satisfactory estimates of the parameters of the long-run demand function, but one must not conclude, on this basis, that they never have done, nor ever will do, so.

In short, the issues discussed in this chapter do not give grounds for a destructively nihilistic attitude about the possibility of satisfactory empirical work in monetary economics. Rather they raise a series of warnings about taking empirical results at face value, about naively believing that the facts can be trusted to speak for themselves. The facts cannot be so trusted, but they can still tell us a great deal if their message is interpreted in the light of the considerations we have discussed in this chapter. One cannot be more specific than this without dealing with the outcome of particular studies, and it is to this task that the next and final part of this book is devoted.

four

THE EMPIRICAL EVIDENCE ON THE DEMAND FOR MONEY

chapter 9

An Overview of the Evidence

THE ISSUES TO BE ADDRESSED

Earlier chapters of this book have generated various questions worth asking about the demand-for-money function. The most important are:

1. Is the rate of interest an important variable in the function?
2. In assessing the responsiveness of the demand for money to market rates of interest, is it important to pay attention to variations in the own rate of return on money?
3. Is it ever the case that the interest elasticity of demand for money becomes infinite, or unstable over time, as the Keynesian theory of the speculative demand for money predicts?
4. Does any particular interest rate appear to be more relevant for the demand for money than others?
5. What influence does the expected rate of inflation exert on the demand for money?
6. Is the demand for money measured in nominal terms proportional to the price level?
7. Should income or wealth, or perhaps both, be included in the demand-for-money function?
8. Does the level of wage rates play a role in determining the demand for money as theories of the transactions and precautionary demand for money suggest?
9. Are there significant economies of scale in money holding as these same theories of the transactions and precautionary demand for money imply?
10. Is institutional change an important factor influencing the demand for money over time?

11. Are there any important instabilities in the behavior of the demand for money which the above-mentioned factors leave unexplained?

A SUMMARY OF THE EVIDENCE

As the reader may expect, the answers that can be given to the above questions vary in quality from quite confident to extremely tentative. An endemic difficulty in testing propositions about economic behavior is that it is impossible to hold "other things equal" and investigate only one issue at a time. The world does not provide data in such a convenient form. In testing a particular relationship, it is necessary to assume something about the nature of other relevant relationships. One cannot deal with the influence on the demand for money of the rate of interest using data generated by an actual economy without also including a variable such as income or wealth in the function fitted to the data, and the outcome of such a test may critically depend on which of these other variables is chosen and on the particular form of functional relationship chosen for fitting. Moreover, different tests address econometric issues such as identification and simultaneity with different degrees of seriousness, and there is always a chance that the outcome of a particular test will depend on the econometric technique employed. It turns out that the answers one obtains for many of the questions posed above are insensitive to this kind of problem. Regardless of the other variables used, of the form of the functional relationship fitted, and the econometric techniques used, the results are essentially the same, and this is true for an encouraging number of issues.

The importance of the rate of interest for the demand for money is now established beyond any reasonable doubt, and the evidence is only a little less clear that the interest elasticity of demand for money never becomes infinite. Although problems of instability have arisen, particularly in more recent studies of the demand for money, these do not seem to be related in any important way to factors associated with the so-called speculative motive for holding money.[1] At the same time studies that have directly confronted the issue find that the own rate of return on money has a measurable effect on the demand for money. The evidence is not clearcut on the choice between a long and a short interest rate for inclusion in the demand-for-money function. Some studies point one way, and others another. However, there is evidence that in recent years the rates of return on such close substitutes for money as (for example, in the United States) savings and loan association shares have been of particular importance. Furthermore, for open economies such as Britain and Canada, foreign interest rates appear to be relevant measures of the opportunity cost of holding money.

There seems to be little doubt that the expected inflation rate influences the demand for money under conditions of hyperinflation and also during

[1] However, in a recent study Slovin and Sushka (1983) have shown that in the United States in recent years variations in the demand for money may be systematically related to the variability of the interest rate, a factor associated with Tobin's extension of speculative demand for money analysis.

rapid inflations such as those widely experienced in Latin America. Though most earlier studies could not find a role for the expected inflation rate during the extremely mild inflations that characterized most advanced economies until the mid-1960s, more recent work in the United States has taken account of the effects of the higher inflation rates experienced since then and has found the expected inflation rate to be important in the demand-for-money function. In any event, inflation has had a marked effect on nominal interest rates in the last 15 years or so, and evidence about the importance of these variables in the function provides strong indirect support for the hypothesis that expected inflation affects the demand for money. As to the role of the price level, a considerable body of evidence gives us little reason to doubt the empirical relevance of the proposition that the demand for nominal balances is proportional to the price level.

If we must choose between the two, then wealth rather than measured income appears to be the superior scale variable for the demand-for-money function. The broader concept of wealth, for which permanent income is frequently a proxy variable, has been more widely used than nonhuman wealth; this has been partly because of the lack of data on which to base nonhuman wealth series for most countries, but there is now some evidence that where series for both variables are available, permanent income performs better than nonhuman wealth.[2]

The Keynesian approach to the theory of the demand for money suggests that both wealth and income might be relevant to the demand for money, the latter being particularly important as far as the transactions and precautionary demand is concerned. It is inherently difficult to get results which find a role for both variables at the same time because wealth and income move closely together and it is hard to distinguish between their separate influences. However, some recent work does suggest that both variables play a role in determining the overall demand for money.[3] Moreover, analysis of the transaction and precautionary motives suggests, as we have seen, that real wages belong in the relationship. Four studies have looked at the role of real wages in the demand-for-money function, and all have found them to be of potential importance. Also, there is an increasing body of evidence that the demand-for-money function is characterized by economies of scale, and this result too points to the importance of transaction and precautionary motives. The fact that economies of scale turn up most frequently when the demand for narrowly defined money is studied strengthens this conclusion.

[2] However, as the reader will have already noted from the previous chapter, it can be difficult to distinguish between cases in which the demand for money reacts to changes in measured income with a distributed lag and those in which it reacts to permanent income but in which the latter variable itself reacts to measured income with such a lag. This issue is addressed on p. 140.

[3] The difficulties here are compounded by the presence of an interest rate in the demand-for-money function, because the product of some wealth variable and the interest rate is in itself interpretable as the income stream associated with the wealth variable in question. This matter is potentially important in the context of interpreting the role of the dividend price ratio in the demand-for-money function as B. Friedman (1978) has argued. See p. 148.

Finally, it does appear that institutional change is an important factor influencing the demand for money. Although much of the impetus toward investigating this matter has come from the apparent instability in the demand-for-money function that has recently been observed in the United States and elsewhere, such change turns out, with the benefit of hindsight, to have been important for a long time and in a rather wide variety of countries. Moreover, failure to account for it in many early studies of the demand for money obscured the existence of the economies of scale in the function to which we have alluded above. In recent years, even when such change is taken into account, there still remain apparent problems of stability with estimates of the demand-for-money function. These probably have as much to do with the problems of estimating adjustment processes discussed in the last chapter (see p. 111–113) as with difficulties having to do with the underlying long-run demand-for-money function.

With this brief summary of the evidence in mind, let us now turn to the tests that provided it, beginning with the question of the importance of opportunity cost variables in the function.

chapter 10

The Influence of the Opportunity Cost of Holding Money

EARLY WORK ON THE ROLE OF INTEREST RATES

Much empirical work, particularly early work, on the demand-for-money function has taken it for granted that the crucial issue to be investigated is the relationship between the demand for money and the rate of interest. This very Keynesian view of the problem led economists to design tests that concentrated on this variable and were based on quite simple notions about the role of the other variable or variables in the function, hence making their results rather difficult to accept at face value. In early studies of Great Britain by Brown (1939) and of the United States by Tobin (1947) and in a later U.S. study by Bronfenbrenner and Mayer (1960), the distinction between active and idle balances was maintained. It was then assumed that only the demand for the latter was responsive to the rate of interest and that the problem was to measure the degree of responsiveness involved. In order to obtain a measure of idle balances, the following broad procedure was followed (with details differing among studies). It was assumed that the demand for active balances is proportional to the level of income and that, at some time when the ratio of total money holdings to income is at its lowest observed value, idle balances held are equal to zero. This lowest ratio was then postulated as measuring the parameter k in the equation

$$\frac{M_d}{P} = kY + l(r) \tag{10.1}$$

so that, on the assumption that the supply and demand for money are in equilibrium, idle balances could then be measured at other times as being equal to

$$\frac{M_s}{P} - kY$$

and the demand for them related to the rate of interest. Differences between these studies in the precise definitions of the variables used, which need not concern us here, did not prevent them from coming to the conclusion that a distinct negative relationship between the demand for idle balances and the rate of interest could be observed.

These early results rest on quite strict assumptions about the nature of the demand-for-money function. Khusro (1952), in updating Brown's work on Great Britain, found it preferable to treat the ratio of idle balances to liquid assets as varying with the rate of interest, and hence provided the first example of evidence to the effect that some, albeit very narrowly defined, wealth variable plays a role in the demand-for-money function. He also used multiple regression techniques to estimate the value of k, the ratio of active balances to income, rather than using the much cruder method described above and found that this too improved the explanatory power of his equations, which always displayed a significant inverse relationship between idle balances and the interest rate. Bronfenbrenner and Mayer too were troubled by the very strict assumptions about the nature of the demand-for-money function implicit in their initial work and as an alternative postulated that the demand-for-money function was of the form

$$\frac{M_d}{P} = kY - r^{\beta_2} \tag{10.2}$$

so that, with equilibrium assumed between the supply and demand for money, they were able to measure the interest elasticity of the demand for money β_2 by way of the equation

$$\frac{M_s}{PY} = kr^{\beta_2} \tag{10.3}$$

They fitted this to successive pairs of years, relating the change in the logarithm of the ratio of money holdings to income to the change in the logarithm of the interest rate and found again the β_2 was generally negative and that this parameter was a better predictor of the direction of change in the demand for money than the hypothesis that this direction of change is a random variable.[1]

A somewhat similar study by Latané (1954) began with the following demand-for-money function:

$$\frac{M_d}{P} = aY + kYr^{-1} \tag{10.4}$$

from which can be derived

$$\frac{M_d}{PY} = a + kr^{-1} \tag{10.5}$$

Latané found, when using regression analysis, that the parameter b was significantly positive, indicating that the demand for money is negatively related to the rate of interest. He also found that the equation he fitted seemed to have

[1] That β_2 is the interest elasticity of demand for money follows from the argument presented in footnote 6, p. 106 above.

some predictive power over data generated outside the time period to which it was initially fitted.

MORE RECENT RESULTS

The drawback to all the tests just described is that they assume that the demand for money is proportional to the level of income, a postulate that would be challenged by those who regard wealth as a more appropriate variable to include in the function, as well as by those who suspect that there may be economies of scale in money holding. Even so, the consistency with which they point to the importance of the rate of interest as a determinant of the demand for money is impressive, and it is not surprising that other work, which does not rest on such strict assumptions, confirms this result. By and large, this work is based on regression analysis and, although regression analysis does constrain one to use certain functional forms for the relationships under investigation, the limits are not too severe.

One can, and most recent work on the matter has done so, postulate that the demand-for-money function can be approximated by

$$\frac{M_d}{P} = kX^{\beta_1}r^{\beta_2} \tag{10.6}$$

where X stands either for the level of income Y, the level of nonhuman wealth W, or the level of permanent income Y^P, and the β's are elasticities, and let a regression equation simultaneously find the values of both elasticities. Work carried out by Allan Meltzer (1963) for the United States fitted such functions for the period 1900–1958, using all three possible substitutes for X and definitions of money that excluded time deposits at commercial banks, (old M_1) included them (old M_2), and added deposits at mutual savings banks (M_3). Using the rate of interest on 20-year bonds for r, Meltzer found a significant negative relationship between the demand for money, however defined, and the rate of interest, regardless of the other variable included in the function. Moreover, when Meltzer divided his time period up into decades, fitting a separate velocity function to each decade, he found a remarkable similarity in the relationship between the velocity of circulation and the rate of interest for various decades.[2]

The same economist, in a joint study with Karl Brunner (Brunner and Meltzer, 1963) fitted, for a similar time period and also for the United States,

[2] It should be clear that a velocity function is derived from a demand-for-money function by assuming that the demand for money is equal to the supply thereof, dividing both sides by income, and inverting the function. Thus, in general, if

$$M_d = f(X, r)P = M_s$$

then

$$\frac{PY}{M_s} = \frac{PY}{f(X, r)P} = V$$

velocity functions derived from demand-for-money functions that used various permutations and combinations of variables, including income, permanent income, and nonhuman wealth. Rather than rely simply on the outcome of regressions, they used a prediction test. A regression equation was fitted to the first 10 years of their data, and its parameters were used to predict the velocity of circulation in the eleventh year; then the second through eleventh years were used to predict the velocity of circulation in the twelfth year, this process being carried out right through their time series. The average errors in prediction made by the various functions were computed, and it was found that the rate of interest played an important role in allowing accurate predictions to be made, while the interest elasticity of demand for money appeared to remain relatively stable regardless of which other variables were included in the function.

Demand functions like Equation (10.6), using successively a short and a long rate of interest and using permanent income as the other variable, were fitted by Laidler (1966b) to United States data for the period 1892–1960 and again, regardless of whether the definition of money used included time deposits or excluded them, statistically significant negative interest elasticities of demand for money were found. In this test various subperiods (1892–1916, 1919–1940, and 1946–1960) were also used, and it was found that the relationship between either interest rate and the demand for money was much the same in each period. Similar work was carried out on United Kingdom data for the period 1900–1965 (Laidler, 1971), using both measured-income and a permanent-income series constructed using the same weights on measured income as had been used in constructing a permanent-income series for the United States. In both cases interest rate variables proved to have a significant effect on the demand for money, as they did in an earlier study by Kavanagh and Walters (1966), in which a measured-income formulation of the demand-for-money function was tested against data drawn from the years 1877–1961. More recently Bordo and Jonung (1981) have fitted permanent-income formulations of velocity functions, in which they paid careful attention to institutional change, to data for Canada, the United States, the United Kingdom, Norway, and Sweden, for the period 1870–1975 and found interest rate variables to be important. So too did Klovland (1983) in his detailed study of Norway for the period 1867–1980 and Spinelli in his (1980) work on Italy over the period 1867–1965.[3]

NEGATIVE RESULTS ON INTEREST RATE EFFECTS

Of the literally hundreds of studies of the demand for money, of which those cited above are representative, I am aware of only three that have failed to find a significant negative relationship between the rate of interest and the demand for money. Thus, Laidler and Parkin (1970), studying the demand for money in

[3] In addition, we may cite the following studies as finding significant interest rate effects: Macesitch (1970), Clark (1973), Clinton (1973), Poloz (1982) for Canada, Teigen (1971) for Norway, Leponeimi (1966) for Finland, Neihans and Schelbert-Syfrig (1967) for Switzerland, Lewis (1978) for Australia, Adekunle (1968) for a number of less developed countries, Namba (1983) for Japan, Gandolfi and Lothian (1983) for eight advanced countries. The list is far from exhaustive.

Great Britain with quarterly data for the period 1955–1967, found that it did not respond systematically to the treasury bill rate. However, the Bank of England (1970), in a study of almost the same period, found no difficulty in discovering evidence of the importance of other interest rate variables in the function; consideration of the rather special role treasury bills played in the British financial system at that time (a description of which need not detain us here) suggests that Laidler and Parkin's choice of variable was inappropriate. Gray, Ward, and Zis (1976) treated the group of ten major industrial countries as if they were a single economy and, in fitting a demand-for-money function to data generated by them, found a negative coefficient for an interest rate variable. However, the coefficient could not be estimated precisely enough for them to conclude firmly that it was in fact different from zero; thus, their results were indecisive on the matter of the role of the rate of interest in the demand-for-money function rather than definitely suggesting that the variable is not important.

Friedman's (1959) work on U.S. data for the period 1869–1957 presents more subtle problems. He reasoned that since by far the greater part of variations in the rate of interest take place within the business cycle, a demand-for-money function fitted to data that abstract from the cycle, if it is used to predict cyclical fluctuations in the demand for money, should yield errors in prediction related to the rate of interest. He therefore took data on the average values of the variables concerned over each business cycle. The variables used were money defined to include time deposits and permanent income, and to them was fitted a log linear regression whose parameters were then used to predict annual variations in the velocity of circulation. He found no close relationship between the errors of prediction and the rate of interest.

Though Friedman was by no means willing to conclude that this evidence ruled out the rate of interest as an important determinant of the demand for money, the results in question certainly raised grave doubts about the matter, and it is fortunate that a refutation of them was forthcoming. Friedman's test is reliable only if the abstracting from the business cycle that underlies it totally frees the data from the influence of any relationship between the demand for money and the rate of interest. As it happens, for the United States there was a slight downward trend in interest rates over the period involved and, by omitting the interest rate from his cycle average regression, Friedman caused that part of the variation in the demand for money which was the result of this downward trend in the interest rate wrongly to be attributed to variation in the level of permanent income. Thus, he measured the relationship between the demand for money and permanent income erroneously, so that his annual predictions based on it were not reliable. When a test similar to Friedman's was carried out by Laidler (1966b), the rate of interest was included in the cycle average regression, and this inclusion was found to increase the predictive power of the function for annual data, thus confirming the importance of the rate of interest as a determinant of the demand for money.[4] Moreover, in a

[4] It was not possible to obtain interest data for Friedman's entire period, so that the data used began in 1892.

subsequent paper, Friedman (1966) himself acknowledged the interest rate to be an important variable in the function, while his recently published work with Anna J. Schwartz [Friedman and Schwartz (1982)] on the role of money in U.S. and United Kingdom economies over the years 1867–1975 accords a significant role to the interest rate (measured by the rate of change of nominal income) in the demand function.

ECONOMETRIC ISSUES

Now most of the studies cited above either used real-money balances or the velocity of circulation of money as their dependent variable and deal with long periods of data. Hence the arguments advanced in a previous chapter (p. 104) suggest that they probably have coped adequately, if implicitly, with the identification problem. However, a number of studies of U.S. data, notably the relatively early ones by Brunner and Meltzer (1964) for the period 1930–1959 and Teigen (1964) for the period 1929–1959, addressed this and the related simultaneity issue explicitly, while estimating both demand and supply functions for money.

The demand function Brunner and Meltzer used in their study was one that used nonhuman wealth and the long rate of interest and, even with explicit account being taken of the supply-of-money function, they found that the interest elasticity of the demand for money appeared to be close to -0.7. This is essentially the same estimate as Meltzer (1963) obtained in his single-equation study. The wealth elasticity they obtained (about 1.0) was also similar to Meltzer's single-equation estimate. Teigen, using the level of income and a short rate of interest and the lagged money stock, as well as a slightly different specification of the supply function, found an interest elasticity of demand for money of about -0.15. This estimate is very like that obtained by Laidler (1966b) with a single equation. Such results are not peculiar to the United States. For example, Frowen and Arestis (1976) carried out a study of the supply and demand functions for money in West Germany and reported that their estimates of the parameters of the demand-for-money function were relatively insensitive to the extent to which they took explicit account of the presence of the supply function in obtaining them. Moreover, Jonson (1976) estimated a demand-for-money function as one component of a complete econometric model of the United Kingdom for the period 1880–1970. He used Wymer's method of simultaneous estimation, alluded to above (p. 113), and, with the real income elasticity of demand for money constrained to be equal to one, obtained an estimate of the interest elasticity of demand for money that was little different from those yielded by the work of Kavanagh and Walters (1966) and Laidler (1971).

Evidence such as this suggests that as far as investigating the role of the interest rate in the demand-for-money function is concerned, the identification problem is not usually a serious one, nor it would seem is the problem of simultaneity. As the reader will have noted, most of the studies we have cited above have been for rather long periods, over which, as it was argued earlier, such problems were less likely to be important. Moreover, Feige's (1967) study of the United States for the period 1915–1963, which used two-stage least squares estimation (see p. 102 above), obtained an estimate of the interest elasticity of demand for money (as well as of other parameters) that was both significantly negative and of about the same order of magnitude as that obtained by other workers [for example, Laidler (1966b)] using ordinary least squares. Klovland (1983) in his study of Norway for 1867–1980 explicitly tested for simultaneous equations bias and found it negligible. Similar results have been obtained by people working with shorter time spans of data where simultaneity might be expected to be more of a problem. For example, Poloz (1980) and Gregory and McAleer (1981) conclude that simultaneity raises at best minor problems for interpreting recent Canadian data.

Mention was made in the previous chapter of serially correlated residuals. Although these are mainly of concern when lagged dependent variables are in the function, it is nevertheless worth noting that, with the notable exception of Courchene and Shapiro (1964), many early demand for money studies took no account of the problems they raise. However, one or two of the more recent studies cited above, such as Bordo and Jonung (1981), took steps to deal with the problems that might arise from this source. Moreover, Lieberman (1980) reworked an earlier study of U.S. data by Gregory Chow (1966) while taking account of this problem, as Chow did not. He obtained lower quantitative estimates of the interest elasticity of demand than did Chow, but like Bordo and Jonung he still found this parameter to be significantly negative.

THE OWN RATE OF RETURN ON MONEY

The introduction of the own rate of return on money into the picture in no way undermines the robustness of results concerning the importance of the rate of interest in the demand-for-money function. Lee (1967) used such a variable in a study of the effects of the rate of return on such near monies as saving and loan association shares on the U.S. demand for money, while more recently Klein (1974a, b) used his estimates of the competitive rate of return on money described in an earlier chapter (p. 94) in somewhat similar exercises, although for a much longer time period (1880–1970) than Lee. Instead of simply entering the interest differential between money and other assets in his equations, as did Lee, Klein entered the two rates of return separately and in finding that they took coefficients of opposite signs but similar orders of magnitude was able to confirm, rather than take for granted, the appropriateness of using the interest differential as a single variable.

Klein's results are also notable in that they suggest that studies that ignore the own rate of return on money underestimate the sensitivity of the demand for money to the opportunity cost of holding it. When market interest rates rise, so does the own rate of return on money, so that the interest differential between money and other assets changes less than the value of market interest rates. The observed change in the demand for money under such circumstances should, according to Klein's results, be attributed to this relatively smaller change in interest differentials rather than the relatively larger change in the overall levels of interest rates. In this respect Klein's results supplement those of Barro and Santomero (1972), who reached a similar conclusion by including their measure of the own rate of return on demand deposits in an equation fitted to 19 annual observations on the demand for money of the U.S. household sector. Moreover, though Startz (1979) has criticized Klein's estimates of the own rate of return on money, his work has not refuted the basic qualitative result Klein sought to establish, namely that the variable in question does affect the demand for money in the direction economic theory would predict, and that its presence in the demand-for-money function does not undermine evidence on the importance of the rate of return on alternative assets.

THE LIQUIDITY TRAP AND THE STABILITY OF THE INTEREST RATE DEMAND FOR MONEY RELATIONSHIP

The liquidity-trap hypothesis states that at low levels of the rate of interest the demand for money becomes perfectly elastic with respect to that variable. It is not possible to fit directly by regression analysis a function that has a negative slope over part of its range and no slope at all over another part, but less direct tests are not hard to devise. If the liquidity-trap hypothesis is true, it must be the case that the interest elasticity of demand for money becomes greater as the rate of interest falls, since this is the only way it can pass from a finite to an infinite value. There appears to be little evidence that this in fact is the case.

As mentioned above, Bronfenbrenner and Mayer (1960) investigated the interest elasticity of M/PY with respect to the interest rate for successive pairs of annual observations. Over the period they dealt with (1914–1957) they noted no tendency for the interest elasticities they measured to be higher at low rates of interest. A somewhat similar test was carried out by Laidler (1966b). The time period (1892–1960) was divided between the years when the rate of interest was above its average value for the period and those when it was below it. Such a division was made both for the long rate of interest and the short rate, and regressions of the money stock on the level of permanent income and the interest rate were performed for these two sets of data separately. Definitions of money including and excluding time deposits were employed, and hardly any tendency was discovered for the interest elasticity of demand for money to be higher for low-interest observations than for high-interest ones; nor was there any evidence that the function was any less stable at low rates of interest.

A more direct approach to the question was taken by Pifer (1969). He argued that to fit a log linear function to the relationship between the demand for money and the interest rate was to take for granted that the minimum conceivable value for the interest rate is zero because such a constant elasticity demand curve is asymptotic to the horizontal axis. He then noted that an equation that has the form of Equation (10.6) is simply a special case of

$$\frac{M_d}{P} = kX^{\beta_1}(r - r^{\min})^{\beta_2} \tag{10.7}$$

where r^{min} is set equal to zero. The relationship between the demand for money and the rate of interest implicit in such a relationship is asymptotic to r^{min}. He then substituted a series of values for this variable into an equation like Equation (10.7), starting at zero and stopping just short of the lowest value actually observed for r. He argued that if an equation with a positive value for r^{min} fitted his data significantly better than the equation that set that variable at zero, it would be evidence in favor of the liquidity-trap hypothesis. Pifer applied this test, and a variation on it in which the interest rate rather than the quantity of money was treated as a dependent variable, to U.S. data for the period 1900–1958 and found no evidence to suggest that there is any well-defined floor above zero for the value of the interest rate.

Kostas and Khouja (1969), using a method somewhat similar to that of Pifer, again on U.S. data, found some evidence that a long interest rate can take a minimum value above zero, but not a short rate, this phenomenon being important in the late 1940s, however, rather than the 1930s. Their estimation techniques have been criticized by Kliman and Oksanen (1973), and since the late 1940s was precisely the period in which U.S. policy was geared to maintaining the rate of interest on government bonds constant by varying the money supply, there must be some suspicion that Kostas and Khouja discovered a perfectly elastic *supply*-of-money function rather than a perfectly elastic demand function for those years, that for once the identification problem was important. Eisner (1971) and Spitzer (1976), both of whom reworked Pifer's tests with more sophisticated econometric techniques and found evidence of a minimum value for the long interest rate, explicitly expressed concern at the absence of any attempt to confront this issue in their own work.

The liquidity-trap hypothesis arises when it is postulated that a "normal" value for the interest rate plays a role in the demand-for-money function. Starleaf and Reimer (1967) computed such a variable as a geometrically weighted average of present and past values of the actual rate, took the difference between this variable and the current rate, and related the demand for money to this very Keynesian variable. They found virtually no evidence of its importance as far as the United States was concerned. Robert Crouch (1971) examined the behavior of the interest rate over time in the United States. He found no evidence that it tended systematically to return to some normal value and no evidence that any kind of average of its past values was a better predictor of its future value than was its current value. Such evidence as this goes against the very basis of the theory of the speculative demand for money on which the liquidity-trap hypothesis is based, but it is worth noting that, in their elaborate study of the Canadian monetary sector, Courchene and Kelly (1971) found evidence consistent with a "normal" interest rate variable playing a role in asset demand functions, though not to the extent of generating a liquidity trap.

Thus, the evidence on the liquidity trap is not quite clearcut. On the whole, the evidence goes against the hypothesis, but the results of Kostas and Khouja, Eisner, and Spitzer are, on the face of things, in its favor. These results, however, all depend on the use of a long interest rate. There is no sign of a trap when short rates are used, and this suggests that these workers may be dealing with a phenomenon associated with the term structure of interest rates rather than the demand for money. More likely, the fact that long rates were at a minimum in the late 1940s, when monetary policy was geared to keeping such rates low and stable, rather than in the 1930s, when the economy was deeply depressed, points to the possibility that the behavior of the money supply function rather than the demand-for-money function may underlie them. Until these conjectures are investigated explicitly, however, the conclusion to which I subscribe, which was also Keynes's view, that the liquidity-trap hypothesis is of no empirical significance, rests on some degree of personal judgment.

The liquidity-trap hypothesis is closely related to the proposition that the relationship between the demand for money and the rate of interest can be expected to be unstable over time. In fact, this relationship seems to be remarkably well determined. If we consider the United States over the period 1892–1960, the work of Laidler (1966b) shows that the elasticity of demand for money M_2, with respect to the short rate of interest, appears to have varied between roughly -0.12 and -0.15 and, with respect to the long rate of interest, between -0.2 and -0.6. (If M_1 is used instead, the relevant elasticities are -0.17 to -0.20 and -0.5 to -0.8, respectively.) These variations seem small, and when Khan (1974) applied formal econometric tests designed to discover the presence of a structural change in the demand-for-money function over a similar period, he found no sign of any such change. The order of magnitude of the interest elasticity estimates found by Laidler (1971) for the United Kingdom over the period 1900–1964 seem to be similar to those implied by United States data and again show little variation between subperiods. Similarly, Friedman and Schwartz (1982) fitted the same demand-for-money function both to the United States and the United Kingdom over the period 1867–1975 and to various subperiods and found very little variation in their interest elasticity estimates.

Teigen (1964) estimated his supply and demand functions separately for both pre- and post-World War II data for the United States. Though the earlier period is dominated by the 1930s, when the economy was severely depressed, interest rates were remarkably low, and financial markets were extremely unstable, Teigen found no important difference between the two periods in the interest elasticity of the demand for money. Meltzer's (1963) procedure of fitting velocity functions decade by decade revealed a slightly lower interest elasticity of the demand for money in the 1930s than at other times, while Brunner and Meltzer's prediction test produced striking results. They excluded the years 1941–1950 from their data because of the interest rate pegging money supply policy mentioned earlier pursued in those years and still found that regressions weighted heavily with observations taken from the 1930s produced a function that was able to predict the velocity of circulation in the 1950s with no marked falling off in accuracy relative to other predictions they made for other times. Similarly, Laidler's variation on Friedman's test, which employed cycle average data to generate a demand-for-money function then used to predict annual variations in money holding, showed no tendency to be less accurate in its predictions for the 1930s than for other times.

Of more recent studies, only one, Lieberman (1980), finds evidence of a break in the stability of the relationship between U.S. demand for money and the rate of interest during the period to which these earlier studies paid attention. It occurred in 1933 for narrow money, but that is precisely the year in which U.S. authorities began to prohibit the payment of interest on demand deposits, and Lieberman argues that although the underlying demand-for-money function was stable at this time, the resulting change in the behavior of the own rate of return on money gave the appearance of instability in tests that ignored this latter variable. This result is of considerable interest because, as we shall see below, the 1970s have generated a good deal of data that has cast doubt not just on the demand for money-interest rate relationship but on the stability of the function as a whole. Subsequent work has shown that institutional changes can account for some, though not all, of these problems. [See Judd and Scadding (1982a) and p. 149 below]. Lieberman's work suggests that there is nothing new in such a phenomenon.

The evidence cited in the last few paragraphs seems to show that instability in the relationship between the demand for money and the rate of interest has never been a factor of particular importance as far as the economic history of either the United States or the United Kingdom in the present century is concerned. Moreover, work on other countries, such as that of Bordo and Jonung (1981), Klovland (1983), and Spinelli (1980), though it did not explicitly address this issue, gives no reason that such instability has been a problem in economies as diverse as the United States, the United Kingdom, Sweden, Canada, Norway, and Italy. This evidence, like that on the closely related liquidity-trap hypothesis, comes from studies using a variety of data and techniques. Some of the tests cited above used a short rate of interest and a narrow definition of money, others used both broad and narrow money concepts and both short and long interest rates. Functions constrained by wealth, income, and expected income were used in these tests, and the conclusions seem invariant with respect to the many possible permutations and combinations of data involved. Like the conclusion that the rate of interest is an important determinant of the demand for money, the conclusion that the instability hypothesis and related doctrines are of little empirical relevance does not seem to depend in any way on a particular formulation of the demand-for-money function.

THE CHOICE OF INTEREST RATE

The results on the role of interest rate variables in the demand-for-money function are clear enough then. Such variables ought to be included in the relationship; there is little reason to suppose that a liquidity trap exists; and no reason to suppose that there is an inherent instability in the relationship between the demand for money and the interest rate. Which interest rates, however? A short rate or a long rate; the rate of return on some financial asset such as, for example, a savings and loan association share, which may be regarded as a close substitute for money; an interest rate on foreign securities; the rate of return on equity capital; the whole term structure of interest rates; or some combination of the above? As we have already seen, some studies have used one and others another of these alternatives, and for many purposes nothing seems to hinge on the choice. For example, for long runs of U.S. data or British data Laidler (1971) showed that there is no systematic difference between a long and a short rate as far as explanatory power is concerned. Perhaps this result is not too surprising since, as we have suggested earlier, a single interest rate in the function is best interpreted as standing as a representative measure of the rates of return to be earned on holding the many assets that agents could substitute for money in their portfolios rather than as the "correct" indicator of the opportunity cost of holding money.

A good deal of recent work, much of it using postwar data, and the bulk of it for the United States, supports this conjecture. Thus, Heller and Khan (1979) showed that over the period (1960–1976) their measure of the whole-term structure of interest rates performed better than any single interest rate in explaining variations in the demand for money. Hamburger (1966, 1977b) has shown that the addition to a function explaining the U.S. demand for narrow money of the real yield on corporate equity improves its explanatory power significantly, even if that function already contains a long-term bond rate and the savings deposit rate, while his (1977a) work in the United Kingdom and West Germany shows that the yield on foreign securities supplements, rather than replaces, that on domestic assets.

One striking feature of much work is the consistency with which the returns on "near monies" (assets that might themselves be included in some broader measures of money) turn out to be significant in explaining variations in the demand for relatively narrowly defined money. For example, when using old M_2 as his dependent variable, Lee (1967) found the interest differential between time deposits and that on savings and loan association shares important, while in 1969 he found that the yield on corporate equities supplemented rather than supplanted the influence of the rate of return on savings and loan association shares on the demand for narrow money. Goldfeld (1973) found the time deposit rate important when using a narrow definition of money, even when he also included a short-term market interest rate—that on 4–6-month commercial paper—in his equation. Cagan and Schwartz (1975), in comparing quarterly data for 1921–1931 and 1954–1971, found a rate of return on savings deposits (computed as an average of the rates of return offered on a variety of such assets) to be important, particularly in the latter period.

These results are typical of the time series evidence reported by Feige and Pearce (1976) and confirm that generated by several studies of portfolio behavior, surveyed by Feige (1974), which show rates of return on near-money assets to exert a systematic influence on the demand for demand deposits and time deposits at commercial banks. The role of rates of return on money substitutes has not been so closely studied for other countries, but it is worth noting that the Bank of England (1970) found the rate of return on deposits with local authorities an important argument in the demand-for-money function for almost the same time period over which Laidler and Parkin (1970) obtained negative results with the treasury bill rate.

It is not too difficult to sum up the implications of the foregoing evidence. Because rates of interest on a wide variety of assets tend to move together, it is possible to obtain reasonable enough results when studying the demand for money by including just one "representative" rate in the function. This is important because the kinds of models of the macroeconomy in general, and the demand for money in particular, that we discussed in the first two parts of this book often rely on a simplification like this. It is good to know that the simplification in question is not so drastic as to remove those models from all contact with the real world. Nevertheless, it is clear that the real world is more complicated than the models in question, and that in fact money-holding agents treat a rather wide variety of assets as alternatives to money in their portfolios. There is nothing surprising about this; indeed it would be startling had things turned out otherwise. However, it does mean that as the menu of assets available to money holders changes over time, we might expect their behavior vis-a-vis money holding also to change as a result. This is a potentially important point when recent stability problems with the demand-for-money function are analyzed, as we shall see in due course.

THE ROLE OF EXPECTED INFLATION

The significance of the expected rate of inflation as a factor influencing the demand for money is well established. Although Cagan's (1956) study of European hyperinflations has been criticized by Jacobs (1975) for using statistical methods that exaggerated the closeness of the relationship between these variables, there is no reason to believe that Cagan's results are entirely a statistical artifact. Furthermore, despite the fact that Cagan measured the expected inflation rate by applying the error-learning hypothesis, it turns out that error learning was very close to "rational" behavior as a means of forming expectations as far as the inflations he studied were concerned. This is particularly the case with respect to the Weimar Republic's hyperinflation, and in this case Frenkel's (1977) use of the forward premium in the foreign exchange market to measure expected inflation may be considered a pioneering attempt to apply the rational expectations hypothesis to the study of the demand for money. It is noteworthy, therefore, that he found expected inflation so measured to be just as important a determinant of the demand for money as did Cagan.

Numerous other studies of rapid inflations, some using error learning to proxy expected inflation, some using lagged actual inflation, and some not using formal econometrics at all, have all come to the conclusion that variations in the expected inflation rate systematically influence the demand for money. Studies have been made on the Confederacy (Lerner, 1956), a group of 16 Latin American countries (Vogel, 1974), Chile (Harburger, 1963; Deaver, 1970), Argentina (Diz, 1970), Brazil and South Korea (Campbell, 1970), and Nationalist China (Hu, 1971). Moreover, Perlman (1970) has shown that cross-country variations in the proportion of a country's assets held in liquid form are related in a systematic fashion to cross-country variations in the average inflation rate. Although early work on the United States by Selden (1956) and

Friedman (1959) could not find any systematic influence of the rate of inflation on the demand for money, later studies by Shapiro (1973) and Goldfeld (1973) did find one in post–World War II data, regardless of whether the expected inflation rate is measured as some weighted average of past actual rates of inflation or, as in the case of some of Goldfeld's work, generated from opinion survey data. Moreover, it is worth noting that Brown (1939), in his pioneering study of the demand for money in interwar Great Britain, found that variations in the inflation rate influenced the demand for "idle" balances, and that Melitz (1976), in a study of France, found the expected inflation rate a more important opportunity cost variable than any market interest rate.

Quite apart from all this, there is an overwhelming amount of indirect evidence on the issue. As we have seen, there can be no reasonable doubt that variations in rates of interest influence the demand for money, and in every study cited in this chapter at least one of the rate of interest variables used has been the rate of return on a nominal asset.[5] Economic theory suggests that such rates of return should vary systematically with the expected inflation rate, and a large body of empirical evidence, some of which is surveyed in Laidler and Parkin (1975), confirms that they in fact do. These two factors taken together thus imply the existence of an indirect, but nevertheless well determined, channel whereby variations in the expected inflation rate influence the demand for money. Because, for reasons not well understood, variations in nominal interest rates do not fully reflect variations in the expected inflation rate, this particular channel of causation still leaves room for the expected inflation rate to play a direct role in the demand-for-money function over and above that played by nominal interest rates as, for example, the results of Brown, Melitz, Shapiro, and Goldfeld show. All four found a role for the expected inflation rate in a function that also contains a nominal interest rate variable.

CONCLUDING COMMENT

Whether one thinks of the demand-for-money function as being constrained by income, wealth, or permanent income, whether one defines money broadly or narrowly, whether one ignores problems of identification, simultaneity, and autocorrelated residuals, or deals with them; whether one uses a short rate of interest, a long one, a measure of expected inflation, the return on financial intermediaries' liabilities, a foreign interest rate, the return on equity, or even an index of the level and structure of interest rates in general; whether one ignores the own rate of return on money or takes explicit account of it, there is an overwhelming body of evidence in favor of the proposition that the demand for money is stably and negatively related to the opportunity cost of holding it. Of all the issues in monetary economics, this is the one that appears to have been settled most decisively.

[5] Indeed, of the commonly used interest rate arguments in studies of the demand for money, only the dividend price ratio favored by Hamburger (1966, 1978) is a real interest rate that does not encompass the expected inflation rate. [See Laidler (1980), Appendix B, for a brief discussion of this.] However, Hamburger does not use this rate by itself in his work. He always includes a nominal interest rate variable, such as a bond rate, in his functions as well.

chapter 11

Other Variables and the Question of Stability

THE INFLUENCE OF THE PRICE LEVEL

The relationship between the demand for money and the opportunity cost of holding it is a key one as far as the interaction of the quantity of money and the rest of the economic system is concerned. That much is evident from the analysis presented in Part I of this book. It also follows clearly from this analysis that, in the long run, the hypothesis that the demand for money is a demand for real balances, that other things equal the demand for nominal money is proportional to the general price level, is of equally crucial significance for the economy's behavior. Furthermore, all of the theories of the demand for money discussed in Part II imply the truth of this proposition. The hypothesis in question is an important one, then, and has been widely and successfully tested.

Many of the tests we dealt with in the previous chapter took this prediction for granted, and the demand-for-money functions fitted in the course of carrying them out were cast in real terms. That is, the original data on nominal wealth, income, and the money stock were divided through by the price level before being used for regression analysis.[1] The reason for this is as follows. If the demand-for-money function under test is, say,

$$\frac{M_d}{P} = kX^{\beta_1} r^{\beta_2} \tag{11.1}$$

where X stands for the scale variable in the function, one of the pieces of information one requires from the regression is the value of the β's. If it is

[1] It is also worth noting that because most of our theories of the demand for money are concerned with the behavior of the individual agent, one might expect the demand for money in the economy as a whole to grow in proportion to the population. This does indeed appear to be the case, and it is usual in studies of the demand for money to measure relevant variables such as money, wealth, and income in per-capita terms.

taken for granted that the demand for nominal balances is proportional to the price level, this function can be rewritten in nominal terms by multiplying both sides through by P; thus

$$M_d = kPX^{\beta_1} r^{\beta_2} \tag{11.2}$$

This is not the same function as

$$M_d = k(PX)^{\beta_1} r^{\beta_2} \tag{11.3}$$

which is what would be fitted if the data were left in nominal terms, for here β_1 would measure an average of the wealth, or income, elasticity of demand for money and the price level elasticity of the demand for money. The former can, in principle, take any value, while in Equation (11.2) the latter is assumed to be equal to 1.

If the price level elasticity of the demand for money is equal to 1, the estimate of the wealth or income elasticity of the demand for money coming from an expression like Equation (11.3) will be biased toward 1. In order to avoid such a bias, formulations like Equation (11.1) have generally been preferred for empirical work. This procedure is all right so long as one is convinced that the price level elasticity of demand for money is indeed equal to 1. If it is not, to divide an expression like

$$M_d = kP^{\beta_4} X^{\beta_1} r^{\beta_2} \qquad \beta_4 \neq 1 \tag{11.4}$$

through by P yields not Equation 11.1, but rather

$$\frac{M_d}{P} = kP^{(\beta_4 - 1)} X^{\beta_1} r^{\beta_2} \tag{11.5}$$

That is, if Equation (11.4) rather than Equation (11.2) is correct, the demand for real balances will also depend on the level of prices, and the omission of this variable may show itself in instability and poorness of fit in any test that uses data measured in real terms. The fact that such instability has not appeared in a wide variety of studies suggests strongly that the price level elasticity of demand for money is indeed 1 and that the price level does not influence the level of real-money holdings.

The evidence just cited is indirect, and there is an even larger body of indirect evidence bearing on the matter under discussion here which is worth mentioning. The macroeconomic proposition that the demand for money is a demand for real balances is closely related in logic to the microeconomic proposition that equilibrium demands and supplies of goods and services depend only on their *relative* prices and not on the level of money prices. If the latter hypothesis were falsified, then so would be the former, but an extremely large literature in empirical microeconomics bears witness to the fact that successful work in that area is consistent with the proposition that relative prices alone are important. The evidence alluded to here is worth taking seriously, but one always feels more comfortable with a result when indirect support of it is supplemented by directed evidence.

Meltzer's (1963) study is an early source of such direct support. First, he fitted functions (using wealth and income in different formulations) both to data cast in nominal terms and data cast in real terms. That is, he measured β_1 in the context both of an expression like Equation (11.1) and of an expression like Equation (11.3). His results show a distinct tendency for the estimate of β_1 to be closer to 1 in the latter case, as one would predict if the demand for nominal balances were proportional to the price level. Nor did Meltzer stop here; he went on to fit directly to the data a regression based on Equation (11.4), obtaining a direct estimate of β_4. The resulting estimate was, to all intents and purposes, equal to 1. Laidler (1971) carried out a similar test to Meltzer's on United Kingdom and U.S. data, over the period 1900–1965 (a little shorter than Meltzer's) and, with a different specification for the rest of the function, nevertheless obtained similar results on the role of the price level. A variation of such a test is to take an equation like (11.5), already cast in real terms, and estimate β_4–1. The parameter should, of course, not be different from zero. Friedman and Schwartz (1982) did just that to the demand functions fitted to U.S. and United Kingdom data for the years 1867–1975 and did indeed get a zero coefficient. Klovland (1983) reports similar results for Norway for the period 1867–1980.

Long runs of data are particularly suitable to testing the hypothesis that the demand for money is a demand for real balances, because, as we have argued above (p. 104), problems of identification and simultaneous equations bias are likely to be at a minimum in such cases. However, tests have also been performed using shorter data periods as well. For example, Goldfeld (1973), using quarterly data on postwar United States, included the price level in a demand-for-real-balances function and found that the elasticity of demand for real balances with respect to the price level was zero, thus confirming that the coefficient β_4 in Equation (7.11) indeed takes a value of unity. In their study of postwar quarterly British data Laidler and Parkin (1970) followed essentially the same procedure as Meltzer (1963) and obtained similar results, while the Bank of England (1970) produced evidence suggesting that the demand for nominal balances varies in proportion to the price level but perhaps with a lagged response. This latter point is of some importance because Laidler (1971) had trouble reproducing the unit elasticity of demand for nominal balances with respect to the price level when he broke his long 1900–1965 data period into subsections. As we have noted above (p. 104), short period data, being less dominated by secular trends, are more prone to simultaenity problems and biases due to neglect of lag effects than long period data. Laidler's (1971) study paid attention to none of these problems. In any event, even if one could not explain away the above-mentioned anomalous results in such terms, and it would be preferable had our conjectures here been explicitly investigated, it would still be correct to assert that the great bulk of the direct evidence we have cited confirms what the indirect evidence so strongly suggests, namely, that economic theory is correct in asserting that the demand for money is a demand for real balances.

THE CHOICE OF A SCALE VARIABLE

The theoretical arguments set out in Part II of this book tell us that an important issue is whether income, or some wealth variable, or perhaps some combination of the two should play the role of the scale variable in the demand-for-money function. If one casts the issue in "either-or" terms, then the evidence is, as we shall now see, on balance in favor of a wealth variable.

It was explained above (p. 87) that two wealth concepts have been thought to be relevant to the demand for money. First, directly measured data on the value of assets, at least for the U.S. economy, have been aggregated to produce a series for nonhuman wealth for that economy. Second, permanent income, measured as an exponentially weighted average of current and past levels of net national product, has been employed as a proxy for a more inclusive concept which treats the present value of future labor income as part of the current stock of wealth. For long runs of U.S. data, either concept appears to be able to explain more of the variation in the demand for money than current income. To reach such a conclusion, it is necessary to compare the performance of demand-for-money functions, identical except for the presence of wealth in one and income in the other, in the face of identical data and using identical statistical techniques. Such experiments have been carried out, using U.S. data, by Meltzer (1963), Brunner and Meltzer (1963), Chow (1966), and Laidler (1966a, 1971).

Meltzer's basic technique was to perform regressions that contained both income and wealth variables, as well as regressions that contained each separately. He found, first, that wealth (nonhuman wealth in this case) provided a more stable demand-for-money function than income and, also, that if both variables were included in the function, wealth showed itself sufficiently closely related to the demand for money to leave nothing for income to explain. The latter variable turned out to be redundant in the presence of wealth. He also fitted one or two functions using permanent income and found that this variable too explained more than measured income did. These results appear to hold regardless of whether money is defined to include or exclude time deposits, although Courchene and Shapiro (1964) argued that they were not robust when allowance was made for autocorrelated residuals. Chow, for the period 1897–1959, fitted regressions using permanent income and measured income as alternatives and found that as far as the long-run demand-for-money function was concerned, the former variable performed better, although Lieberman (1980) has questioned the reliability of Chow's results, particularly for data generated since 1933.[2]

Strong evidence that wealth (or permanent income) performs better than measured income as a scale variable in the U.S. demand-for-money function

[2] Lieberman replicated Chow's work making explicit allowance for autocorrelation in the residuals of the equation in a way that Chow had not. As we have seen (p. 107), the presence of serially correlated residuals presents special econometric problems when lagged dependent variables are also included in the function, and we have also seen that to measure permanent income using the error-learning hypothesis does just that.

comes from Brunner and Meltzer's (1963) prediction tests mentioned earlier (p. 124). They directly compared functions using income, nonhuman wealth, and permanent income and used both broad and narrow definitions of money. They found that, regardless of the definition of money used, functions containing a wealth variable gave more accurate predictions of the velocity of circulation than those containing income. Just as important, they found that the superior predictive power of wealth was not the product of one short time span, but rather that it characterized the entire period from the beginning of this century. Brunner and Meltzer's conclusion is strengthened by evidence produced by Laidler (1966a), using a rather different technique. Year-to-year changes in the data, rather than their annual levels, were used in the tests, and nonhuman wealth was measured in an indirect way.[3] The function fitted was a linear one, and the results achieved with it were compared to those generated by linear functions relating changes in the demand for money to changes in measured income and changes in permanent income. A short rate of interest was included, and both broad and narrow definitions of money were employed. With either definition of money, wealth and permanent income performed better than measured income, inasmuch as they produced functions that explained more of the variance in year-to-year changes in the demand for money.

Laidler (1971) also carried out tests on British data using measured- and permanent-income variables as alternatives in straightforward log linear functions and found that permanent income provided systematically better results, while Clark's (1973) work on Canada and Klovland's (1983) on Norway both led to a similar conclusion. Diz's (1970) study of Argentina generated evidence in favor of a permanent-income variable, though Deaver's (1970) work on Chile produced results that were indecisive in this respect. The permanent-income series used in all the tests described here was generated by applying the error-learning hypothesis described in Chapter 8 to data on measured income. Though the logarithm of permanent income measured in this way does not have quite the same value that would be obtained by taking a weighted average of past values of the logarithm of measured income—the former being the logarithm of a weighted average of incomes and the latter the weighted average of the logarithms of income—one would certainly be a good approximation of the other. Moreover, there is no reason to prefer one way of generating a permanent-income series to another. If one insists on using error learning, and we shall consider this matter in due course, there is no a priori reason for preferring to express the errors from which we postulate agents to learn as differences rather than ratios.

[3] The change in the public's holding of wealth in any year must be equal to their saving. There is much evidence to suggest that consumption is a constant fraction of permanent income and, since saving is equal to income minus consumption, it should also be equal to measured income minus permanent income (a variable usually known as *transitory income*) plus a constant fraction (1 minus the propensity to consume) of permanent income. Instead of a direct measure of a change in wealth, then, two variables, transitory income and permanent income, were used in the regression and related to changes in money holding.

We saw in a previous chapter that if we supplemented a log linear demand-for-money function of the form

$$(m - p)_t = \beta_0 + \beta_1 y_t^p + \beta_2 r_t + e_t \tag{8.7}$$

with the following, also logarithmic, error-learning formulation for permanent income,

$$y_t^p = \lambda y_t + (1 - \lambda) y_{t-1}^p \tag{8.8}$$

we end up with

$$\begin{aligned}(m - p)_t = {} & \lambda\beta_0 + \lambda\beta_1 y_t + \beta_2 r_t - (1 - \lambda)\beta_2 r_{t-1} + \\ & (1 - \lambda)(m - p)_{t-1} + e_t + (1 - \lambda)e_{t-1}\end{aligned} \tag{8.9}$$

We also saw that this latter equation is very similar, though not identical, to the one obtained by applying the "real adjustment cost" hypothesis to modeling a short-run demand-for-money function in which current income is the scale variable. This procedure would yield, if we substitute y_t for X_t in Equation (8.5) (p. 106),

$$\begin{aligned}(m - p)_t = {} & \beta_3\beta_0 + \beta_3\beta_1 y_t + \beta_3\beta_2 r_t + \\ & (1 - \beta_3)(m - p)_{t-1} + \beta_3 e_t\end{aligned} \tag{8.5}$$

There are problems involved in applying adjustment cost notions to the demand for money; we have discussed them earlier (pp. 109–112) and shall discuss them further below. Setting these aside for the moment, however, the similarity between Equations (6.9) and (6.5) opens up the possibility that the results we have cited so far as to the superiority of permanent income as a scale variable in the demand-for-money function in fact reflect nothing more than the existence of important adjustment lags in a function whose scale variable is, in fact, measured income. A number of studies [Teigen (1964), de Leeuw (1965), Bronfenbrenner and Mayer (1960), and Goldfeld (1973) for the United States and Fisher (1968) for Great Britain to cite but a few examples] included a lagged dependent variable in what they regarded as a measured-income formulation of the function and found it to play an important role.

The issue of distinguishing between these two conceptually very different but observationally rather similar hypotheses may be addressed by noting that, in principle at least, the adjustment lag model and the permanent-income hypotheses may be treated as complementary. If we replace y_t with y_t^p in Equation (8.5), substitute in Equation (8.8), and perform the Koyck transformation, we get

$$\begin{aligned}(m - p)_t = {} & \lambda\beta_3\beta_0 + \lambda\beta_3\beta_1 y_t + \beta_3\beta_2 r_t - \beta_3(1 - \lambda)\beta_2 r_{t-1} \\ & + (2 - \beta_3 - \lambda)(m - p)_{t-1} - \\ & (1 - \beta_3)(1 - \lambda)(m - p)_{t-2} + \beta_3 e_t + (1 - \lambda)\beta_3 e_{t-1}\end{aligned} \tag{11.6}$$

The parameters of the model from which Equation (11.6) is derived may be estimated by a technique known as "constrained least squares" whose details need not concern us here. The use of this technique, combined with two-stage least squares to cope with simultaneity, to study the demand for money was pioneered by Feige (1967) who employed a narrow definition of money, and annual data for the United States for the period 1915–1963.[4] He found that the parameter β_3 was just about equal to 1, implying that no adjustment lag was present in the data but that the parameter λ took a value of about 0.4. The rather long expectation lag implicit in this estimate was completely consistent with the one generated by Friedman in his consumption function work and subsequently used in constructing the permanent-income series employed in earlier studies of the demand for money described above. In addition, Feige found that the permanent-income and interest elasticities of demand yielded by his study were completely consistent with those produced by earlier work. In short, his study provided striking confirmation of the superiority of permanent income over measured income as an argument in the demand-for-money function.

More recently, Feige's results have received support from Kohli (1981) who simultaneously estimated a consumption function and a demand-for-money function for Canada using quarterly data for the period 1955–1976. He found that the same value for λ served well in both equations. Furthermore, Spinelli (1980) carried out work modeled on Feige's for Italian annual data for the years 1867–1965 with essentially similar results, namely that permanent income effects provide a better explanation of lags in the relationship than do adjustment mechanisms. Khoury and Myhrman (1975) obtained similar results with Swedish data, and Calliari et al. (1983), using quarterly data for 1961–1980 for Italy, with a broad (M_3) definition of money, while finding both adjustment and expectation lags present, were able to identify the latter as the longer one.

Not all of the work that has followed up Feige's lead has produced such strong results. Thus, Laidler and Parkin (1970) applied Feige's techniques to quarterly British data for the years 1955–1967 and found evidence consistent with the presence of both expectation and adjustment lags in the demand-for-money function, the former probably being longer than the latter, though the difficulties they encountered in finding a role for the interest rate in the function (see p. 125) made their results on this issue difficult to interpret. Laidler (1980) applied similar techniques to quarterly U.S. data for the period 1953–1978 and, as far as narrow money was concerned, found the simple adjustment lag hypothesis taken alone sufficient to explain the data, though an expectations lag did marginally better with broad money. Results which show that the permanent-income hypothesis has no extra explanatory power relative to the adjustment lag notion, as far as postwar U.S. data are concerned, have led some workers [for example, Goldfeld (1973)] to conclude that it is safe to accept the latter, apparently simpler, formulation as a basis for further work.

This last-mentioned conclusion may have been premature, because, as we have seen above (pp. 88–89), the error-learning hypothesis is very restrictive in

[4] It will be noted that the use of the Koyck transformation to generate Equation (11.5) has introduced a moving average process into its error term. Feige did take steps to cope with this problem in his econometric work, but other workers, for example Laidler and Parkin (1970), although they noted the problem, preferred to assume that it was unimportant.

the way it links expected income to past experience and is hard to square with the idea of rational expectations. It is therefore noteworthy that when Shapiro (1973) and Goldfeld himself (1973) applied econometric techniques that permit somewhat more flexibility in dealing with lag patterns than is permitted by the particular formulations of the expectations and adjustment mechanisms used by Feige, they both found that the demand for money is slower to respond to real income than to other variables. Even if it is necessary to postulate some kind of short-run adjustment when dealing with quarterly data, then, the evidence is still consistent with the view that permanent income has a role to play in the relationship.

The discussion so far has cast the choice of scale variable in "either-or" terms, but we have seen in Part II of this book that certain approaches to explaining the demand for money would accord a role to both variables at once. In a Keynesian view of the world transactions and precautionary money holdings might vary with current income and expenditure, but cash held for portfolio reasons would be related to some wealth variable. There is a certain amount of evidence in favor of this view.

For example, Meyer and Neri (1975) developed Feige's analysis with a view to refining the notion of "expected income." We have seen that the error-learning hypothesis produces a series that is a geometrically weighted average of current and past income levels. Meyer and Neri argued, on the basis of statistical forecasting theory, which is closely related to the rational expectations notion, that such a series is indeed a good representation of a "long-run normal" income level and hence a good proxy variable for wealth. They also suggested that what we could call "short-term expected" income should be distinguished from long-term normal or permanent income, that such a variable may, for transactions reasons, be important in the demand-for-money function, and that it can be measured in the following way. The value of permanent income at any moment is the value that people expect their actual income eventually to converge on, but there is no reason for them to expect that convergence to be immediate. If convergence is slow, short-term expected income will lie between current income and permanent income; the difference between expected income and current income might be a proportion of the difference between permanent income and current income. Thus, with the variables in logarithms, and y^e as the log of short-term expected income we have

$$y_t^e - y_t = d(y_t^p - y_t) \tag{11.7}$$

so that

$$y_t^e = dy_t^p + (1 - d)y_t \tag{11.8}$$

Meyer and Neri included expected income thus defined as a scale variable in the demand-for-money function fitted to annual U.S. data. A technique similar to that used by Feige enabled them to estimate the value of d, along with the other parameters of the function. Had the value of d turned out to be 1, this result would have implied that the expected-income variable is not operationally significant and that permanent income is the appropriate scale variable for the function; had it turned out to be equal to 0, the implication would have been that measured income is the appropriate scale variable. In fact, when a narrow definition of money was used, the value of d turned out to be clearly between these extremes. Though it fell in the same range when a broad definition of money was used, it was in fact closer to 1 in this case. These results suggest that short-term income expectations affect the demand for narrow money, but that once we begin to include assets less readily usable as a means of exchange in our measure of money, wealth becomes an increasingly important factor. Since narrow money is a component of broader money, it follows that, at least as far as the latter is concerned, both wealth and short-term expected income belong in the demand function.

This conclusion gets further support from the work of B. Friedman (1978) who, contrary to Goldfeld's (1973) result, found that nonhuman wealth could usefully be added to a function explaining the demand for narrow money in the United States. It also gets support from a recent study by Grice and Bennett (1984) of the demand for sterling M_3, a broad United Kingdom monetary aggregate. For the period 1963–1978 they found that both financial wealth and expenditure—clearly a transactions proxy that would be closely related to short-term expected income—were important arguments in the function they fitted. Note that the results just cited do *not* say that income, or some other transactions proxy, is after all a preferable variable to wealth in the demand-for-money function. What they say is that such a variable might usefully stand alongside wealth as a scale variable.

The results of all this work on the appropriate scale variable to include in the demand-for-money function are easily summarized. The evidence is overwhelming that current income taken alone is inadequate unless appropriate allowance is made for lags in the response of money holdings to variations in income. Such a lagged response seems in part to reflect the adaptation of income expectations to experience, though not necessarily through a simple error-learning mechanism, and points to the appropriateness of using some permanent- or expected-income variable in the function. However, recent work suggests that once due allowance is made for the role of wealth in the demand-for-money function, there is still some variation left over that can be explained by a transactions proxy variable, such as current, or at least short-term, expected income. This is particularly the case where narrower definitions of money are concerned.

THE REAL WAGE, ECONOMIES OF SCALE, AND INSTITUTIONAL CHANGE

The evidence we have summarized above suggests that it is unwise to neglect explicit analysis of transactions and precautionary motives for money holding. Studies of the role of the wage rate, interpreted as a proxy variable for the brokerage fee, which plays a key role in transactions and precautionary theories of the demand for money, tend to confirm this conclusion. There have been four such studies.

The first of them, by Dutton and Gramm (1973), used U.S. annual data for the period 1919–1958 and also included an interest rate and nonhuman wealth in the function. A variety of alternative measures of wealth was employed, all of which differed from that employed by Meltzer in excluding government debt (see p. 87), while a variety of interest rate variables were employed. The wage rate proved to have a systematic positive effect on the demand for money, regardless of precisely which other variables were included in the function. In Karni's (1974) study, data for a slightly longer time period (1919–1968) were used, and the model of the demand for money that underlay the empirical function was more closely related to an explicit inventory-theoretic approach to the demand for money. Here too, however, Karni found a wage variable (real hourly earnings) to have a systematic influence on the demand for money. Diewert (1974) fitting a complete model of households' demand for consumption and money, and labour supply, found the level of wages to affect the demand for money, as also did Phlips (1978). Of course, one would like to see the importance of the wage variable investigated across a far wider variety of specifications of the demand-for-money function than these before concluding definitely that this work has unearthed another important factor influencing money holding, but the results cited here are nevertheless highly suggestive and open up an interesting line for future research.

The evidence on the existence of economies of scale in money holding, another prediction of transactions and precautionary theories, also favors these approaches. It is true that if one looks at earlier studies of long runs of U.S. annual data such as Friedman (1959), Laidler (1966b, 1971), and Meltzer (1963), or of long runs of British data such as Kavanagh and Walters (1966) and Laidler (1971), or of data for such countries as Chile (Hynes, 1967) and Argentina (Diz, 1970), one has the impression that economies of scale in money holding are nonexistent. Broader definitions of money on the whole produce higher estimates of the income or wealth elasticity of the demand for money than narrower ones, but it is a fair generalization to say that unity puts a lower bound on the range of the estimates yielded by the above-cited studies.

However, as already noted, several of these studies, and in particular some of those on the United States, also presented estimates of the demand-for-money function for subperiods, and these results seem to show that the elasticity in question has fallen over time. Thus Laidler (1971), using annual data for the United States, estimated that the permanent-income elasticity of demand for money defined to include time deposits was 1.39 for the period 1900–1916, 1.28 for 1919–1940, and 0.65 for 1946–1965. For Great Britain, also using broad money, the relevant estimates were 1.24, 0.79, and 0.68 for the same time periods. These results are representative of a considerable body of evidence. Furthermore, studies using a narrow definition of money have found a more pronounced tendency for income or wealth elasticities of demand to lie below unity. In particular, the existence of economies of scale in the post-World War II demand-for-money function for both Great Britain and the United States is confirmed by several studies of quarterly data; see, for example, Shapiro (1973) and Goldfeld (1973) for the United States and Laidler and

Parkin (1970) and the Bank of England (1970) for Great Britain. The results for 13 countries surveyed by Fase and Kure (1975) were all generated by postwar quarterly data and show a heavy preponderance of evidence that economies of scale exist. Moreover, a multicountry study by Boughton (1979) shows evidence of economies of scale in the demand for narrow money over the years 1960–1977, though not for broad money. Such results are not affected by the precise specification of the demand function fitted.

At first sight it may seem appropriate to conclude on the basis of such evidence that the nature of the demand-for-money function has changed over time, so that economies of scale that did not exist, say, before World War I are now important particularly for narrow-money concepts. Bordo and Jonung (1981), in their study of five advanced countries, show that this conclusion may be misleading. They argue that in this earlier period institutional change, which involved a widening of the proportion of national income going through the market sector, was taking place. The effects of this change were of course correlated with the growth of real permanent income, and if they are ignored, the permanent-income elasticity of demand for money in this earlier period appears to be greater than unity. When these effects are allowed for, by introducing the institutional variables mentioned (p. 97) into the function, they turn out to add to the relationship's explanatory power and to reduce estimates of the permanent-income elasticity of demand for money to below unity. Klovland's (1983) work on Norway confirms this result, and the work of Friedman and Schwartz (1982) in the United States and the United Kingdom is at least not inconsistent with it. Although the latter do not introduce explicit measures of institutional change into their equations, they nevertheless acknowledge its importance.[5] In short, the earlier studies cited at the outset of this section were perhaps misleading on the matter of economies of scale. Holding institutional factors constant, these economies have probably always been present in the demand-for-money function. However, they are a more important characteristic of demand functions for narrowly defined money than for broader concepts. This is of course consistent with transactions and precautionary motives being of particular significance in determining the demand for narrow, as opposed to broad, money.

RECENT INSTABILITY OF THE DEMAND-FOR-MONEY FUNCTION

The discussion so far will have given the reader the impression that empirical work has taught us a great deal about the nature of the demand-for-money function, and indeed it has. However, it would be wrong to leave the impres-

[5] Rather, Friedman and Schwartz adjust their data prior to estimation for the effects of such change in pre–World War I United States and employ dummy variables to allow for once-and-for-all shifts of the relationship at other times. It should be noted that Bordo and Jonung investigated the potential influence of overall uncertainty about economic matters as measured by the variability of real income per head but found this to have a measurable influence only in the case of the United Kingdom.

sion that in the process of learning about the demand for money we have not encountered setbacks from time to time, or that the puzzles those setbacks have generated have all been definitively solved. The fact is that a decade ago it was possible to be much more confident about the robustness of our knowledge of the demand-for-money function than it is now. The reason for this is to be found in evidence generated over the last 10 years, notably in the United States, but in other countries as well, evidence which shows that certain widely accepted formulations of the demand-for-money function have performed very badly indeed in recent years.

The problem developed, as far as the United States was concerned, in the years 1972–74, when the demand for money began to grow much more slowly than would have been expected on the basis of past relationships; and this has been followed, more recently, by an equally unexplained upward shift of the demand for money in 1981–82. "The Case of the Missing Money," as Goldfeld (1976) aptly termed it, may be described as follows. By the early 1970s it was widely accepted, particularly among economists working in the Federal Reserve System, that a certain formulation of the demand-for-narrow-money function was to be preferred for policy-related analysis. This formulation used current real income as its scale variable, a nominal interest rate as an opportunity cost variable, and because it was typically employed to deal with quarterly data, it was cast in "short-run" terms: that is, a lagged value of the dependent variable of the relationship, real balances, was added to the right-hand side of the relationship to account for adjustment phenomena. Such a function had been shown [for example, by Goldfeld (1973)] to fit data from the 1950s and 1960s at least as well as any other, but in the mid-1970s it began to fail a certain kind of prediction test by an increasing amount.

The test in question involved fitting the function to an initial time period and then using the parameters thus obtained to forecast the demand for money beyond the end of the sample. In making forecasts, new observations of real income and the interest rate were of course introduced, but the value of the lagged dependent variable utilized, rather than being an actual observation, was instead the value of the demand for money the equation itself had predicted in the previous period. Such "dynamic simulations," as they are called, of the relationship produced a systematic and increasing overprediction of the demand for money after 1974. In a dynamic simulation once a relationship overpredicts the value of its dependent variable, the error in question is compounded over time as it is fed back period after period into the value of the lagged dependent variable. However, there is more to the "missing money" puzzle than the simple arithmetic of dynamic simulation. Laidler (1980) showed that if a "static simulation," which uses the actual instead of the previously predicted value of the lagged dependent variable, is carried out for a function very like the one Goldfeld used, the breakdown of the relationship, though less dramatic, is still readily observable. However, it takes the form of a once-and-for-all shift rather than a cumulative collapse. The puzzle here is a real one, and though the United States suffered from the problem first of all, instability in previously satisfactory formulations of the demand-for-money functions plagued other economies too as the 1970s progressed.

As Judd and Scadding's (1982a) survey of the U.S. literature on this problem shows, there has been no shortage of attempts to explain these difficulties, and they may be grouped into three categories. First, there are those that suggest that the basic demand-for-money functions that generated the puzzle was mis-specified to begin with. Second, there are those that suggest that, although it might have been properly specified for the 1950s and 1960s, the relationship in question needs to be modified to take account of the institutional change that took place in the 1970s. Finally, there are those that suggest that the fundamental problem lies not with the specification of the long-run function, but with the modeling of the adjustment process of the short-run relationship.

Perhaps the most obvious potential mis-specification in the demand function under discussion here involves its using current income rather than wealth or permanent income as a scale variable. The evidence discussed earlier in this chapter suggests that current income is almost certainly the wrong variable to use. However, that same evidence also suggests that current income does have a role to play in explaining the demand for narrow money, and Goldfeld's "missing money" was narrowly defined. Furthermore, we have seen that measuring permanent income with the error-learning hypothesis gives us a form for the short-run demand-for-money function very like that actually used by Goldfeld (see p. 108 above), and Laidler (1980) was able to confirm that instability of the function after 1974 could not be attributed to the use of current rather than permanent income. Of course, some other means of measuring permanent income more in accordance with notions of rational expectations might make more of a difference here, but this possibility remains uninvestigated.

If the scale variable of the function is not seriously mis-specified, the opportunity cost variable might well be. In the previous chapter we have seen that although a single bond or bill rate serves well enough in many formulations of the function, it does seem possible to do better with a little effort. Thus, Heller and Khan's (1979) function, which attempted to relate the demand for money to the whole-term structure of interest rates was fitted to the period 1960–1976 and did not appear to create any special problems of goodness of fit for these later years. However, simulation tests similar to Goldfeld's carried out by Porter and Mauskopf (1978) and cited by Judd and Scadding (1982a) suggest that this particular line of enquiry does not solve the problem at hand.

As early as 1966 Hamburger argued that the dividend-price ratio ruling in the stock market should be included in the demand-for-money function. Stock market prices fell dramatically in the 1972–74 period, while dividends did not, and Hamburger was able to show (1977b) that his version of the demand-for-money function generated little or no sign of a missing money puzzle. This result could be a coincidence, and as Judd and Scadding note, citing Hafer and Hein (1979), it does seem to depend rather specifically on Hamburger's assuming an income elasticity of demand for money of unity in his tests. However, the more recent, and to some equally puzzling, increase in the demand for money in 1982–83 has also been associated with a marked fall in the dividend price ratio, as Hamburger (1983) has been quick to point out.[6] Recent work by Slovin and Sushka (1983) shows that changes in the variability of interest rates in the 1970s might also have a role to play in explaining these phenomena. Since such variability is a plausible proxy variable for the riskiness of holding bonds, a factor that Tobin's approach to modeling the demand for money suggests belongs in the function, this postulate, like Hamburger's, is a suggestion worth further attention. Certainly this line of enquiry is more promising than that which attributes shifts in the demand for money to changes in the variability of the price level. Klein (1975) developed such a measure and in 1977 showed that over the period 1880–1973 it seemed to have a systematic positive influence on the demand for money. Unfortunately, as Laidler (1980) showed, this relationship completely broke down after 1974 and cannot be used to solve the "missing money" puzzle.[7]

We have already noted that the "missing money" puzzle involved a narrow (old M_1) definition of money. If the problem was to be completely resolved by attributing it to the absence of the dividend price ratio, or the variability of interest rates, we might expect to find a broader monetary aggregate such as old M_2 behaving in a similar manner in the 1970s. After all, bonds and equity are just as much alternative assets to broad money as they are to narrow money. However, though there is some evidence of instability in the demand for broad money over the 1970s, it is much less pronounced than in the case of narrow money, as Laidler (1980) showed. Closely related, the work of Barnett (1980) shows that the use of Divisia indices of money in the study of the demand for money makes no real difference as far as narrow aggregates are concerned, but a considerable difference for broader concepts.[8] These facts suggest that the source of shifts in the demand for narrow money be sought, at least in part, in institutional changes within the banking system.

In this context, it has been noted that with the rapid inflation and high market interest rates of the 1970s, the United States banking system, which has been prohibited from paying any explicit interest on demand deposits and has

[6] Although it has already been argued that the scale variable in the demand function is probably not to blame for the "missing money" puzzle, it is worth noting that B. Friedman (1978) has shown that much of the variation in Hamburger's dividend price ratio over the relevant period was in the price term. Hence, he argues that this variable may well be picking up the effects on wealth of variations in the stock market rather than in the opportunity cost of holding money. He then shows that there is evidence to suggest that the addition of wealth to Goldfeld's equation improves its performance after 1974. It would be of interest to see if this argument is supported by data drawn from the 1981–1982 episode.

[7] For a discussion of theoretical and statistical problems involved in distinguishing between the effects on the demand for money of the expected inflation rate and its variability, see Eden (1976).

[8] This is perhaps not surprising, since narrow-money concepts are aggregates of assets all of which are readily acceptable means of exchange. In this sense, the "moneyness" of the aggregate should not change much as its composition varies. However, broader aggregates encompass a much wider variety of assets, and changes in their composition can have a significant effect on their overall "moneyness." Thus, at a time of rapid change in the financial sector, the meaning of broader aggregates is much more subject to change than that of the narrower ones.

been subject to a ceiling on the interest it could pay on time deposits, was given particularly strong incentives to find ways of providing assets to its customers that furnished them with services similar to those yielded by more traditional forms of bank accounts, while evading the regulations on interest payments. Such institutional innovations, once induced, would remain in place so that one might expect to find a *permanent* downward shift of the demand-for-money function to be associated with the *temporary* appearance of high nominal interest rates. Enzler Paulus and Johnson (1976) were among the first to investigate the presence of such a ratchet effect in the relationship between the demand for money and nominal interest rates and they found evidence in favor of this hypothesis. Moreover, Garcia and Pak (1979) claim to have isolated an important factor contributing to it in the emergence of large-scale use by firms of repurchase agreements as a means of holding liquid assets.

Such results as these certainly provide a plausible approach to the "missing money" puzzle, and they are consistent with the evidence discussed above on the role of institutional change in influencing the demand for money, not least that developed by Lieberman (1980) in the context of the effects of the introduction of a prohibition on interest payments on demand deposits in 1933. Such effects are nothing new, as we have seen. Nevertheless, the particular explanation discussed here hinges on the existence of a rather special set of regulations within the U.S. banking system. If institutional change in response to those regulations was all there was to recent problems of stability with the demand-for-money function in the United States, then one would not have expected other countries, where such regulations were not in place, to have encountered stability problems with their own demand-for-money functions. However, they have, not least Canada where, it should be noted, regulations governing the payment of interest on various classes of deposits are essentially nonexistent. One possibility here is that changes in technology, largely associated with a rapid increase in the availability of low-cost computers and associated devices, has brought changes to the nature of the banking system which would have occurred regardless of the regulatory environment.

Another, complementary to the foregoing, explanation of instability in the demand-for-money function focuses on the interaction of the conduct of monetary policy and the adjustment processes underlying the short-run demand-for-money function. As the reader will recall, in Chapter 8 it was argued that to the extent that it is appropriate to capture short-run adjustment processes by adding a lagged dependent variable to the demand-for-money function, the relationships underlying the adjustment coefficients so obtained should be interpreted as reflecting mechanisms linking changes in the price level to changes in the supply of money, rather than costs encountered by individual economic agents in adjusting their portfolios. Furthermore, as the work of Gandolfi and Lothian (1983) has shown, in the cases of quarterly data for no fewer than eight advanced economies (the United States, the United Kingdom, the Netherlands, Japan, Italy, Germany, France, and Canada) over the period 1957–1976, estimates of the adjustment coefficients in question are very sensitive to the way in which the autocorrelation structure of the residuals from the relevant regression equations is specified. Since that autocorrelation structure itself might plausibly be thought of as reflecting adjustment processes of some unspecified kind, the implication of this evidence is that the interaction of prices and the money supply is complicated, volatile, and ill understood.[9]

In light of the above arguments, in the 1970s, when money supply behavior was, in comparison to earlier years, extremely volatile in a large number of countries, it would not be surprising if econometric devices for dealing with such adjustment, which worked in those earlier years, began to break down. A number of workers [Carr and Darby (1981), Laidler (1980), Judd and Scadding (1982b), and Gordon (1983)] have investigated or discussed this potential source of instability in demand-for-money functions, mainly for the United States, though Carr and Darby's work extends to the same eight countries dealt with by Gandolfi and Lothian. The details of the functions postulated and statistical techniques used vary quite widely among individual studies, but all of them place particular emphasis on explicitly modeling short-run adjustment as involving the responses of endogenous variables, in particular the price level (but also sometimes interest rates and output [see Laidler (1980)], to changes in the money supply, rather than as simply reflecting the movement of real balances over time in response to changes in the arguments of the demand-for-money function.

The studies in question have met with mixed success, and it would be wrong to claim that they have made a systematic contribution toward clearing up puzzles concerning the stability of the demand-for-money function in the seventies and early eighties. However, it would also have been wrong to expect them to do so, at least in the usual sense of obtaining from them alternative models of adjustment processes to those conventionally used whose parameters remain stable over time. The basic hypothesis at stake in the just-cited work is that recent instability in the demand-for-money function stems from a failure of economists working on the relationship properly to model the transmission mechanisms that lie between money supply changes and the endogenous variables of the macroeconomic system. Such mechanisms form the subject matter of Part I of this book, and one important point made there (p. 31) was that they were likely to be volatile, with their structure interacting with the conduct of monetary policy. Such a conclusion emerged because, following Robert E. Lucas (1976), we argued that the behavior of economic agents which underlies the mechanisms in question depends on those agents' expectations about the conduct of the very policy to which they are responding. It is suggestive that of the above-cited approaches to modeling adjustment processes in the context of the demand for money that of Carr and Darby (1981) has been one of the more successful. (On this see Laidler, 1980, pp. 247–253.) Carr and Darby's model explicitly distinguishes between expected and unexpected changes in the nomi-

[9] As has been noted, Laidler (1980) found evidence of a shift in the demand-for-money function in the United States in around 1974, but he also found that after that date the autocorrelation pattern in the residuals from the relevant equation changed. This latter result is at least consistent with the postulate that something in the dynamic adjustment mechanisms at work in the economy changed at around the same time.

nal money supply and attributes a different response on the part of prices to the two types of change.

The implication of the above argument is not necessarily that Carr and Darby have found a correct way of modeling adjustment processes because certain aspects of their approach are open to question.[10] Rather, and much more generally, it is that some, at least, of the apparent instability we have observed in demand-for-money functions over the last decade might be more than a statistical artifact reflecting omitted variables or mis-specified adjustment processes. Perhaps it reflects instead a form of instability that is always going to be inherent in the transmission mechanism of monetary policy at times when the conduct of policy is itself unstable and hence hard to anticipate. Without wishing to downplay the significance of omitted variables or institutional change as explanations for puzzles in the behavior of the demand for money in recent years, it is the above line of argument, bringing us as it does face to face with certain fundamental and general issues in empirical macroeconomics, that raises the most significant questions for monetary economists.[11] If it is valid, it suggests that the search for stable adjustment mechanisms in the context of the "short-run" demand-for-money function is inherently futile.

CONCLUDING REMARK

We have now completed our survey of the evidence on the various questions concerning the demand-for-money function we set out at the beginning of Chapter 9. It remains now briefly to assess the significance of this evidence both for the theories of the demand for money discussed in Part II of this book and for the macroeconomic framework described in Part I. These matters are the subject of the next, concluding, chapter of this book.

[10] Specifically, Carr and Darby have the price level respond immediately and fully to expected changes in the money supply, but only slowly, and with a distributed lag, to those which are unexpected. This aspect of their work raises problems because it is hard to see how the economy can simultaneously be characterized by sufficient price level flexibility to permit instantaneous adjustment to expected monetary changes and sufficient stickiness to prevent instantaneous adjustment to unexpected changes once they have, in fact, taken place and are therefore known to have done so. Their work has also been severely criticised on econometric grounds by MacKinnon and Milbourne (1984).

[11] Some of the issues involved here are addressed by Jonson (1976b) and Laidler (1982, Chapter 3; 1984).

chapter 12

Tentative Conclusions

INTRODUCTION

As we have seen in the last two chapters, by no means all of the issues raised by macroeconomic theory in general and theories of the demand for money in particular have been settled by empirical work. Nevertheless, on some matters a sufficient amount of evidence does seem to point in a particular direction that it is permissible to come to tentative conclusions about them. The adjective *tentative* must be stressed, however, because no matter how well established a particular set of results might now appear, there always exists a real possibility that evidence generated in the future will cast doubt on them. Not the least important lesson that monetary economists have learned over the last decade from the "missing-money" puzzle and related problems discussed at the end of the preceding chapter is that our knowledge of how the real world works, though by no means nonexistent, is fragile. That being said, we have learned some important lessons from empirical work and the next two sections of this chapter will be devoted to setting out what seem to be the most important of them. It will be convenient to begin with questions about the nature of the demand-for-money function itself.

IMPLICATIONS OF THE EVIDENCE FOR THEORIES OF THE DEMAND FOR MONEY

The basic question to be asked here is whether or not it pays to base a model of the demand for money on careful and explicit analysis of the motives that lead people to hold money. Let us consider the speculative motive first. This analysis does not seem to have produced anything in the way of predictions that are both unique to the approach in question and empirically important. It tells us that the rate of interest belongs in the demand-for-money function, but so does nearly every other piece of analysis we have considered, while its use of wealth as a scale variable for the demand-for-money function does not set it apart from simpler asset-demand approaches to the theory of the demand for money such as that of Friedman. Its specific predictions about the likelihood of instability in the demand for money–rate of interest relationship and about the possibility of a "liquidity trap" appearing, particularly when the economy is deeply depressed, receive little support from empirical evidence. Moreover, the very existence of assets whose capital value does not vary with the rate of interest, but which pay a return to their holders at a rate higher than that borne by commercial bank liabilities—assets such as savings and loan association shares in the United States, building society deposits in Great Britain, or those deposits with trust companies in Canada on which checks cannot be drawn, to give but three examples—suggests that speculative motives cannot dominate the demand for money. If they did, commercial bank liabilities, particularly demand deposits, would not be held in any large amount by the public when, from the point of view of satisfying this motive, apparently perfect substitutes exist that pay more interest.

Matters are different when it comes to theories of the transactions and precautionary demand for money. Several predictions specific to these approaches have been confirmed by much of the evidence discussed above. Though there have been only four studies of the matter—it does seem that wage levels, standing as a proxy for time and trouble brokerage costs, play a role in determining the demand for the narrowly defined money, which is particularly relevant in the context of models of transactions and precautionary demand. Furthermore, we have noted earlier that the superiority of wealth or permanent income to current or short-term expected income as a scale variable in the relationship is more marked in studies that use a broader definition of money. This suggests that there exists a demand function for those assets readily usable as a means of exchange which is distinct from the relationship governing the demand for less liquid assets. Studies such as those of Laidler (1966a) and Goldfeld (1973) were able to identify separate and stable demand functions for time deposits, and the portfolio studies surveyed by Feige and Pearce (1976) found the degree of substitutability between narrow money and other assets to be rather limited in scope. These facts add further weight to the above conclusion.

The key prediction of transactions and precautionary theories is that there should exist economies of scale in money holding, particularly where narrow money is concerned. We have seen that empirical evidence from a number of countries is in favor of this prediction where data for the post–World War II period are concerned. There is less support for data generated in earlier times, but there are a number of reasons to believe that the earlier evidence understates the importance of such economies of scale and that we should hesitate to regard it as casting doubt on their existence. First, as Fried (1973) has argued, when an economy's income grows over time, two factors affecting the transactions and precautionary demand for money will vary. First, the planned volume of transactions will go up and, other things being equal, if money is held for transaction purposes, one would expect the ratio of money holdings to income to fall as a result of this. However, at the same time the level of wages will increase, and, as the opportunity cost of time thus rises, one would expect the volume of money holding associated with any planned volume of transactions to rise. These two forces will operate in opposite directions on the money/income ratio as an economy's income rises, and there is nothing to rule out the effect of rising wages, of an increasing brokerage fee, swamping the economies of scale associated with a growing transactions volume. The appropriate way to investigate this suggestion is to include a wage rate variable as well as some other scale variable in the demand-for-money function in order to sort out their relative contributions to variations in money holding. We have seen that Dutton and Gramm, Karni, Diewert, and Phlips did just this, and Karni who fitted his function with and without a wage rate variable found that, with a wage rate variable included, the wealth elasticity of demand for money fell significantly below unity.

The above argument is highly suggestive, but it does not account for the discrepancy between prewar and postwar results on economies of scale, nor does it account for the steady downward drift over time of the permanent-income elasticity of demand for money that has characterized the demand functions of a number of countries. The most plausible explanation of these phenomena rests on the observation that with the passage of time monetary systems have become more sophisticated. As we have seen, Bordo and Jonung (1981) concluded, after studying this phenomenon in five countries, that estimates of the permanent-income elasticity of demand for money obtained from late-nineteenth and early-twentieth century data are biased upward, if proper account is not taken of institutional change when they are derived.

Cagan and Schwartz (1975), building on a suggestion of Alvin Marty (1961), have considered a property of institutional change in the United States that would account both for the fact that economies of scale are more apparent there in post–World War II demand functions than for earlier periods and that the change in question is more clearcut in the context of narrow money. They argue that one consequence of post–World War II growth of financial intermediaries was a shift in emphasis within the pattern of motivation underlying money holding in the United States. When mutual savings banks, savings banks, and savings and loan associations were relatively unimportant, people held bank liabilities not just for transactions and precautionary motives but also as a convenient way of storing wealth in a liquid form. Asset motives for holding money can now just as easily be satisfied by holding the liabilities of financial intermediaries and, as these institutions have become important, there has been a transfer of funds to their liabilities, leaving money holding satisfying only transactions and precautionary motives. According to the above argument, in the postwar period money holding came to be motivated mainly by the transactions and precautionary considerations that lead to economies of scale in money holding in a way that it was not in the prewar period. The reader will note that, to the extent that the "missing-money" puzzle of the 1970s is explicable in terms of institutional developments, the arguments advanced in that context are very similar to those of Marty and Cagan and Schwartz and suggest that such institutional change is an ongoing phenomenon that continues to influence the demand-for-money function.

One piece of evidence that might be thought to go against the conclusion that specific consideration of transactions and precautionary motives adds to our understanding of the demand for money is the poor performance of current income relative to permanent income or wealth as a scale variable. As we have seen, advocates of the transactions motive have tended to treat current income as a proxy for transactions. Here, the problem probably lies more in the nature of the proxy relationship between current income and transactions than in any fault with the underlying theory. There is no compelling reason to believe that current income should be a good proxy variable for transactions. Indeed, the fact that modern theorizing on the matter suggests that permanent rather than current income is the main determinant of consumption enables a plausible argument to be mounted that the latter variable is, after all, to be associated with transactions motives at least as much as with a more generalized asset demand for money; Feige advanced just such an argument as long ago as 1967.

To sum up then: although one can get a long way toward specifying an empirically satisfactory demand-for-money function without being concerned with the role money plays in the economy and the effect that might have on agents' attitudes toward holding it, it does seem that one can get further by taking specific account of transactions and precautionary motives. Thus, of all the theoretical approaches set out in Part II of this book, these will most likely repay efforts at further theoretical refinement.[1]

IMPLICATIONS OF THE EVIDENCE FOR MACROECONOMICS

Let us now turn to what we have learned about the macroeconomic model set out in Part I of this book and its relevance to the actual economy. The evidence on the relationship between the demand for money and the rate of interest described earlier allows a major issue to be settled, because neither of the extreme possibilities whose implications were discussed in Part I turns out to have much empirical content. It is not true that the demand for money is unrelated to the rate of interest, nor does it seem to be the case that the function becomes perfectly elastic with respect to the rate of interest at any relevant level of the short rate. It follows from this that although changes in the money supply will shift aggregate demand and cause changes in output and prices, so will so-called real shocks involving fluctuations in private sector investment, for example. Moreover, when it comes to the design of macroeconomic policy, the evidence implies that, in order to assess the effect that some given change in government expenditure, tax rates, or the money supply will

[1] The reader interested in contemporary debates about the proper analytical foundations for monetary theory will note that this conclusion lends strong support to the view of McCallum (1982) that the efforts of Sargent and Wallace and their associates (see, for example, 1982) to ground monetary theory in an "overlapping generations" framework where the asset they call "money" is a pure store of value is fundamentally misconceived.

have on the economy, one must make use of a complete model of the economy and not concentrate solely on one sector of it.

The fact that the demand for money is systematically related to the opportunity cost of holding it has important implications for the interaction of the quantity of money and the price level in inflationary situations. The model discussed in Part I of this book predicts that if output is fixed at an exogenous full-employment level, the price level changes in proportion to the quantity of money. This "neutral money" conclusion was derived in the context of a once-and-for-all change in the level of the nominal money supply. It would be a short step from this result to the conclusion that the inflation rate—the percentage rate of change of the price level—always equals the percentage rate of growth of the money supply; but, in light of the evidence just cited, such a conclusion would be a misleading oversimplification.

It is certainly true that if real balances are to remain constant while the nominal quantity of money grows, the price level must rise at the same rate as the quantity of money. Thus, holding real balances constant, an increase in the rate of monetary expansion will lead to an equal increase in the inflation rate. However, if the demand for real balances is inversely related to the expected rate of inflation, and if the expected rate of inflation varies with the current rate, it is not valid to assume that real balances remain constant when the rate of monetary expansion, and hence the inflation rate, increases. They will fall, so that, for a while after the increase in the rate of monetary expansion, prices will rise more rapidly than nominal balances. The inflation rate will "overshoot" its long-run equilibrium value. It is only when real balances have fallen to a level compatible with an inflation rate equal to the new rate of monetary expansion that such an equilibrium inflation rate can in fact be generated. There is no a priori reason to suppose that the time which must elapse for such a state of affairs to be reached will be short or that the path by which the inflation rate approaches its long-run equilibrium value after initially overshooting it will be smooth and monotonic.

Indeed it cannot be taken for granted that the equilibrium in question will ever be reached. If the demand for money is very sensitive to the expected inflation rate, and if the latter variable is very sensitive either to actual inflation or to the rate of monetary expansion itself, then a self-generating inflation resulting from a so-called flight from money is at least a logical possibility. Empirical work in the demand for money–expected inflation rate relationship suggests that it is not usually sensitive enough for inflation to become self-generating [see, for example, Cagan (1956)], but if the time path the inflation rate takes toward a new equilibrium value after the rate of monetary expansion changes depends on the behavior over time of the money-holding public's expectations about the inflation rate, then the other less extreme possibilities noted above cannot be ruled out as being empirically important. Thus, Dutton (1971), following up Cagan's (1956) analysis, was able to show that if inflation expectations were formed by an error-learning process, and if all other variables affecting the demand for money remained constant, a cyclical time path for the inflation rate after a once-and-for-all change in the rate of monetary expansion was a distinct empirical possibility.

Permitting other variables, such as output, to vary with the inflation rate, and allowing for the fact that the formation of expectations about inflation is likely to be a good deal more complex than a simple error-learning process, only make it more likely that the interaction of money and inflation in the real world will be complex. One very important, albeit negative, conclusion follows from this. The fact that it is difficult to observe a close relationship between fluctuations in the monetary expansion rate and the inflation rate on a quarter-by-quarter or even year-by-year basis does not mean that monetary expansion can be ruled out as a major cause of inflation. Such a relationship should only be observable when the expected rate of inflation is more or less constant and when other variables affecting the demand for money are not changing very much, and the real world seldom if ever generates such simple experiments for us.

Now it is of the very essence of the foregoing argument that the influence of money on the price level takes place *over time.* This observation highlights one of the most obvious shortcomings of the model set out in Part I when confronted with empirical evidence, namely its comparative static nature. The foregoing argument illustrates the weakness of this approach with reference to the role of inflation in the analysis, but problems also arise when we replace (or supplement) current income by permanent income as a scale variable in the demand-for-money function, as so much evidence suggests we should. To appreciate what is involved here, consider the following simple (indeed over-simple except as an illustration) model of Walters (1965) in which the price level is fixed, the demand for money depends only on permanent income, and the latter is related to measured income by an error-learning mechanism. We may write

$$\left(\frac{M_s}{P}\right)_t = \left(\frac{M_d}{P}\right)_t = kY_t^p \tag{12.1}$$

and

$$Y_t^p = \lambda Y_t + (1 - \lambda)Y_{t-1}^p \tag{12.2}$$

Substituting Equation (12.2) into Equation (12.1), applying the Koyck transformation, and rearranging gives

$$Y_t = \frac{1}{k\lambda}\left(\frac{M_s}{P}\right)_t - \frac{(1 - \lambda)}{k\lambda}\left(\frac{M_s}{P}\right)_{t-1} \tag{12.3}$$

Suppose that in time t the money supply is increased and thereafter held constant. The effect will be to increase Y_t by $1/k\lambda$ times the change in M_s. But, because $Ms_{t+1} = Ms_t$ income in $t + 1$ will be given by

$$Y_{t+1} = \frac{1}{k\lambda}\left(\frac{M_s}{P}\right)_{t+1} - \frac{(1 - \lambda)}{k\lambda}\left(\frac{M_s}{P}\right)_t = \frac{1}{k}\frac{M_s}{P_t} \tag{12.4}$$

and the change in income between $t - 1$ and $t + 1$ will be just $1/k$ times the change in the money supply. In short, when the money supply is changed in a model such as this, income initially changes by *more* than the ultimate amount. The effect of introducing an expectations lag into the demand-for-money function is to speed up rather than slow down the economy's initial reaction to an exogenous change in the money supply, and for reasons that are obvious enough once we think about them. Equation (12.1) tells us that the level of permanent income must adjust to keep the supply and demand for money in equilibrium when the supply changes, but Equation (12.2) tells us that the only way in which at time t the level of permanent income can be changed is for current income to change by a greater amount. Thereafter, if there is no further change in the money supply, there can be no further change in permanent income, but Equation (12.4) implies that for this to be the case measured income must fall back to the new level of permanent income and remain there.

The foregoing analysis was chosen for purely illustrative purposes.[2] Clearly, the rate of interest belongs in the demand-for-money function, and if we take note of this factor, we have to look at the behavior of the rest of the economy to see how income will respond both in the short run and in the long run to a change in income, because in such a case the interest rate will also adjust to help keep the demand and supply of money in equilibrium. The extent to which the level of expenditure in the economy reacts to interest rate changes will in turn determine the manner in which the initial effects of a monetary change are spread between interest rate changes and output changes. If expenditure is relatively insensitive to interest rate changes and responds only slowly to them, most of the initial impact of a change in the quantity of money will be on the level of interest rates, with income changes coming only later; and this is to say nothing of the implications that arise if the price level also changes as income varies; nor is it to mention that, as we have argued time and again in this book, error learning is very simple, and indeed probably too simple, description of the interaction of current and permanent income.

INTERPRETING RECENT INSTABILITY IN THE DEMAND-FOR-MONEY FUNCTION

The discussion so far in this chapter has been carried on without reference to the problems that empirical work on the demand for money has generated in the last 10 years and which were discussed at the end of the previous chapter. It is important to keep a sense of proportion about these difficulties because they have not cast doubt on all we thought we had learned from earlier work. In particular, recent evidence gives us no reason to doubt that the demand for

[2] The reader should note that, as a matter of algebra, an "overshooting" result similar to the above follows from a model in which the short-run demand-for-money function contains a lagged dependent variable motivated by an adjustment lag. Such results have been developed, for example by Tucker (1966) and Laidler (1973). Nevertheless, though algebraically correct, such results make economic nonsense in a model in which the money supply is exogenous, as the reader of p. 111 will suspect. This latter conclusion is established in Laidler (1982, Chapter 2).

money is systematically related to the opportunity cost of holding it, that the demand for nominal money is proportional to the general price level, that current income alone is probably an inadequate scale variable in the relationship, and so on. Rather, recent evidence has shown us that when we allow for the effects of the above-mentioned variables on the demand for money, there still remain certain systematic shifts that need to be explained. Moreover, the shifts in question seem to be particularly marked when dynamic simulation tests (see p. 146) are used to investigate the function's stability. Two lines of enquiry are particularly promising in the context of these problems, and each one of them has rather general implications for the manner in which we think about the role of money in the macroeconomic system.

First, we have seen that institutional change is a plausible explanation of at least some of the changes that have taken place in the demand-for-money function in a number of countries over the last decade. Furthermore, recent work on earlier periods suggests that such change has been influencing the demand-for-money function for virtually as long as recorded data permit the problem to be investigated. That this should be the case is not really surprising. It has already been noted that transactions motives seem to be particularly relevant to explaining the demand for money, and we have also seen (p. 46) that Irving Fisher long ago pointed to the importance of institutional and technical factors as determinants of the aggregate transactions demand for money in an economy.[3] However, if this result is unsurprising, it nevertheless has important implications for the way in which we think about monetary policy issues, because institutional change, which has been a recurring phenomenon in the past, is also likely to be such in the future.

Any monetary authority seeking to ensure that the behavior of the money supply over time is consistent with low and stable inflation and steady growth in real income must constantly be on the look out for institutional change so that it can adapt to the behavior of the supply of whatever monetary aggregate it is controlling to the shifts in demand such change might bring. This in turn means that suggestions for removing discretion from monetary authorities by seeking to legislate a preannounced manner of behavior for a chosen monetary aggregate, forevermore into the future, simply do not provide a viable way of ensuring monetary stability. This is not just because institutional change is unpredictable, although it often is, particularly when it results from technological innovations. It is also because any attempt to impose some sort of monetary rule on the system will itself be likely to provoke reactions on the part of those particularly affected by it. As was noted above, some of the innovations in the U.S. financial system that took place in the 1970s were probably partly a

[3] However, as was noted, Fisher's work on the quantity theory represents a summing up of a long-standing tradition in monetary economics—albeit with much novelty in matters of detail—rather than an original contribution that had no forerunners. Many economists had discussed the role of institutional factors before Fisher. Indeed, Bordo and Jonung, whose (1981) paper has been referred to frequently in this book, associate their investigations with the work of Knut Wicksell (1898; translated into English in 1936). Wicksell, too, was by no means the first to discuss such matters.

side effect of regulation. This is not to say that monetary authorities should not announce their policy plans, nor that they should give up any attempt to control the growth of the money supply, defined one way or another, but it is to say that "Goodhart's Law"—that any monetary aggregate chosen as a policy instrument will quickly see its significance in the financial system change—requires that they constantly monitor the private sector's response to their actions and allow for it in their own behavior.[4]

The 1970s, which generated so many of our concerns about the stability of the demand-for-money function, was also a decade of considerable turbulence in the conduct of monetary policy. The second promising line of enquiry into the causes of shifts in the demand for money referred to above starts from the simple proposition that it is unlikely that this was simply a matter of coincidence. As was argued in Part I of this book, we want to know about the demand function for money in the first place so that we may make predictions about the effects of changes in the money supply on variables, such as interest rates, real income, and prices. At times when the supply of money is fluctuating rapidly, so too will these variables fluctuate. We have seen that the interaction of the supply of money with the variables determining the demand for it is inherently dynamic, that it takes place over time. We have also seen, both as an analytic and an empirical matter, that the behavior of expectations about the time path of prices and output plays a key role in the mechanisms linking the supply of money to the variables it influences. Moreover, the rational expectations idea suggests that the very behavior of those expectations will be influenced by the behavior of the money supply. Thus, when the money supply fluctuates a great deal and in an unpredictable manner, not only ought we to expect the arguments of the demand-for-money function to fluctuate a great deal, but we ought also expect the dynamic mechanisms through which the money supply influences those variables to be unstable and unpredictable, and hence at least difficult and perhaps impossible to model empirically.

Though the foregoing argument is about the stability over time of the transmission mechanism that links the behavior of the money supply to the variables monetary policy influences, it is of direct relevance to the question of the stability of the demand-for-money function. The demand-for-money relationships that have given us most trouble over the last decade or so have been so-called short-run ones, relationships that include a lagged dependent variable among their arguments; and their difficulties have been most evident in the face of dynamic simulation tests, in which the lagged dependent variable plays a critical role. It was argued in Chapter 8 (p. 112) that the lagged dependent variable is needed in such a relationship to allow for the fact that the adjustment over time of the price level in the face of monetary disturbances is slow. This interpretation has been advanced or discussed recently in one form or

[4] Goodhart's law is named after Dr. Charles Goodhart of the Bank of England and reflects his frustration with the difficulties encountered by that institution in coping with institutional change in the United Kingdom. The proposal that money growth be tied down by a rule is associated with Milton Friedman (1960) in particular, and the implications of institutional change for such proposals are discussed in more detail in Laidler (1982, Chapter 5).

another by Carr (1983), Carr and Darby (1981), Coats (1982), Gordon (1983), Judd and Scadding (1982a), Laidler (1980, 1982), and Motley (1983). If it is valid—and I find it hard to argue that the debate about the question is settled as yet, regardless of my personal views on the issue—it follows that we have been trying to capture, in one coefficient on the lagged dependent variable, the whole of the complex dynamic mechanism linking money and prices. In light of the argument of the preceding paragraph it is hardly surprising that equations containing such a term have performed badly over the last decade or that their dynamic properties seem to be a particular source of difficulty.

CONCLUDING COMMENT

A chapter which is itself a summing up needs no long concluding section. Nevertheless, one implication of the preceding argument, obvious though it may be, needs to be addressed explicitly. Our discussion of the dynamics of the short-run demand-for-money function and their relationship to the transmission mechanism of monetary policy and the implications of the rational expectations notion for their stability and predictability has been cast in terms of empirical problems that have been encountered with data generated by the 1970s and early 1980s. However, the discussion in question is quite general in nature. It is relevant to any time and place, although it is likely to be of particular importance in periods of instability in monetary policy. The last decade or so has certainly been such a period, but it is by no means the only one for which we have data.

If the arguments we have considered above are valid, they ought to have readily observable implications for other times and places as well—the United States in the 1930s, for example, or Britain in the 1920s.[5] Moreover, even data generated by more tranquil times might turn out to be open to reinterpretation in matters of detail in their light. Though it would be surprising if work on these matters radically altered some of the more robust conclusions we have developed in this book—about the stability of the demand for money-interest rate or demand for money–price level relationships, or about the presence of economies of scale in the function in the context of narrower money concepts—one cannot be sure of such things until the issues have been explicitly addressed. Thus, the reader is reminded of the significance of the word *tentative* in the title of this chapter.

[5] A recent and as yet unpublished paper by Hafer (1982) takes up the question of the stability of the U.S. demand-for-money function in the 1930s using newly developed quarterly data and finds that there were problems, particularly in 1933, the year that saw the most spectacular of the banking collapses of that decade. Recall that Lieberman (1980) also reported instability arising in that year, although he attributed it to regulatory changes.

Bibliography

Adekunle, J. O. 1968. "The Demand for Money: Evidence from Developed and Less Developed Countries," *I.M.F. Staff Papers,* 15 (July), 220–266.

Akerlof, G. 1973. "The Demand for Money: A General Equilibrium Theoretic Approach," *Review of Economic Studies,* 40 (January), 115–130.

Artis, M. J. and Lewis, M. K. 1976. "The Demand for Money in the United Kingdom, 1963–1973," *Manchester School,* 44 (June), 147–181.

Axilrod, S., et al. 1977. "The Impact of the Payment of Interest on Demand Deposits," Board of Governors of the Federal Reserve System.

Bank of England. 1970. "The Importance of Money," *Bank of England Quarterly Bulletin,* 10 (June), 159–198.

Barnett, W. 1980. "Economic Monetary Aggregates: An Application of Index Numbers and Aggregation Theory," *Journal of Econometrics,* 14 (September), 11–48.

Barro, R. J. 1974. "Are Government Bonds Net Wealth?," *Journal of Political Economy,* 82 (November/December), 1095–1118.

———. 1977. "Unanticipated Money Growth and Unemployment in the United States," *American Economic Review,* 67 (March), 101–115.

———. 1978. "Unanticipated Money, Output, and the Price Level in the United States," *Journal of Political Economy,* 86 (August), S49–80.

———. 1984. *Macroeconomics* (New York: John Wiley).

Barro, R. J. and Santomero, A. J. 1972. "Household Money Holdings and the Demand Deposit Rate," *Journal of Money, Credit and Banking,* 4 (May), 397–413.

Baumol, W. J. 1952. "The Transactions Demand for Cash: An Inventory Theoretic Approach," *Quarterly Journal of Economics,* 66 (November), 545–556.

Becker, W. and Bental, B. Undated. "Regulation Q and the Effective Rate of Return on Demand, Savings, and Time Deposits," University of Minnesota.

Bordo, M. and Jonung, L. 1981. "The Long-Run Behaviour of the Income Velocity of Money in Five Advanced Countries 1879–1975—An Institutional Approach," *Economic Inquiry,* 19 (January), 96–116.

Boughton, J. 1979. "Demand for Money in Major OECD Countries," *OECD Economic Outlook* (January), 35–57.

Bronfenbrenner, M. and Mayer, T. 1960. "Liquidity Functions in the American Economy," *Econometrica,* 28 (October), 810–834.

Brown, A. J. 1939. "Interest, Prices and the Demand for Idle Money," *Oxford Economic Papers,* 2 (May), 46–69.

Brunner, K. and Meltzer, A. H. 1963. "Predicting Velocity: Implications for Theory and Policy," *Journal of Finance,* 18 (May), 319–354.

———. 1964. "Some Further Evidence on Supply and Demand Functions for Money," *Journal of Finance,* 19 (May), 240–283.

———. 1967. "Economies of Scale in Cash Balances Reconsidered," *Quarterly Journal of Economics,* 81 (August), 422–436.

Cagan, P. 1956. "The Monetary Dynamics of Hyperinflation," in M. Friedman (ed.), *Studies in the Quantity Theory of Money* (Chicago: University of Chicago Press).

Cagan, P. and Schwartz, A. J. 1975. "Has the Growth of Money Substitutes Hindered Monetary Policy," *Journal of Money, Credit and Banking,* 7 (May), 137–160.

Calliari, S., Spinelli, F., and Verga, G. 1984. "Money Demand in Italy: A Few More Results," *Manchester School,* 52 (June) 141–159.

Campbell, C. D. 1970. "The Velocity of Money and the Rate of Inflation: Recent Experience in South Korea and Brazil," in D. Meiselman (ed.), *Varieties of Monetary Experience* (Chicago: University of Chicago Press).

Carlson, J. A. and Parkin, J. M. 1975. "Inflation Expectations," *Economica,* NS42 (May), 123–138.

Carr, J. 1983. "Demand for Money: A Reinterpretation," University of Toronto (mimeo).

Carr, J. and Darby, M. 1981. "The Role of Money Supply Shocks in the Short-Run Demand for Money," *Journal of Monetary Economics,* 8 (September), 183–199.

Chow, Gregory, 1966. "On the Long-Run and Short-Run Demand for Money," *Journal of Political Economy,* 74 (April), 111–131.

Clark, C. 1973. "The Demand for Money and the Choice of a Permanent Income Estimate: Some Canadian Evidence 1926–1965," *Journal of Money, Credit and Banking,* 5 (August), 773–793.

Clinton, K. 1973. "The Demand for Money in Canada 1955–1970: Some Single-Equation Estimates and Stability Tests," *Canadian Journal of Economics,* 6 (February), 53–61.

Clower, R. W. 1967. "A Reconsideration of the Microfoundations of Monetary Theory," *Western Economic Journal,* 6 (December), 1–8.

Clower, R. W. and Howitt, P. W. 1978. "The Transactions Theory of the Demand for Money: A Reconsideration," *Journal of Political Economy,* 86 (June), 449–466.

Coats, W. L., Jr. 1982. "Modelling the Short-Run Demand for Money with Exogenous Supply," *Economic Inquiry,* 20 (April), 222–239.

Cockerline, J. P. and Murray, J. D. 1981. "A Comparison of Alternative Methods of Monetary Aggregation: Some Preliminary Evidence," Bank of Canada Technical Report 28.

Cooley, T. F. and Leroy, S. F. 1981. "Identification and Estimation of Money Demand," *American Economic Review,* 71 (December), 825–844.

Courchene, T. J. and Kelly, A. K. 1971. "Money Supply and Money Demand: An Econometric Analysis for Canada," *Journal of Money, Credit and Banking,* 3 (May), 219–243.

Courchene, T. J. and Shapiro H. T. 1964. "The Demand for Money: A Note from the Time Series" *Journal of Political Economy,* 42 (October), 498–503.

Crouch, R. L. 1971. "Tobin vs. Keynes on Liquidity Preference," *The Review of Economics and Statistics,* 53 (November), 368–371.

Deaver, J. V. 1970. "The Chilean Inflation and the Demand for Money," in D. Meiselman (ed.), *Varieties of Monetary Experience* (Chicago: University of Chicago Press).

DeLeeuw, F. 1965. *The Demand for Money, Speed of Adjustment, Interest Rates and Wealth,* Staff Economic Studies, Board of Governors of the Federal Reserve System, Washington, D.C.

Diewert, W. E. 1974. "Intertemporal Consumer Theory and the Demand for Durables" *Econometrica,* 42 (May), 497–516.

Diz, A. C. 1970. "Money and Prices in Argentina 1935–62," in D. Meiselman (ed.), *Varieties of Monetary Experience* (Chicago: University of Chicago Press).

Dutton, D. S. 1971. "The Demand for Money and the Price Level," *Journal of Political Economy,* 79 (September–October), 1161–1170.

Dutton, D. S. and Gramm, W. P. 1973. "Transactions Costs, the Wage Rate, and the Demand for Money," *American Economic Review,* 63 (September), 652–665.

Eden, B. 1976. "On the Specification of the Demand for Money: The Real Rate of Return versus the Rate of Inflation," *Journal of Political Economy,* 84 (December), 1353–1360.

Edgeworth, F. Y. 1888. "The Mathematical Theory of Banking," *Journal of the Royal Statistical Society,* 51, 113–127.

Eisner, R. 1971. "Non-linear Estimates of the Liquidity Trap," *Econometrica,* 39 (September), 861–864.

Entzler, J., Johnson, L., and Paulus, J. 1976. "Some Problems of Money Demand," *Brookings Papers on Economic Activity,* 1, 261–280.

Fase, M. M. G. and Kure, J. B. 1975. "The Demand for Money in Thirteen European and Non-European Countries: A Tabular Survey," *Kredit und Kapital,* 3, 410–419.

Feige, E. 1964. *The Demand for Liquid Assets: A Temporal Cross Section Analysis* (Englewood Cliffs, N.J.: Prentice-Hall).

———. 1967. "Expectations and Adjustments in the Monetary Sector," *American Economic Review,* 57 (May), 462–473.

———. 1974. "Alternative Temporal Cross-Section Specifications of the Demand for Demand Deposits," in H. G. Johnson and A. R. Nobay (eds.), *Issues in Monetary Economics* (London: Oxford University Press).

Feige, E. L. and Pearce, D. K. 1976. "Substitutability between Money and Near Monies: A Survey of the Time Series Evidence," SSRI Workshop Series 7617, University of Wisconsin, Madison, Wis. (mimeo).

Fisher, D. 1968. "The Demand for Money in Britain: Quarterly Results 1951 to 1967," *Manchester School,* 36 (December), 329–344.

Fisher, I. 1911. *The Purchasing Power of Money* (New York: Macmillan).

Flavin, M. A. 1981. "The Adjustment of Consumption to Changing Expectations about Future Income," *Journal of Political Economy,* 89 (October), 974–1009.

Frenkel, J. 1977. "The Forward Exchange Rate, Expectations and the Demand for Money: The German Hyperinflation," *American Economic Review,* 67 (September), 653–670.

Fried, J. 1973. "Money, Exchange and Growth," *Western Economic Journal,* 11 (September), 285–301.

Fried, J. and Howitt P. W. 1983. "The Effects of Inflation on Real Interest Rates" *American Economic Review,* 73, (December), 968–980.

Friedman, B. M. 1978. "Crowding Out or Crowding In? The Economic Consequences of

Financing Government Deficits," *Brookings Papers on Economic Activity,* 3, 593–641.

Friedman, M. 1956. "The Quantity Theory of Money, A Restatement," in M. Friedman (ed.), *Studies in the Quantity Theory of Money* (Chicago: University of Chicago Press).

———. 1957. *A Theory of the Consumption Function* (Princeton, N.J.: Princeton University Press for the NBER).

———. 1959. "The Demand for Money—Some Theoretical and Empirical Results," *Journal of Political Economy,* 67 (June), 327–351.

———. 1960. *A Program for Monetary Stability* (New York: Fordham University Press).

———. 1966. "Interest Rates and the Demand for Money," *Journal of Law and Economics,* 9 (October), 71–85.

———. 1969. "The Optimal Quantity of Money," in *The Optimal Quantity of Money* (London: Macmillan).

———. 1977. "Time Perspective in Demand for Money," *Scandinavian Journal of Economics,* 79, 397–416.

Friedman, M. and Schwartz, A. J. 1970. *The Monetary Statistics of the United States: Estimates, Sources, Methods* (New York: Columbia University Press for the NBER).

———. 1982. *Monetary Trends in the United States and the United Kingdom* (Chicago: University of Chicago Press for the NBER).

Frowen, S. F. and Arestis, P. 1976. "Some Investigations of Demand and Supply Functions for Money in the Federal Republic of Germany 1965–74," *Weltwirtschaftliches Archiv,* 112, 136–164.

Gandolfi, A. E. and Lothian, J. R. 1983. "International Price Behaviour and the Demand for Money," *Economic Inquiry,* 21 (July), 295–311.

Garcia, G. and Pak, S. 1979. "Some Clues in the Case of the Missing Money," *American Economic Review,* 69 (May), Papers and Proceedings, 330–334.

Gilbert J. C. 1953. "The Demand for Money: The Development of an Economic Concept," *Journal of Political Economy,* 61 (April), 144–159.

Goldfeld, S. M. 1973. "The Demand for Money Revisited," *Brookings Papers on Economic Activity,* 3, 577–638.

———. 1976. "The Case of the Missing Money," *Brookings Papers on Economic Activity,* 3, 683–730.

Goldman, S. M. 1974. "Flexibility and the Demand for Money," *Journal of Economic Theory,* 9 (October), 203–222.

Goodfriend, M. (in press). "Reinterpreting Money Demand Regressions", K. Brunner and A. H. Meltzer (eds.) *Carnegie-Rochester Conference Series,* Amsterdam, North Holland.

Goodhart, C. E. A. 1982. "Disequilibrium Money—A Note," Bank of England (mimeo).

Gordon, R. J. 1983. "The 1981–82 Velocity Decline: A Structural Shift in Income or Money Demand?" in FRB San Francisco *Monetary Targeting and Velocity.*

Gray, M. R. and Parkin, J. M. 1973. "Portfolio Diversification as Optimal Precautionary Behaviour," in M. Morishima et al. *Theories of Demand, Real and Monetary* (London: Oxford University Press).

Gray, M. R., Ward, R. J., and Zis, G. 1976. "World Demand for Money," in J. M. Parkin and G. Zis (eds.), *Inflation in the World Economy* (Manchester: University of Manchester Press).

Gregory, A. W. and McAleer, M. 1981. "Simultaneity and the Demand for Money in

Canada: Comments and Extensions," *Canadian Journal of Economics,* 14 (August), 488–496.

Grice, J. and Bennett, A. In press. "Wealth and the Demand for £M3 in the United Kingdom 1963–1978," *Manchester School.*

Hafer, R. W. 1982. "The Stability of the Short-Run Demand for Money Function 1920–1939," FRB of St. Louis Research Paper 82-009.

Hafer, R. W. and Hein, S. E. 1979. "Evidence on the Temporal Stability of the Demand for Money Relationship in the United States," *Federal Reserve Bank of St. Louis Review,* 61 (December), 3–14.

Hamburger, M. J. 1966. "The Demand for Money by Households, Money Substitutes and Monetary Policy," *Journal of Political Economy,* 74 (December), 600–623.

———. 1977a. "The Demand for Money in an Open Economy: Germany and the United Kingdom," *Journal of Monetary Economics,* 3 (January), 25–40.

———. 1977b. "The Behaviour of the Money Stock: Is There a Puzzle," *Journal of Monetary Economics,* 3 (July), 265–288.

———. 1983. "Recent Velocity Behaviour, The Demand for Money and Monetary Policy" in FRB San Francisco *Monetary Targeting and Velocity.*

Harberger, A. C. 1963. "The Dynamics of Inflation in Chile," in C. F. Christ et al. *Measurement in Economics: Essays in Mathematical Economics and Econometrics in Memory of Yehuda Grunfeld* (Stanford, Calif.: Stanford University Press).

Heller, H. R. and Khan, M. 1979. "The Demand for Money and the Term Structure of Interest Rates," *Journal of Political Economy,* 87 (February), 109–129.

Hendry, D. F. and Ericsson, N. R. 1983. "Assertion Without Empirical Basis: An Empirical Appraisal of Friedman and Schwartz' Monetary Trends in the . . . United Kingdom," in Bank of England Panel of Academic Consultants, *Monetary Trends in the United Kingdom* Panel Paper 22.

Hendry, D. F. and Mizon, G. 1978. "Serial Correlation as a Convenient Simplification, Not A Nuisance, A Comment on A Study of the Demand For Money by the Bank of England," *Economic Journal,* 88 (September), 549–563.

Hicks, J. R. 1935. "A Suggestion for Simplifying the Theory of Money," *Economica,* 2 (February), 1–19.

Hu, T. W. 1971. "Hyperinflation and the Dynamics of the Demand for Money in China 1945–1949," *Journal of Political Economy,* 79 (January–February), 186–195.

Hynes, A. 1967. "The Demand for Money and Monetary Adjustments in Chile," *Review of Economic Studies,* 34 (July), 285–294.

Jacobs, R. L. 1975. "A Difficulty with Monetarist Models of Hyper-inflation," *Economic Inquiry,* 13 (September), 332–360.

Johnson, H. G. 1963. "Notes on the Theory of Transactions Demand for Cash," *Indian Journal of Economics,* 44 (172), part 1 (July), 1–11.

———. 1969. "Inside Money, Outside Money, Income Wealth and Welfare in Monetary Theory," *Journal of Money, Credit and Banking,* 1 (February), 30–45.

Johnston, J. 1972. *Econometric Methods* (New York: McGraw-Hill).

Jonson, P. D. 1976a. "Money and Economic Activity in the Open Economy: The United Kingdom 1880–1970," *Journal of Political Economy,* 84 (September–October), 979–1012.

———. 1976b. "Money Prices and Output: An Integrative Essay," *Kredit und Kapital,* 4, 499–518.

Jonson, P. D., Moses, E., and Wymer, C. 1976. "A Minimal Model of the Australian Economy," Reserve Bank of Australia Discussion Paper 7601. Also in *Conference in Applied Economic Research,* Sydney, RBA 1977.

Judd, J. and Scadding, J. 1982a. "The Search for a Stable Money Demand Function: A Survey of the Post-1973 Literature," *Journal of Economic Literature,* 20 (September), 993–1023.

———. 1982b. "Financial Change and Monetary Targeting in the United States," in *Interest-Rate Deregulation and Monetary Policy,* Asilomar Conference, FRB of San Francisco.

Kanniainen, V. and Tarkka, J. 1983. "The Demand for Money: Mircrofoundations for the Shock Absorption Approach," Bank of Finland (mimeo).

Karni, E. 1972. "A Note on the Transactions Money Demand and the Term Structure of Interest Rates," Ohio State University, Division for Economic Research, Report 7232.

———. 1974. "The Value of Time and the Demand for Money," *Journal of Money, Credit and Banking,* 6 (February), 45–64.

Kavanagh, N. J. and Walters, A. A. 1966. "The Demand for Money in the United Kingdom 1877–1961: Preliminary Findings," *Bulletin of the Oxford University Institute of Economics and Statistics,* 28 (May), 93–116.

Keynes, J. M. 1923. *A Tract on Monetary Reform* (London: Macmillan).

———. 1930. *A Treatise on Money* (London and New York: Macmillan).

———. 1936. *The General Theory of Employment, Interest, and Money* (London and New York: Macmillan).

Khan, M. 1974. "The Stability of the Demand for Money Function in the U.S. 1901–1965," *Journal of Political Economy,* 82 (November–December), 1205–1220.

Khoury, M. and Myhrman, J. 1975. "Econometric Analysis of the Demand for Money in Sweden: 1909–1968," University of Stockholm (mimeo).

Khusro, A. M. 1952. "An Investigation of Liquidity Preference," *Yorkshire Bulletin of Economic and Social Research,* 4 (January), 1–20.

Klein, B. 1974a. "The Competitive Supply of Money," *Journal of Money, Credit and Banking,* 6 (November), 423–454.

———. 1974b. "Competitive Interest Payments on Bank Deposits and the Long-Run Demand for Money," *American Economic Review,* 64 (December), 931–949.

———. 1975. "Our New Monetary Standard: The Measurement and Effects of Price Uncertainty 1880–1973," *Economic Inquiry,* 13 (December), 461–484.

———. 1977. "The Demand for Quality Adjusted Cash Balances: Price Uncertainty in the U.S. Demand for Money Function, *Journal of Political Economy,* 85 (November), 691–716.

Kliman, M. L. and Oksanen, E. H. 1973. "The Keynesian Demand for Money Function: A Comment," *Journal of Money, Credit and Banking,* 5 (February), 215–220.

Klovland, J. T. 1983. "The Demand for Money in Secular Perspective: The Case of Norway 1867–1980," *European Economic Review,* 22 (July), 193–218.

Knoester, A. 1979. "Theoretical Principles of the Buffer Mechanism, Monetary Quasi-Equilibrium and its Spillover Effects," Erasmus University, Rotterdam.

Kohli, U. R. 1981. "Permanent Income in the Consumption and the Demand for Money Functions," *Journal of Monetary Economics,* 7 (March), 227–238.

Kostas, P. and Khouja, M. W. 1969. "The Keynesian Demand for Money Function: Another Look and Some Additional Evidence," *Journal of Money, Credit and Banking,* 1 (November), 765–777.

Koyck, L. M. 1954. *Distributed Lags and Investment Analysis* (Amsterdam: North-Holland).

Laidler, D. 1966a. "Some Evidence on the Demand for Money," *Journal of Political Economy,* 74 (February), 55–68.

———. 1966b. "The Rate of Interest and the Demand for Money—Some Empirical Evidence," *Journal of Political Economy,* 74 (December), 545–555.

———. 1969. "The Definition of Money: Theoretical and Empirical Problems," *Journal of Money, Credit and Banking,* 1 (August), 508–525.

———. 1971. "The Influence of Money on Economic Activity: A Survey of Some Current Problems," in G. Clayton, J. C. Gilbert, and R. Sedgwick (eds.), *Monetary Theory and Policy in the 1970s* (London: Oxford University Press).

———. 1973. "Expectations, Adjustment and the Dynamic Response of Income to Policy Changes," *Journal of Money, Credit and Banking,* 4 (February), 157–172.

———. 1980. "The Demand for Money in the United States—Yet Again," in K. Brunner and A. H. Meltzer (eds.), *On The State of Macroeconomics, Carnegie-Rochester Conference Series in Public Policy,* Amsterdam, North Holland Vol. 12.

———. 1981. *Introduction to Microeconomics,* 2nd ed. (Deddington: Philip Allan. New York: Halstead Press).

———. 1982. *Monetarist Perspectives* (Deddington: Philip Allan. Cambridge, Mass.: Harvard University Press).

———. (1984). "The Buffer Stock Notion in Monetary Economics," *Conference Proceedings, Supplement to the Economic Journal,* 94 (March) 17–34.

Laidler, D. and Parkin, J. M. 1970. "The Demand for Money in the United Kingdom 1956–1967: Preliminary Estimates," *Manchester School,* 38 (September), 187–208.

———. 1975. "Inflation—A Survey," *Economic Journal,* 85 (December), 741–809.

Latané, H. A. 1954. "Cash Balances and the Interest Rate—A Pragmatic Approach," *Review of Economics and Statistics,* 36 (November), 456–460.

Lee, T. H. 1967. "Alternative Interest Rates and the Demand for Money: The Empirical Evidence," *American Economic Review,* 57 (December), 1168–1181.

———. 1969. "Alternative Interest Rates and the Demand for Money—Reply," *American Economic Review,* 59 (June), 412–417.

Leponiemi, A. 1966. *On the Demand and Supply of Money: The Evidence from the Quarterly Time Series in the United States, the United Kingdom and Finland* (Helsinki: The Finnish Economic Association).

Lerner, E. 1956. "Inflation in the Confederacy 1861–65," in M. Friedman (ed.), *Studies in the Quantity Theory of Money* (Chicago: University of Chicago Press).

Lewis, M. 1978. "Interest Rates and Monetary Velocity in Australia and the United States," *Economic Record,* 54 (April), 111–126.

Lieberman, C. 1980. "The Long Run and Short Run Demand for Money, Revisited," *Journal of Money, Credit and Banking,* 12 (February), 43–57.

Lucas, R. E., Jr. 1973. "Some International Evidence on Output Inflation Trade-Offs," *American Economic Review,* 63 (June), 326–334.

———. 1976. "Econometric Policy Evaluation," in K. Brunner and A. H. Meltzer (eds.), *The Phillips Curve and the Labor Market, Carnegie-Rochester Conference Series,* Vol. 1 (Amsterdam: North-Holland).

Macesich, G. 1970. "Supply and Demand for Money in Canada," in D. Meiselman (ed.), *Varieties of Monetary Experience* (Chicago: University of Chicago Press).

Marty, A. 1961. "Gurley and Shaw on Money in a Theory of Finance," *Journal of Political Economy,* 69 (February), 56–62.

Mason, W. 1976. "The Empirical Definition of Money: A Critique," *Economic Inquiry,* 14 (December) 525–538.

Matthews, R. C. O. 1963. "Expenditure Plans and the Uncertainty Motive for Holding Money," *Journal of Political Economy,* 71 (June), 201–218.

McCallum, B. T. 1983. "The Role of Overlapping Generations Models in Monetary Economics," in K. Brunner and A. H. Meltzer (eds.), *Money, Monetary Policy and Financial Institutions,* Carnegie-Rochester Conference Series, Vol. 18.

MacKinnon J. G. and Milbourne R. D. 1984. "Monetary Anticipations and the Demand for Money," *Journal of Monetary Economics,* 13 (March), 263–74.

Melitz, J. 1976. "Inflationary Expectations and the French Demand for Money 1959–70," *Manchester School,* 44 (March), 17–41.

Meltzer, A. H. 1963. "The Demand for Money: The Evidence from the Time Series," *Journal of Political Economy,* 71 (June), 219–246.

Meyer, P. A. and Neri, J. A. 1975. "A Keynes-Friedman Money Demand Function," *American Economic Review,* 65 (September), 610–623.

Michaelson, J. B. 1973. *The Term Structure of Interest Rates* (New York and London: Intext).

Milbourne R. D., Buckholtz P., and Wasan M. T. 1983. "A Theoretical Derivation of the Functional Form of Short-Run Money Holdings," *Review of Economic Studies,* 50 (July), 531–542.

Motley, B. 1983. "Dynamic Adjustment in Money Demand," FRB San Francisco (mimeo).

Mussa, M. 1975. "Adaptive and Regressive Expectations in a Rational Model of the Inflationary Process," *Journal of Monetary Economics,* 1 (October), 423–442.

Muth, J. R. 1961. "Rational Expectations and the Theory of Price Movements," *Econometrica,* 29 (July), 313–335.

Namba, S. 1983. "The Stability of the Demand for Money and the Choice of Financial Intermediate Targets—An Empirical Study on the Monetary Aspects of Japan," Tokyo, Bank of Japan (mimeo).

Niehans, J. and Schelbert-Syfrig, H. 1966. "Simultaneous Determination of Interest and Prices in Switzerland by a Two-Market Model for Money and Bonds," *Econometrica,* 34 (April), 408–413.

Orr, D. 1970. *Cash Management and the Demand for Money* (New York and London: Praeger).

Parkin, J. M. and Bade, R. 1984. *Modern Macroeconomics* (New York: Prentice-Hall).

Patinkin, D. 1965. *Money, Interest and Prices,* 2nd ed. (New York: Harper & Row).

———. 1969. "The Chicago Tradition, The Quantity Theory, and Friedman," *Journal of Money, Credit and Banking,* 1 (February), 46–70.

Perlman, M. 1970. "International Differences in Liquid Assets Portfolios," in D. Meiselman (ed.), *Varieties of Monetary Experience* (Chicago: University of Chicago Press).

Pesek, B. P. and Saving, T. R. 1967. *Money, Wealth and Economic Theory* (New York: Macmillan).

Phlips, L. 1978. "The Demand for Leisure and Money" *Econometrica,* 46 (September), 1025–43.

Pifer, H. W. 1969. "A Nonlinear, Maximum Likelihood Estimate of the Liquidity Trap," *Econometrica,* 37 (April), 324–332.

Pigou, A. C. 1917. "The Value of Money," *Quarterly Journal of Economics,* 37 (November), 38–65.

Poloz, S. 1980. "Simultaneity and the Demand for Money in Canada," *Canadian Journal of Economics,* 13 (August), 407–420.

———. 1982. *The Demand for Money in a Multicurrency World.* Ph.D. dissertation, University of Western Ontario.

Porter, R. D. and Mauskopf, E. 1978. "Cash Management and the Recent Shift in the Demand for Demand Deposits," Board of Governors of the Federal Reserve System (unpublished).

Santomero A. M. and Seater, J. J. 1981. "Partial Adjustment and the Demand for Money," *American Economic Review,* 71 (September), 566–78.

Sargent, T. J. and Wallace, N. 1982. "The Real Bills Doctrine Versus the Quantity Theory: A Reconsideration," *Journal of Political Economy,* 90 (December), 1212–1236.

Saving, T. 1971. "Transactions Cost and the Demand for Money," *American Economic Review,* 61 (June), 407–420.

Selden, Richard. 1956. "Monetary Velocity in the United States," in M. Friedman (ed.), *Studies in the Quantity Theory of Money* (Chicago: University of Chicago Press).

Shapiro, A. A. 1973. "Inflation, Lags, and the Demand for Money," *International Economic Review,* 14 (February), 81–96.

Slovin, M. B. and Sushka, M. E. 1983. "Money, Interest Rates and Risk," *Journal of Monetary Economics,* 12 (September), 475–482.

Spindt, P. A. 1983. "Money is What Money Does: A Revealed Production Approach to Monetary Aggregation," Federal Reserve Board Special Studies Paper 177.

Spinelli, F. 1980. "The Demand for Money in the Italian Economy 1867–1965," *Journal of Monetary Economics,* 6 (January), 83–104.

Spitzer, J. J. 1976. "The Demand for Money, the Liquidity Trap and Functional Forms," *International Economic Review,* 17 (February), 220–227.

Starleaf, D. 1970. "The Specification of Money Demand-Supply Models Which Involve the Use of Distributed Lags," *Journal of Finance,* 25 (June), 743–760.

Starleaf, D. R. and Reimer, R. 1967. "The Keynesian Demand Function for Money: Some Statistical Tests," *Journal of Finance,* 22 (March), 71–76.

Startz, R. 1979. "Implicit Interest in Demand Deposits, *Journal of Monetary Economics,* 5 (October), 515–534.

Teigen, R. 1964. "Demand and Supply Functions for Money in the United States," *Econometrica,* 32 (October), 477–509.

———. 1971. "The Demand for Money in Norway 1959–1969," *Statokonomisk Tidsskrift,* 3, 65–99.

Tobin, J. 1947. "Liquidity Preference and Monetary Policy," *Review of Economics and Statistics,* 29 (May), 124–131.

———. 1956. "The Interest Elasticity of Transactions Demand for Cash," *Review of Economics and Statistics,* 38 (August), 241–247.

———. 1958. "Liquidity Preference as Behavior towards Risk," *Review of Economic Studies,* 25 (February), 65–86.

Tucker, D. 1966. "Dynamic Income Adjustment to Money Supply Changes," *American Economic Review,* 56 (June), 433–449.

———. 1971. "Macroeconomic Models and the Demand for Money Under Market Disequilibrium," *Journal of Money, Credit and Banking,* 3 (February), 57–83.

Vogel, R. C. 1974. "The Dynamics of Inflation in Latin America, 1950–1969," *American Economic Review,* 64 (March), 102–114.

Walters, A. A. 1965. "Professor Friedman on the Demand for Money," *Journal of Political Economy,* 73 (October), 545–551.

Weinrobe, Maurice D. 1972. "A Simple Model of the Precautionary Demand for Money," *Southern Economic Journal,* 39 (July), 11–18.

Whalen, E. L. 1966. "A Rationalisation of the Precautionary Demand for Cash," *Quarterly Journal of Economics,* 80 (May), 314–324.

Wicksell, K. 1898. *Interest and Prices* [trans. R. F. Kahn. 1936. (London: Royal Economic Society)].

Working, E. 1927. "What Do Statistical Demand Curves Show," reprinted (1953) in Stigler, G. J. and Boulding, K. E. (eds.), *Readings in Price Theory* (London: Allen and Unwin).

Index

Adaptive expectations hypothesis. *See* Expectations
Adekunle, J. O., 124n
Adjustment processes, 105–110, 111, 113, 140–142, 149–151, 160–161
Aggregate demand, 23, 24–32, 34
  and interest elasticity of demand for money, 25–27
  as rectangular hyperbola, 26
Aggregate expenditure, 10, 15, 16, 17
Aggregate supply, 27–29, 30, 101n
  and capital accumulation, 29
  and population growth, 29
  in the short run, 30
Akerlof, G., 112
Arestis, P., 126
Artis, M. J., 112n
Axilrod, S., 94

Bade, R., 31n
Bank of England, 125, 132, 137, 145
Barnett, W., 84, 148
Barro, R. J., 31n, 35, 62n, 82n, 90n, 93, 94, 95, 128
Becker, W., 94
Bennett, A., 86, 143
Bental, B., 94
Bonds, 11, 34, 41, 48, 51–52, 55, 60–61, 64, 70
  riskiness of, as determinant of demand for money, 69–77, 96
  20-year corporate, 91, 95
Bordo, M., 97, 124, 127, 131, 145, 154, 159n
Boughton, J., 145
Brokerage fee, 60–64, 64n, 65–69, 143, 153, 154
Bronfenbrenner, M., 121, 122, 128, 140
Brown, A. J., 121, 122, 134
Brunner, K., 63n, 123, 126, 130, 138–139
Budget constraint, 55–56, 72
Buffer stock approach, 105n. *See also* Adjustment processes

Cagan, P., 94, 95, 96, 132, 133, 154, 155, 156
Calliari, S., 141
Cambridge approach to monetary theory, 47–50
Capital gain, 48, 51–52, 56, 71
Carlson, J. A., 95n
Carr, J., 112n, 150, 151, 161
Chow, Gregory, 106n, 127, 138
Clark, C., 124n, 139
Clinton, K., 124n
Clower, R., 41n, 63n
Coats, W. L., 112n, 161
Cockerline, J. P., 85
Commercial paper, 4- to 6-month, 91, 95, 132
Consumption, 8–10, 23, 24
  income as determinant of, 8–9, 16–17
  wealth as determinant of, 34–35
Cooley, T. F., 101, 103
Courchene, T. J., 127, 129, 138
Credit cards, 46
Currency, 81, 82, 83, 84

Darby, M. R., 112n, 150, 151, 161
Deaver, J. V., 133, 139
de Leeuw, F., 140
Diamond, P., 70n
Diewert, W. E., 96, 144, 153
Diminishing marginal rate of substitution, 55, 56
Divisia index, 84, 85, 148
Diz, A. C., 133, 139, 144
Dutton, D. S., 96, 144, 154, 156

Economies of scale in money holding, 63–64, 119, 143–145, 153–154
Edgeworth, F. Y., 64n
Eisner, R., 129
Employment, full, 27–29, 31, 34, 47, 101n
Entzler, J., 149
Equation of exchange, 45
Ericsson, N. R., 113n
Error-learning hypothesis, 88–89, 94–95, 108, 133, 139, 140–142, 147, 156–157
Exchange rates
  fixed, 6n
  forward premium as measure of expected inflation, 96
Expectations, 31, 49, 52, 88–90, 133–134, 141–142, 150, 157
  adaptive, 88–89, 94
  rational, 89, 95, 133, 142, 147, 160
  survey data on, 95, 134
Expectations lags, 108–109, 140–141
Expected income. *See* Permanent income

Fase, M. M. G., 145
Feige, E. L., 93, 127, 132, 141, 142, 153, 155
Financial innovation, 81–82, 84, 85, 148–149, 159–160. *See also* Institutional changes in the banking system
Fiscal policy, 16–17, 33, 54
Fisher, D., 140
Fisher, Irving, 59, 159
  approach to quantity theory, 44–47, 48, 49–50, 54, 97
Flavin, M. A., 89n
Frenkel, J., 96, 133
Fried, Joel, 62n, 85n, 91n, 153
Friedman, B., 119n, 143, 147n
Friedman, Milton, 54, 55n, 59, 84n, 85n, 92, 103, 104, 105, 113n, 125, 126, 130, 134, 137, 140, 144, 145, 153, 160n
  modern quantity theory of, 54–58
Frowen, S. F., 126

Gandolfi, A. E., 124n, 149, 150
Garcia, G., 149
Gilbert, J. C., 42

Goldfeld, S. M., 95, 132, 134, 137, 140, 141, 142, 143, 144, 146, 147, 148n, 153
Goodfriend, M., 110n
Goodhart, C. E. A., 112n, 160n
Goodhart's law, 160
Gordon, R. J., 150, 161
Government debt, 34–35, 87
Government expenditure, 8, 9, 10, 16, 17, 23, 24, 155
Gramm, W. P., 96, 144, 154
Gray, M. R., 64n, 125
Gregory, A. W., 127
Grice, J., 86, 143

Hafer, R. W., 147, 161n
Hamburger, M., 92, 132, 134n, 147, 148
Harberger, A. C., 133
Hein, S. E., 147
Heller, H. R., 92, 132, 147
Hendry, D., 113
Hicks, Sir J. R., 40n
Howitt, P., 63n, 85n, 91n
Hu, T. W., 133
Hynes, A., 144
Hyperinflation, 94, 96, 118–119, 132

Identification problem, 99–101, 103, 112, 126, 129
Income
  as determinant of consumption, 8, 9, 16–17
  as determinant of demand for money, 11, 12, 25–26, 47, 49, 52–53, 60, 62–63, 67–68, 102, 119, 121, 123, 138–143, 144, 147, 153, 155, 158, 159
  disposable, 8–9, 16
  distribution of, 63, 97
  equilibrium level, 9–10, 11–17, 20–21, 23–25, 28–29
  measures of, 86
  permanent income, 88, 89–90, 108, 119, 124, 125, 138–142, 144, 145, 147, 153, 154, 155, 158
  transitory, 139n
Indifference curves, 71–76
Inflation
  as determinant of demand for money, 57–58
  expected rate of, 94–96, 118–119, 133–134, 156–157
  and interest rates, 96, 119
Instability of the demand for money. *See* Stability
Institutional changes in the banking system, 148–149, 154–155, 159. *See also* Financial innovation
Interest rate
  demand deposits and, 93–94
  as determinant of demand for money, 11–12, 13–14, 17–18, 33, 49, 50–54, 56–57, 60–61, 66–68, 69–77, 90–92, 102, 118, 121–126, 127–133, 134, 148, 149, 155, 158–159
  as determinant of investment, 9, 10
  elasticity of demand for money and, 17–21, 25–27, 29, 53, 106n, 124, 126, 127, 128–133
  empirical evidence, 118, 121–126, 128–133
  equilibrium level of income and, 9, 10, 11–21, 28
  expected level, 51–52
  long rates, 91, 92, 118, 124, 126, 128, 129–133
  normal level, 52–54
  opportunity cost of holding money and, 11, 48, 56, 90–92, 93–94, 121–126, 131–133, 147
  riskiness of bonds and, 69–77, 148
  short rates, 91, 92, 118, 124, 126, 128, 129–133, 155
  stability, 118n, 130–131
  term structure of, 91, 130, 147

Investment, 8, 9, 14, 17, 23, 24, 30, 33
interest rate as determinant of, 9, 10. *See also* Interest rate
IS curve, 10, 11–17, 20–21, 23–25, 27, 33, 34–35

Jacobs, R. L., 133
Johnson, H. G., 35, 59n, 85n
Johnson, L., 149
Johnston, J., 102n
Jonson, P. D., 112n, 113n, 126, 151n
Jonung, L., 97, 124, 127, 131, 145, 154, 159n
Judd, J., 94, 112n, 131, 147, 150, 161

Kanniainen, V., 112n
Karni, Edi, 62n, 92, 96, 144, 154
Kavanagh, N. J., 124, 126, 144
Kelly, A. K., 129
Keynes, J. M., 50, 71n
Keynesian theory, 50–54, 56n, 69
later developments in, 59–77
precautionary motive, 64–69
speculative motive, 69–77
transactions motive, 59–64
Khan, M., 92, 130, 132, 147
Khouja, M. W., 92, 129
Khoury, M., 141
Khusro, A. M., 86, 122
Klein, B., 93, 94, 97, 127, 128, 148
Kliman, M. L., 129
Klovland, J. T., 97, 124, 127, 131, 137, 139, 145
Knoester, A., 112n
Kohli, U. R., 141
Kostas, P., 129
Koyck, L. M., 108n
Koyck transformation, 108, 109, 140, 141n, 157
Kure, J. B., 145

Labor
demand for, 27–28
supply of, 27–28
Laidler, D., 27n, 31n, 35, 84n, 92, 97, 110n, 112n, 124, 125, 126, 127, 128, 130, 132, 134, 137, 138, 139, 141, 144, 146, 147, 148, 151n, 153, 158n, 161
Latané, H. A., 122
Lee, T. H., 93, 127, 132
Leponiemi, A., 124n
Lerner, E., 133
Leroy, S. F., 101, 103
Lewis, M. K., 112n, 124n
Lieberman, C., 127, 131, 138, 149, 161n
Liquidity, 41, 85, 96
Liquidity trap, 29n, 53–54, 92, 118, 128–131, 153
LM curve, 12–15, 17, 19–21, 23–25, 27, 30, 33, 34
Lothian, J. R., 124n, 149, 150
Lucas, R. E., Jr., 31, 89n, 150

M1, 84, 130, 148
M2, 84, 130, 148
McAleer, M., 127
McCallum, B. T., 155n
Macesich, G., 124n
MacKinnon, J. G., 151
Marshall, A., 47, 50, 54, 55
Marty, Alvin, 61n, 154, 155
Mason, W., 84n
Matthews, R. C. O., 71n
Mauskopf, E., 147
Mayer, T., 121, 122, 128, 140
Melitz, J., 134
Meltzer, A. H., 63n, 87, 123, 126, 130, 137, 138–139, 144
Meyer, P. A., 142
Michaelson, J. B., 91n
Milbourne, R. D., 109, 151
"Missing money," 146–149. *See also* Stability of the demand for money function
Mizon, G., 113n
Modern quantity theory, 54–58
Monetary policy, 13–14, 20–21, 25, 28–30, 112, 149, 150, 151

Money
  empirical definition of, 81–86
  as a means of exchange, 11, 41, 42, 50, 81–82, 105
  opportunity cost of holding, 11, 48, 55, 56, 60, 93–94, 104, 118, 121–134, 156
  own rate of return on, 93–94, 118, 127, 131
  predictable market value of, 41, 42
  supply of, 6, 11, 23, 45, 63, 95, 99–101, 112, 129, 155, 158, 159, 160
  velocity of circulation of, 44–47, 49, 123, 124, 125, 126, 130, 139
Money market certificates, 84
Money market mutual funds, 83, 84
Moses, E., 113n
Motley, B., 161
Murray, J. D., 85
Mussa, M., 95n
Muth, J. R., 89
Myhrman, J., 141

Namba, S., 85, 124
Neri, J. A., 142
Neutral money, 29, 156
Niehans, J., 124n
"NOW" accounts, 81–83, 84, 93

Oksanen, E. H., 129
Opportunity cost of holding money, 11, 48, 55, 56, 60, 93–94, 104, 118, 121–134, 156
  measures of, 90–92
Orr, D., 64n

Pak, S., 149
Parkin, J. M., 31n, 64n, 95n, 110n, 124, 125, 132, 134, 137, 141, 145
Patinkin, D., 34, 35, 64n
Paulus, J., 149
Pearce, D. K., 132, 153
Perlman, M., 133
Pesek, B., 35
Phlips, L., 96, 144, 154
Pifer, H. W., 128, 129
Pigou, A. C., 47, 49, 50, 54, 55
Poloz, S., 92, 124n
Porter, R. D., 147
Precautionary motive, 50, 52–53, 64–69, 83, 119, 142, 143, 144, 145, 153–155
Price level
  as determinant of demand for money, 11, 12, 13, 21, 22, 23, 31, 34–35, 48, 57–58, 64, 69, 101, 135–136, 159
  downward flexibility, 34–35
  empirical evidence, 135–137
  expected rate of change, 57–58
  fixed, 8–21, 30–31, 47, 111
  flexible, 22–29, 47. *See also* Wage-price flexibility
  fluctuations, 41, 48
  indexes of, 85–86

Quantity theory, 44–58
  Cambridge approach, 47–50
  Fisher, Irving, version of, 44–47, 48, 49–50, 54
  Friedman, Milton, modern quantity theory, 54–58

Ratchet effect, 149
Rational expectations hypothesis. *See* Expectations
Regression analysis, 98, 107, 123
  constrained least squares, 140
  two-stage least squares, 102–103, 127, 140
Reimer, R., 129
Residual autocorrelation, in demand for money functions, 107–108, 113, 127, 138, 149–150
Riskiness of bonds, as determinants of demand for money, 69–77

Santomero, A. J., 62n, 93, 94, 109, 128
Sargent, T. J., 155n
Saving, T. R., 35, 62n
Saving and loan association shares, 83, 91, 118, 127, 131, 132, 153
Scadding, J., 94, 112n, 131, 147, 150, 161
Schelbert-Syfrig, H., 124n
Schwartz, Anna J., 84n, 103, 104, 105, 113n, 126, 130, 132, 137, 145, 154, 155
Seater, J. J., 109
Selden, R., 133
Shapiro, A. A., 95, 127, 134, 138, 142, 144
Simultaneity, 102–103, 104, 126–127
Slovin, M. B., 96, 118n, 148
Speculative motive, 51, 52–53, 56n, 69–77, 82–83, 92, 118, 129, 152–153
Spindt, P. A., 85
Spinelli, F., 124, 131, 141
Spitzer, J. J., 129
Stability of the demand for money function, 33, 54, 95, 118, 120, 128–131, 136, 145–151, 160
Starleaf, D. R., 112n, 129
Startz, R., 94, 128
Sushka, M. E., 96, 118n, 148

Tarrka, J., 112n
Taxes, 16–17, 23, 34–35, 155
Teigen, R., 124n, 126, 130, 140
Time deposits, 82, 83, 84, 93, 94, 124, 125, 128, 132, 149
Tobin, J., 59, 62n, 69, 71n, 121, 148
Transactions motive, 41–42, 44–54, 59–64, 81–82, 86, 109, 119, 142, 143–144, 145, 153–155, 159
Treasury bills, 3-month, 91, 125
Tucker, D., 158n

Uncertainty, 41, 42, 51, 64, 69
Unemployment, 8, 29
Utility, 40–42, 70

Velocity of circulation of money, 44–47, 49, 123, 124, 125, 126, 130, 139
Vogel, R. C., 133

Wage-price flexibility, 28, 29, 32
Wage rate as determinant of demand for money, 62, 68, 96, 119, 143–144, 153, 154
Wallace, N. W., 155n
Walters, A. A., 112n, 124, 126, 144, 157
Ward, R. J., 125
Wealth. *See also* Income, permanent
  allocation of, between two assets, 70–77
  defined, 55–56
  as determinant of consumption, 34–35
  as determinant of demand for money, 48, 49, 52–53, 55–58, 119, 122, 138–139, 142, 143, 144, 146, 153
  human, 56, 57, 87, 138
  measures of, 86–88
  nonhuman, 56, 57, 86, 119, 124, 126, 138–139, 143
Wealth effect, 29n, 34–35, 74
Weinrobe, M. D., 64n
Whalen, E. L., 64n
Wicksell, K., 159n
Working, E., 99n
Wymer, C., 113, 126

Zis, G., 125